The Investor's Guide to Understanding Accounts

The Investor's Guide to Understanding Accounts

10 crunch questions to ask before investing in a company

Robert Leach

HARRIMAN HOUSE LTD

43 Chapel Street
Petersfield
Hampshire
GU32 3DY
GREAT BRITAIN

Tel: +44 (0)1730 233870
Fax: +44 (0)1730 233880

email: enquiries@harriman-house.com
web site: www.harriman-house.com

First published in Great Britain in 2004
Reprinted in 2006

Copyright Harriman House Ltd

The right of Robert Leach to be identified as Author has been asserted in accordance
with the Copyright, Design and Patents Act 1988.

ISBN 1-8975-9727-4

British Library Cataloguing in Publication Data
A CIP catalogue record for this book can be obtained from the British Library.

Printed and bound by Graficas Cems, Navarra, Spain

About the author

Robert Leach

Robert Leach FCCA FIPPM ACertCM is a chartered certified accountant, private investor and author of over 30 books. His titles include *How to Make Money on the Stock Exchange* (Foulsham), *Financial Times Guide to Your Company Pension* and *Allied Dunbar Guide to Financial Planning for the Over 50s*. For two years he was a judge of the Stock Exchange Awards for best published accounts. He is the author of the looseleaf works *Payroll Factbook* and *Tax Factbook* published by Sweet & Maxwell. He also writes for newsletters, magazines, newspapers and anyone else who will pay him. He is a local councillor, church organist and member of General Synod. He lives in Epsom with his wife, three children, and a harpsichord bought from his meagre royalties.

At the time of writing this book, the author held small shareholdings in Abbey National, AstraZeneca, Atlantic Caspian, Bolton Group, BP, BT, Cadbury Schweppes, Chorion, Crown Sports, GlaxoSmithKline, Lloyds TSB, National Grid, Pharmagene, PlaneStation, Prudential, Pursuit Dynamics, Royal Bank of Scotland, Sainsbury, Scottish & Newcastle, SiRViS iT, Tesco, Urbium, and Wilshaw.

Contents

Part III

Aerospace, AIM companies, Airlines, Alcohol and breweries, Automobiles, Banks, Business services, Chemicals, Construction, Construction materials, Engineering, Food manufacturing, Food retailing, Football clubs, Household goods, Insurance, Internet companies, Investment trusts, Leisure industry, Media, Mines, Oil industry, Pharmaceuticals, Property, Retailers, Shell companies, Technology companies, Telephone companies, Television companies, Tobacco companies, Utilities, Wholesalers & distributors

Part IV

Part V

Supporting information from outside the accounts   **199**

Updating the information in the accounts
Independent research
Directors' dealings

Part VI

Summary   **207**

10 signs of a company in good health
10 signs of a company in trouble
Key accounting ratios and measures

Appendices

Index

I Why you cannot afford to ignore company accounts

Introduction

Company accounts and the annual report tell you:

- how much profit the company has made
- how it made that profit
- how much the company is worth
- how the directors view the year
- what the directors expect for the future

and much more, all of which can help you to decide whether to invest.

However, sifting through the mass of information requires knowledge of what to look for, how to use it when found, and what it all means. This book aims to help you understand how to analyse numbers and how to apply that analysis to investment decisions.

By law, all shareholders must receive a copy of the company's accounts. For larger companies these are often printed in glossy A4 format, almost like a brochure, with the front section containing the reports, and the accounts starting halfway through. Much of this book is concerned with explaining those numbers, including a basic tutorial at the start of Part IV. However the written reports are also important, and therefore form part of the discussion.

Numbers in accounts rarely mean much on their own. A net profit before tax of £200,000 or a share price of 50p tells you nothing about whether the company represents a good investment.

First, you must make sure that you are looking at the right accounts. You should be looking at **consolidated accounts**. Almost all businesses are now structured as a holding company which owns subsidiaries, some of which may themselves own sub-subsidiaries. Consolidated accounts treat all this group of companies as if they were one single company. It is in this group that you have invested. The accounts for the holding company itself must be published by law, but you can generally ignore them. Where accounts have columns or separate pages marked 'company' and 'consolidated' (or 'group'), it is the latter in which you are interested.

The main method for interpreting accounts is the **ratio**, though sometimes you need to understand about the basic figures. The accounts are the raw material for which ratios act as the tools. Which ratios you use depends on the company and what you wish to check. Just as a toolkit contains many tools only some of which you use for any particular job, so this book contains a kit of ratios, only some of which are needed to consider particular companies.

A ratio is simply one figure in the accounts divided by another, such as dividing profit by number of shares to give earnings per share. The answer rarely means much on its own. In most cases, the figure must be compared with similar companies.

Sometimes a ratio becomes one of the figures in another ratio, such as price/earnings ratio when the share price is divided by earnings per share.

Some ratios are in such common use that companies and providers of stock information calculate them for you. Common ratios include:

- gearing
- earnings per share
- dividend cover
- price/earnings ratio
- dividend yield

Other ratios are widely used in the accounting profession to understand the accounts. These include:

- gross margin
- acid test

These ratios and others are explained and discussed in detail later in the book.

Understanding the ratios

A ratio is not an end in itself, but a means to an end, namely forming an opinion about the company from its accounts.

To assist in this process, the major part of this book is structured under ten basic questions which all investors should ask about a company:

1.	Is the company growing?
2.	Are costs under control?
3.	Does it make a profit?
4.	How much cash does it have?
5.	Is its market value supported by assets?
6.	Is it using debt wisely?
7.	Are there any hidden nasties?
8.	Is management good enough?
9.	Can I expect a reliable income?
10.	Are there any threats to my interests?

The ratios and other comments under each question will help you come to an answer for each question.

For management there are obvious answers wanted for each question (no for 7 and 10, and yes for the rest). However there are no obvious answers for investors.

> **The best share investment in the world is in a company which you think will perform better than the market thinks.**

Even if you conclude that a company is likely to perform badly, it could still be a good investment if the market thinks that it will perform even worse.

Investment analysts are always at a disadvantage in that they must rely on historic data which may not prove a reliable indicator for the future.

However remember that you are trying to find shares which you think will perform better than the market thinks they will. Both you and the market have the same disadvantage in having to rely on historic data. So, to some extent, the disadvantages cancel each other out.

The ratios and other comments in this book are intended to help you determine how a company is likely to perform, and how the market expects it to perform.

However understanding accounts is more than calculating a few ratios. It is first necessary to narrow down your choice of company, as suggested in Section 2.1. It is recommended that you consider companies in three stages:

- review the accounts, using ratios and comparators;
- then read the narrative reports to compare your conclusions and seek explanations;
- then read coverage in the press, newsletters and on websites to compare your conclusions against other commentators.

Sometimes the accounts seem to be saying one thing when the reality is different. This book contains examples where the reality is different from the initial perception gained by following ratios alone.

It is good practice to identify three reasons for investing in a particular company. When you have identified those reasons, write them down. Review the company periodically. If you still believe in those reasons, continue holding the share. Only sell when you no longer believe the reasons.

You can always gain free hands-on experience by operating a dummy portfolio. You go through the process of share picking without buying the shares. You can monitor the shares as if you had bought them, to give you experience of how well you can pick them.

All this is in addition to the normal good advice about investing in shares:

Investing in shares - general advice

- only invest in what you understand;

- do not borrow money to invest;

- do not invest money in shares if you need it for a specific date (such as for buying a house or paying for a holiday);

- be prepared to see your investments go down sometimes;

- monitor share performance;

- be prepared to sell to take profits and cut losses;

- do not grieve over losses. If your emotional constitution cannot stand losses, buy National Savings instead and give this book to the Oxfam shop;

- run a dummy portfolio if you have not invested before, and then start a real portfolio cautiously, not using all your capital;

- do not feel possessive or sentimental about your shares. If it is time to sell them, do so;

- remember shares have not made you a profit until you have received a cheque from the stockbroker;

- never believe that you are a whizz investor. You should outperform unit trusts, but only because you are not paying their charges.

What business?

Ratios are of limited value by themselves. It is necessary to understand the nature of the business as what may be a healthy ratio for a supermarket can be an unhealthy ratio for a construction company.

For this reason, Part III makes some observations about particular trade sectors. Although much of the book deals with big companies, the principles apply equally to small companies. It is here that research can pay off. All the big companies are analysed by at least 50 analysts every day. It is among the unanalysed small and medium-sized companies that you may find a real bargain. Peter Lynch, a successful money manager, made a fortune from investing in an obscure hosiery company called Hanes in the 1970s when his wife raved about the tights they made.

Reliability of accounts

You also need to consider the reliability of the accounts, particularly since the Enron scandal.

Accountancy is an art not a science. The figures you read are, to some extent, reflections of opinion as well as fact. Part IV of the book considers the reliability of accounts, and how you may be able to detect anything suspicious. Part V looks at how you may obtain supporting information.

You should also appreciate that companies do not live in a vacuum but in a world where politicians make decisions, events happen, values and fashions change and economies perform with the same limited expectations as the weather. This aspect is considered in general in Section 2.10, and in relation to specific sectors in Part III. However no such consideration can ever be complete. In general, external economic factors affect companies similarly and therefore may often be ignored in some comparisons.

So should I invest in shares at all?

A share is the part ownership of a business. When you own a share in Sainsbury's, you own part of the company. With the other shareholders, you own the whole company. That means that some of the profit on every tin of baked beans sold belongs to you, and will come to you, either as a dividend or an increase in the share price.

The accounts are the record of how well the managers have run the business for you; whether they have been good stewards of your investment.

Shares are the ideal long-term investment for the private individual. They provide two sorts of income – dividends and capital growth; they are simple to understand and to monitor, and they provide the highest levels of return and the lowest level of cost.

This may seem a strange claim when the stock market has lost half its value in the three years to 2002. However even the depressed market cannot stop shares being long-term value. Someone given £130 worth of free shares in Abbey National (now called Abbey) in 1988 would find that they were worth "only" £420 in 2003, having had £75 in dividends in 2002. Such shares would have been given to someone with at least £200 in an account in 1988, worth about

£250 in 2003. Abbey National was regarded as one of the worst performing shares in 2003, as its value fell by more than two-thirds from a peak of £14 to just over £4. Even for such a poor performing share in such a poor performing market, the investor has an annual income of over 50% his original investment and has seen that investment more than treble.

Another way of considering shares in a bear market is to consider what happened to houses in the recession of 1991/92. Some property prices fell by 25% or more, as many house-owners faced negative equity – the balance owed on the mortgage exceeding the value of the house. If those property owners held their nerve and sat tight, they could have seen their property value treble in the next ten years.

The stock market is not always volatile. It was largely static between 1938 and 1952, and between 1968 and 1982. It crashed between 1972 and 1974, in 1987, and between 1999 and 2003.

For shares, this can be seen as a law of economics. Wealth is simply the capitalisation of products and services, as represented by services and tangible products. The commercial sector is where this wealth is created. Shares are the wellspring of wealth. Some prefer unit trusts as a safer investment. All that the fund managers do is to invest the funds in shares and cream off some profit. The wealth is still coming from the same stream, but further from the spring. That is why pensions, unit trusts, life policies and many other forms of investment have also done badly during the bear market.

In the year to April 1998, the London stock market rose by 44%, but the average increase in unit trusts was a mere 12%. Only two out of 1588 funds out-performed that market. Over three-quarters of managed funds routinely fail even to match the market, despite the hype about star fund managers.

Even those investments which appear unrelated to shares – such as property, gilts and gold – have their return indirectly funded by shares, as they provide both the benchmark to measure such investments and the wealth to buy them.

Aim of this book

There have been several experiments where a random selection of shares, chosen by such methods as throwing darts at *The Financial Times*, has been measured against unit trusts. Over a long term, a minimum of ten years, such a random selection consistently outperforms managed funds.

This is simply because of fees. The combination of capital growth and dividends can produce income growth of 12% from shares, even including periods of bear markets. Suppose a fund manager takes a modest 1% a year in commission, so that you only receive 11%. Over 30 years, £100 will have grown to £3,000 at 12% but only to £2,300 at 11%.

Fund managers find it hard to beat the market, simply because they are the market. Some managers perform better than others, but much of such variation can be put down to random distribution rather than to any skill. But over a long period, none of them can outperform the market sufficiently to make up for the lost return represented by their fees.

You can beat the market because you can be more informed, more adventurous and pay less in fees. This book will not guarantee that you will succeed, but should help the process. Good luck.

Robert Leach

PART

II

The 10 tests that a set of accounts must pass

1.   Is the company growing?

2.   Are costs under control?

3.   Does it make a profit?

4.   How much cash does it have?

5.   Is its market value supported by assets?

6.   Is it using debt wisely?

7.   Are there any hidden nasties?

8.   Is management good enough?

9.   Can I expect a reliable income?

10. Are there any threats to my interests?

Is the company growing?

Relevant to
All fundamental investors

Underlying worry
'Is the company selling a product/service that people want to buy?'

Sources of sales

What does the company do?

This is the first question every investor must ask about a potential investee. You cannot make any sensible investment decision, nor understand the accounts, until you have a clear answer in your mind.

Many times, companies have substantial interests in related businesses. Marks & Spencer does not just sell knickers and marmalade. It has a substantial and growing business in the financial sector. Tesco has an insurance business which frequently comes top in rates for life insurance. Sainsbury's owns a bank.

Suppose you are considering investing in Whitbread, which *The Financial Times* lists under 'leisure and hotels'. Do you know what the company does? Logging on to its website, which has an excellent section for investors, you can see that its main businesses are:

*   Whitbread Hotels (the most rooms for any hotel business);
*   Travel Inn;
*   Pub chains;
*   Beefeater restaurants;
*   Pizza Hut (joint venture);
*   Costa coffee shops;
*   David Lloyd Leisure (sports centres);
*   Britvic (soft drinks).

Immediately you can start to identify possible good investments. Where do you eat? Who owned the hotel you chose for your last holiday? Did you have a good meal at Beefeater or Pizza Hut? What do your friends think of them? Where are Britvic drinks sold?

Sometimes companies have odd combinations of activities. Burndee Investments sells fixed caravans and ladies' tights. Cosalt sells lifejackets, fish nets and school uniforms. Chorion exploited rights in children's books and ran nightclubs, until the latter was demerged into Urbium. Initial Link, the overnight and same-day parcel service, is owned by Rentokil, the pest control company.

Many companies in various sectors own substantial amounts of property, which may not be obvious from your experience as a consumer of their products and services, but which significantly changes their investment profile.

Conversely, some companies may appear to be bigger than they are. Pubs may be branded with the name of a brewer but be owned by a franchisee.

Plain common sense in this area can be valuable. If a company says it is marketing a popular soap, go to the chemist and see how many are being sold. Indeed, see if you find it on sale. Investors can become deluded. During the Wall Street Crash in 1929, many individuals continued to pour money into companies even though they knew they were laying off staff. From its low in 1932, the American stock market did not recover until 1954. In 1991, investors continued to buy shares in Polly Peck without wondering how such spectacular profits were made from tinned pineapple and cardboard boxes.

Above all, do not buy shares just because everyone else is. In 1719 people bought shares in South Sea Company which soared in price from £100 to £1,050 even though it did nothing for eight years. It crashed in 1720. Something similar happened 280 years later with Boo.com (see Part III).

If you want to invest in interesting companies there are still some pioneering innovative ideas. Stanelco is developing a packet of dried soup where the packet dissolves in the water with the soup. Syence Skin Care develops cosmetics acceptable under Islamic law.

Sometimes companies change their scope. Wiggins Group moved from being a property company to an out-of-town airport operator, and changed its name to Planestation. London & Boston Investments has moved from investments to covert surveillance. Companies can move within their sector, such as when Haynes Publishing diversified from motor handbooks to a sex manual. At least they both involve stripping down to fit bodywork together.

And sometimes it is difficult to know in what you are investing. In the early 2000s, troubled engineering company Invensys was forced to sell so many businesses to reduce its debt, that it was difficult for investors to know what would be left.

How do I start choosing companies?

The London Stock Exchange currently lists 1,770 UK companies and 430 overseas companies. These are the biggest of the 12,400 public companies in the

UK (in March 2002) which in turn were the biggest of the 1,491,500 registered companies. You need a way to narrow the field quickly.

Only buy shares in companies you understand. If you are an engineer or chemist consider engineering companies or chemical companies. Here is a quote about future prospects from the 2002 accounts of Shire Pharmaceuticals:

ADDERALL XR is now well established as a leading once-daily ADHD treatment and, in its first year of launch, has become the preferred choice of top-prescribing physicians for the patients in the US. In conjunction with continued growth of our key revenue streams, including the relaunch of CARBATROL, and three pending product registrations (ADDERALL XR – adults in the US, FOSRENOL (lanthanum carbonate) – US/EU, XAGRID – EU), our sales and marketing organisation is poised to continue driving the performance of Shire's revenues.

If you have a clue what this means, you can make a judgment about whether it is worth investing in it. Exactly how you apply your knowledge to different types of business is explained in Part III.

In 18th century London it was possible to buy shares in companies for transmuting animals, curing lunatics, melting sawdust, perpetual motion machines and "a company for carrying on an undertaking of great advantage, but nobody to know what it is". The last company raised £2,000 in five hours selling shares at £2. The law on company prospectuses is tighter now.

Another good starting point is to look at what is selling in supermarkets, what products your family and friends enthuse about, what comments friends make about the companies they work for, and which company is building new premises. You already know these companies have the potential for success. Some analysis on their accounts will assist you in deciding whether to invest. Always start by asking "what does the company do?". If it sells widgets, find out what a widget is.

If the company serves consumers, you can try dealing with the company. Do you get good service when you call, or do you get a machine asking you to press buttons on the telephone before a voice tells you that your call is important, so someone will speak to you in 12 minutes? Companies tend to treat customers and investors the same way. Consider this quote from *Investors Chronicle* of 13 February 2004, "With Greene King pubs, punters always know they can expect honest fare in traditional surroundings. And the offering to investors is similarly solid and dependable."

Some companies you may reject on ethical grounds. Between 10% and 25% of the market is usually excluded by ethical investors, depending on their exact criteria.

Look at the website. It should promote both the company's products or services *and* have investor information readily available.

Then obtain the annual report; Appendix 1 explains how. First impressions are usually right. The report is, literally, selling the company. A good example is Reckitt Benckiser accounts for 2000. The cover is attractive (particularly as the picture is just a pile of plastic bottle tops) with the punchy slogan "over 9 million products sold every day". The inside cover shows these products: Dettol, Lysol, Vanish, Resolve, Calgon, Finish, Electrasol, Veet etc. The opposite page gives financial highlights: net revenue, operating profit, profit before tax, profit after tax, diluted earnings per share, and dividend per share.

This is a good combination of sales and finance, which drive every successful business. You should be wary of companies which talk only of their products or only of finance. And do not touch companies which have more than three photographs of any director. The opening pages should explain what the company is about. The official narrative reports usually follow next, before the accounts. This in itself does not mean that Reckitt Benckiser is a good share to buy, but it does mean that you should seriously consider the company.

Only when you have filtered down the companies are you ready to start analysing the accounts. You will find that Reckitt Benckiser has improved operating profit to 18.3%, but this is still behind competitors Colgate Palmolive at 21.9% and Proctor & Gamble at 20%, but Reckitt has set itself a growth target of 5% a year. These are the key questions for a household products company, but we are racing ahead.

How does the company compare?

Each business sector has its own particular financial profile, as explained in Part III.

The problems of intra-sector comparison can be avoided by comparing companies with their peers in the same sector. For example, BAE Systems is the fourth largest defence contractor in the world, but from 1999 to 2004 it underperformed the market by 53%. The company can get the orders but cannot get profits from them. If that continues, there may be pressure for management change.

This does not make BAE a poor investment, but it means that you would have to form the opinion that the company will improve more than the market thinks it will.

What are the company's different sales divisions?

It should be possible from the report to the accounts to determine the various activities of the company.

Few companies venture into a completely new area. One rare exception was when Sketchley diversified from dry cleaning into maintaining telegraph poles. Otherwise, the divisions are usually related in that one division will not only generate its own profit but contribute to the profits of other divisions. A common example is a store offering financial products which not only make their own profit, but also encourage customers to buy the store's products.

An investor should look for this synergy between divisions.

In the 1970s, diversification was a fashion among businesses. There was a saying "if you want a pint of milk, buy a cow", and so companies sought to replace contractors with in-house facilities. Instead of hiring cleaners, the company would set up a cleaning company to clean its own premises and offer the service to other companies. In general, this amount of diversification proved too much for a single management. The more obscure and small bits typically were poorly managed and of uneconomical scale. So the fashion swung back to 'zero-basing', which means sticking to what the company knows. You should consider how far the company has diversified and how far it is zero-based.

Which parts of the business are growing and which are contracting?

What is segmental reporting?

Companies are required to provide segmental reporting under statement of standard accounting practice SSAP 25, issued in June 1990.

The different parts of a business for which segmental reporting is appropriate are determined either as a geographical area or according to the class of business. So a company operating in the US and UK may provide segmental reports for each country. A company selling products and financial services may provide segmental reports for each activity.

For most companies, it is possible to analyse trading activities into an almost infinite number of segments. The standard therefore restricts disclosure to reportable segments. The basic requirement of a reportable segment is that it:

- differs significantly from other sectors in terms of return, risk, growth or development potential for investors;
- represents at least 10% of the turnover, profits or assets of the company;
- is distinguished from other segments by geographical area or class of business.

For each segment, the accounts must disclose:

- turnover;
- 'result' (broadly net profit before interest and tax);
- costs (with an appropriate apportionment of common costs);
- net assets; and
- associated undertakings.

Where a company provides segmental reporting it must analyse its whole business into segments. So the totals for each segment must equal the total shown in the consolidated accounts.

Segmental reporting should be seen as an adjunct to the directors' report. This report will talk of growth and decline in its various markets. Look to see if the directors regard the market as sufficiently discrete to justify a segmental report. Some simple analysis, such as comparing "results" with previous years will see how credible is the directors' view.

Insurance company Prudential is an example where segmental reporting is useful. Its 2003 accounts show that sales rose by 8% in Asia but fell by 30% in the USA.

What are its discontinued operations and why were they discontinued?

Discontinued operations must be accounted for separately in the profit and loss account. However the law does not state that details must be given of the discontinued operations.

Where this entry appears in the profit and loss account, and is for a significant amount, you should look elsewhere in the accounts to identify which operations have been discontinued, and why.

You should consider the information offered critically. Is this simply an activity which has come to the end of its natural life, or is better supplied in another way? Reports rarely ask why, if it is now considered necessary to "concentrate on core activities" (a common excuse), did they buy the business in the first place.

One answer is that a company only wanted part of the business. When Racal bought Decca, it wanted the navigation side. The record business was sold.

Are sales geographically spread?

In business, geography is considered at two main levels. The internal level looks at how well the business supplies the home market. The external level looks at its exports.

Geographical spread may be indicated by segmental reporting, as explained above. However a more subtle indication may be given by looking at the group structure and seeing what companies there are for specific countries. Most businesses find it convenient to set up a subsidiary company in each territory where they operate. It can be revealing to see what is said about them in the directors' report and other text.

Sometimes companies deliberately withhold this information. Calibration company Renishaw keeps quiet about what it sells, where and when, to keep competitors in the dark. However half-yearly accounts show that the company makes most of its profits in the second half of the year.

Is there a seasonal sales pattern?

Businesses are more seasonal than is generally realised. For example, about one third of retail jewellery is sold in the four weeks before Christmas.

For the long term, you need to consider what the company is doing about seasonality. Is it diversifying into off-season activities? A classic example was Wall's which sold ice cream in summer and hot dogs in winter.

Seasonality also needs to be considered in terms of when the year-end is, as it impacts on the balance sheet. If a company prepares its balance sheet towards the end of its busy season, it will have plenty of cash and a healthier looking balance sheet which may not properly represent its general working condition.

A good indication of seasonality comes from looking at 'cash' in current assets on the balance sheet, and 'interest paid' in the profit and loss account. Some businesses prepare their balance sheet just after their main season when they have the most cash. There are good practical reasons why a company wants to prepare its financial statements promptly after its busiest season, so that in itself should not be regarded as suspicious. However it can hide the fact that the company has lean months. A significant figure for interest paid when a company shows plenty of cash is a good indication of lean seasons. You then need to consider whether the company has sufficient resources to continue through the next lean season.

Seasonality relates to the business, not to the everyday calendar. So clothing wholesalers will be selling summer clothes in winter, and winter clothes in summer. Winter clothes are more expensive and therefore generate more revenue.

Business focus

Historically, has it stuck to its knitting?

Any departure from existing products and existing trading methods should be questioned. Developing new products and methods are signs of a healthy company. However what may be thus represented may in truth simply be another desperate ploy to conceal poor trading.

The commonest reason for a big company suffering is that it has lost its way. Over decades the company develops vast management experience in its chosen area and decides that it can conquer the world by moving into other areas. Suddenly it finds that it does not have the management expertise to cope with these new areas. Clark's, the shoe-makers, tried various forms of diversification up to the 1980s. It concluded that it should stick to what it knows best – selling shoes.

The management term for sticking to your knitting is **zero-basing**. Be suspicious of companies which decide they are going into completely new areas to conquer the world.

The lessons from Marconi

Marconi was a cash-rich conglomerate from the well-run GEC whose wide range of electrical products were in every home. Chairman Lord Simpson boasted that he was spending the cash pile carefully accumulated over 30 years as fast as he could. He attempted to move into global telecommunications. Marconi's annual report for 2000 said "The internet boom is a high-tech gold rush, a latter day Klondike of bits and bandwidth. In that earlier gold rush, some prospectors struck it rich. Some went broke. But the people who consistently profited were the ones who supplied the prospectors with the picks, shovels and maps. That is Marconi's starting position."

At first, things went well. Marconi won contracts in the UK, Australia, China, France, Holland and Belgium, in addition to providing internet infrastructure for companies such as Cable & Wireless, UUNET Technologies, Level 3 Communications, MCI/WorldCom and Qwest. The share price rose on Klondike excitement.

In 2001, the dotcom bubble suddenly burst. On 17 May 2001 Marconi issued good results, albeit with qualifications about "scarcity of capital to finance network development" and "slowdown in orders for communications equipment across the whole industry". Later that year, the company wrote down the value of its acquired companies by £3.5 billion, and Simpson went (with a big pay-off).

The share price crashed on 4 July 2001, 48 days later, falling a record 54% in one day, one tenth of all its shares changed hands, and the company was valued at one tenth of its value of ten months earlier.

A Marconi share was worth £8.85 on 16 May 2000, and was expected to double. Three years later that share was worth 0.8p. A subsequent series of share consolidations means that 1 Marconi share in 2004 represents 3,000 shares of 2000. Marconi shares have been worth up to £6 during 2003, but this is the equivalent of 0.2p for a 2000 share. A Marconi investor from 2000 has lost 99.98% of his investment.

What is the company's policy on acquisitions and disposals?

Companies grow in two ways: organically and acquisitively. Organic growth is when a company grows from within by reinvesting some of its profits. Acquisitive growth is when it grows by acquiring new businesses.

Both forms of growth can be healthy, but acquisitive growth is more risky. Marconi was a healthy trading company with a pile of cash. It was brought to the brink of bankruptcy by acquiring businesses at inflated prices which added little to the value of the business.

A healthy policy is to acquire businesses which fit into the existing structure, such as complementing the existing product range and buying out competitors.

All acquisitions carry a price. The old shareholders must be paid off. If the acquiring company does not use cash, it must either borrow money or issue new shares. If it borrows money, it must generate sufficient profit to repay the loan plus earn a similar profit to the existing business. If it issues shares, your holding is diluted. This is only in your interest if the new business is more profitable than the old one.

In other words, acquisitive growth is only in your interests if the acquisition is already *more* profitable than the existing business, or can easily be made so.

What do the Chairman and the Directors say about the future direction of the company?

They will say that the future is rosy. The chairman's or directors' report sometimes say the past year has been bad. ICI chief executive John McAdam described the profit performance as "unsatisfactory", but that was his first year. But the directors report which *predicts* a disastrous year has probably yet to be written.

In January 2002, when Marconi shares had lost 97% of their peak value and were fast sinking into oblivion, chief executive Mike Parton wrote, "the third quarter outcome shows good progress towards our debt and cost reduction targets against the background of a difficult market. It is with regret that we have announced the need for further cost and job reductions, but we are all the more determined not to be dependent on improvement in the market to return the group to profitability."

Your function as an investor is to test the inevitable optimism for credibility. You do this by asking "why?"

If the company has had "a difficult year" in "adverse trading conditions", why will next year be any better?

Directors usually blame bad results on difficult trading conditions, even though there has yet to be a single year which has not been good for some business. It is a rarity, but a report which admits that the company made mistakes probably indicates a better prospect than one which blames trading conditions. A company which admits mistakes will certainly learn from them and seek to prevent further mistakes, which makes it a better investment than one which blames the weather.

The future sales outlook

Is the company's sales growth sustainable?

A company is like a baby; a steady growth is healthy, but rapid growth or no growth is unhealthy. Companies and unit trusts which top the charts one year are often at the bottom next year. Shooting stars quickly look like black holes. Some of the most successful investors have found steady growth companies and simply stuck with them.

A simple example of growth study is Debt Free Direct, a company which specialises in helping people who are seriously in debt. It screens out the irresponsibles in favour of the unfortunates. The company secures 95% of its income from IVAs (Individual Voluntary Agreements) for which it receives a sign-up fee of around £2,700 each plus £75 a month for the lifetime of the IVA, usually five years. Thus the company ended 2003 knowing exactly where £4m future revenue was coming from. Its longer-term future depends on how far the UK consumer remains profligate.

One possible measure is to compare market share with stock share. Stock share is the percentage of the sector's market capitalisation represented by the company's market capitalisation. If market share is significantly bigger than stock share, this represents a growing company. For example Northern Rock secured 8.2% of mortgage lending in the year to 2003, though it represents only 4.8% of stock share.

What do the Chairman and Directors say about the past year and the future?

There are certain expressions to look out for in reports:

in accordance with our expectations

This means that the company has performed badly. If it had performed well, the directors would be bragging about it. Instead, a bad performance is excused by saying that they expected it to be bad for some reason, and the management really is competent because it could see this coming. Don't believe it.

in difficult market conditions

A company which is properly diversified should be able to deal with all market conditions. Alternatively, a company should be able to ensure that seasonal sales are sufficient for the whole year.

cost reductions

The question to ask here is "if a cost can be cut now, why was it not cut sooner?" At best, this is a belated admission that the company has been overspending.

More likely, it is recognition of the desperate situation of the company. The cuts are likely to go beyond fat, and to start cutting into the essential organs of the body. This means reduced sales and reduced capacity for improvement.

In most businesses, particularly service companies, the main cost is staff. So significant cost reductions can only be achieved by losing staff. This means people needing a job, possibly with a grudge, ready to be snapped up by competitors or to band together and form a new competitor with all their inside knowledge.

Prudent control of overheads is an essential element of financial management. However the annual report does not boast about saving £5,000 a year by buying envelopes more cheaply. If cost reductions make it to the annual report, they are having a fire sale.

consolidating our activities

This is the income equivalent to cost reductions. And the question to ask is similar: "If the products are not worth selling now, why were they considered worth selling in the first place?" At best, it means that the company has over-diversified.

Is their view of the past year consistent with the accounts?

Look at the profit and loss account. If it shows a loss, question any ebullient optimism in the chairman's report.

There is an exception, for start-up companies which are still on 'cash burn' (see page 83). There you should look for a reducing loss.

Do they say anything about the current and future competitive environment?

Competition does not kill a healthy business. However competition is wider than just simply other suppliers of the same product.

A food shop is not just competing with other food shops, but with restaurants and suppliers of prepared meals. They compete with internet suppliers, wholesalers and supermarkets.

Do they say anything about external threats?

The absence of any comment about external threats means either that the company does not have any, or that it is too daft to know what they are.

You should form your own view on the external threats, and consider which applies. Some comments on the subject are included in Section 2.10.

Are costs under control?

Relevant to
All fundamental investors

Underlying worry
'Even if its sales are growing, has it got the other half of the equation right?'

Comparison to sales

Are Cost of Sales growing or contracting as a % of Sales, and why?

Formula: Turnover less Cost of sales = Gross profit
                 Gross profit less Overheads = Net profit

Formula: **Percentage Cost of sales = Cost of sales ÷ Turnover**

There are three elements to making a profit:

> turnover, *less*
> costs, *less*
> overheads.

The shareholder is primarily concerned that the first is as big as possible, and the second two as small as possible. This question looks at the second of the three.

This is usually the easiest of the three to control. 'Cost of sales' is an accounting term which refers to the direct costs of making the items which contribute to turnover. It is traditionally divided between materials and labour.

Any expenditure which is not a cost of sale is an expense. The distinction is not always as clear cut as may seem. For example, electricity will usually be part of a cost, but may not always be so attributed. Some marginal services such as packing and inspection are sometimes included. Few items of expenditure can wholly be attributed either as a cost or an overhead, as each item usually includes an element of each. Supervision and storage are generally regarded as overheads, yet there will come a time when additional production requires additional overheads, which then take on the nature of a cost.

The punchline to all this is that there is no clear distinction between costs and overheads, so you should not get too concerned about small differences.

A high cost base can create a gearing effect in the sensitivity between turnover and profit. (Gearing is explained in detail in Section 2.6.) Consider two companies in the same sector with a turnover of £10 million but cost bases of £9 million and £5 million. They each manage to increase turnover by 10% on the same cost base.

	High cost base	Low cost base
Turnover	£10 million	£10 million
Cost base	£9 million	£5 million
Profit	£1 million	£5 million
Turnover + 10%	£11 million	£11 million
Cost base	£9 million	£5 million
Profit	£2 million	£6 million
Increase in profit	+100%	+20%

The two obvious points to make are, firstly, that gearing works both ways; a reduction in turnover will have a similarly greater effect on the high cost base company. Second, the low cost base is and remains the more profitable company. For the investor, the greater profitability of the second company will already have been factored into the share price. If you believe a high cost base company, such as supermarket Somerfield, is likely to increase turnover as well as low cost base Tesco does (and we make no comment), Somerfield will give you the greater earnings growth.

Are items correctly defined?

Sometimes companies have been imaginative in what they have regarded as turnover or operating profits. Until 2002, support services company Interserve treated the sale of properties as operating profit.

Are Distribution Costs and Administrative Expenses growing or contracting as a % of Sales, and why?

A company in decline will often have expenses growing faster than profit or turnover. To find out, you should look for 'net operating costs' or whatever figure appears between turnover and operating profit. You can compare this figure with that for the previous year.

The main component parts of net operating costs will be found in the notes to the accounts. You simply divide the figure for one year by the same figure for the previous year. These figures are compared with figures for turnover.

Be circumspect on what conclusions you draw from the results. There are often different reasons why what appears to be bad news could have a better explanation.

When you have drawn some conclusions from the accounts, see what the directors' report, chief executive's report and other text says. Use this to interpret your conclusions. Then look for press comment to see how far they agree with you.

It is important to follow this order, otherwise the comment or text will influence the initial conclusions you draw from your reading of accounts. An example of the process is given below from a set of accounts selected at random.

Example: Scottish & Newcastle plc

For example, from Scottish & Newcastle's accounts for 2003, the net operating costs are £4,149.9 million against £3,659.8 million in 2002. This represents a 13.4% increase, which looks quite large. Operating profit was £385.3 million against £458.4 million, a decrease of 15.9%.

This is beginning to look serious – a 13.4% increase in costs against a 15.9% drop in operating profit. So what is causing the problem? Turnover is £4,535.2 million against £4,118.2 million, an increase of 10.1%, which is healthy except that expenses grew faster. Including joint ventures, turnover grew by an even healthier 18.7%.

Against net operating costs, the column marked 'notes' says 4, so we look at 4 for a breakdown of these costs. Raw materials have increased by just 2.7% from £1,145.4 million to £1,175.9 million. This would indicate that the company's procurement policy is very good. Staff costs rose by 9.6% which, again, is less than turnover, indicating a good employment policy.

Custom and excise duties have increased by 32.9% from £813.9 million to £1,082.2 million. This makes up about half the increase in operating costs. This is not explained anywhere. Although stocks of finished goods are up, the amount is nothing like enough to explain the increase.

So some of the additional costs have been generated by increasing stocks. However the large increase is not obvious from the accounts. Perhaps the operating and financial review will help. This notes the 18.7% increase in turnover and boasts that operating profit rose 22.1% from £538.9 million to £657.9 million. However neither of these figures appears in the profit and loss account, and there is no obvious way of seeing where they came from. Buried in paragraph 3 is the telling comment that "if we exclude acquisitions and disposals, then turnover would have grown 2.3% and operating profit would have grown 0.9%". Why? "Additional costs arising from the implementation of the UK supply chain reorganisation which was slower and more expensive than previously anticipated [sic]".

The picture is emerging from the accounts of a business not really growing and with a patchy record on controlling costs.

All this was written without checking press comment on the company. In 2004, this refers to a "struggling group" forced to cut costs, and ripe for a takeover.

Extraordinary and exceptional items

How extraordinary are the extraordinary items?

If we could find any, we would tell you. The author has managed to find just one, which is approximately one more than he expected to find. Extraordinary items were in effect outlawed in 1992 when Financial Reporting Standard FRS 3 was introduced.

FRS 3 defines an extraordinary item as "possessing a high degree of abnormality which arises from events or transactions that fall outside the ordinary activities of the reporting entity and which are not expected to recur". FRS 3 later refers to their "extreme rarity". The standard cannot think of a single example. When pressed on the matter in 1992, ASB chairman Sir David Tweedie said that "Martians walking through the streets" was extraordinary.

Before 1992, extraordinary items were quite common and appealing, as they were excluded from reportable profit. So if a business made a net loss of £100,000 but could find a transaction which made £150,000 of extraordinary loss, it could add that to the reportable net loss, showing a net profit of £50,000, and subtract the extraordinary loss from that figure. Many extraordinary losses were just extra ordinary losses.

Extraordinary items are still encountered in accounts prepared under non-UK accounting standards, though even those are abandoning the concept of extraordinary items. The US accounting standards ruled that losses arising from the terrorist attack on 11 September 2001 were *not* extraordinary.

The one extraordinary item found in UK published accounts is in the unaudited accounts for the six months to 31 October 2003 of property company Bolton Group (International) Ltd. The company is suing its former director for his alleged sale at undervalue of the company's main asset, held by a subsidiary, to a company run by the director's personal friend. The extraordinary item is a profit figure of £263,000 "owed to the previous subsidiary companies which is no longer payable". This extraordinary item turns a net loss of £188,000 into a net profit of £75,000.

It would seem that this is a correct classification. A director flogging off the company's assets cheap is highly abnormal. An illegal activity is clearly outside the scope of normal trading activities, and clearly cannot recur.

If you do encounter an extraordinary item, read the story.

How exceptional are the exceptional items?

They are not. As far as the investor is concerned, there is no such thing as an exceptional item. It is just another expense that the business has incurred, another reduction in the profit which funds your dividends and the company's future growth.

FRS 3 defines an exceptional item as "material items which derive from events or transactions that fall within the ordinary activities of the reporting entity and which individually or, if of a similar type, in aggregate, need to be disclosed by virtue of their size or incidence if the financial statements are to give a true and fair view".

In practice, an exceptional item is usually a loss, though it is possible for it to be a profit.

The accounting requirement for an exceptional item is that it is shown separately on the face of the profit and loss account. It is still included in the same totals and sub-totals, so the existence of exceptional items does not affect any of the ratios in this book.

The profit and loss account for Wilshaw plc to 31 March 2002 shows:

	£'000
gross profit	4,885
other operating expenses	(4,435)
continuing operations before exceptional items	767
exceptional operating expenses	(268)
continuing operations after exceptional items	499
discontinued operations	(49)
profit on ordinary activities before interest	450

The company has made a profit before interest of £450,000. However the exceptional item highlights that there were £268,000 worth of exceptional operating expenses, and a £49,000 loss on discontinued operations. Without these items, the company would have made £767,000 operating profit, which is 70% more. So these items are significant to understanding the accounts.

The details are found in the notes to the accounts, where we find that the £268,000 relates to "compensation payments and other costs associated with the reduction in the head office function". In the previous year £500,000 was paid for the same exceptional item. The financial review states that this arose from the sale of two businesses, which generated an exceptional profit of disposal proceeds.

Wilshaw has honestly accounted for and explained what has happened. Showing the exceptional item separately allows you to see how much profit the company has made this year (including the exceptional item) and how much profit the normal trading activities of the company are (excluding the exceptional item).

A disposal of a business is probably the only properly genuine exceptional item.

Other costs commonly described as exceptional are reorganisation costs and writing off goodwill. In truth, the former means that the company employed too many people or was badly run in the first place. The second means that the company paid too much for an acquisition. Far from being something to ignore in the current accounts, these "exceptional items" represent too much profit in previous years' accounts.

Some companies have acquired a reputation for their fondness for exceptional items.

Accounting standards require that costs associated with the millennium bug and introduction of the euro should be treated as exceptional items, though it is difficult to see what is exceptional about having a computer and accounting system which can cope.

Depreciation

What is the company's depreciation policy, and what is its significance?

The depreciation policy is stated in the notes to the accounts. It usually appears in note 1 'principal accounting policies', but may appear against a note number for depreciation in either the balance sheet or profit and loss account.

A good example of a depreciation policy is given in Pharmagene plc accounts for 2002:

> The cost of tangible fixed assets is their purchase cost, together with any incidental costs of acquisition.
>
> Depreciation is calculated so as to write off the cost of tangible fixed assets on a straight-line basis over the expected useful economic life of the assets concerned. The principal annual rates used for this purpose are:
>
> | | |
> |---|---|
> | Fixtures and fittings: | 5-10 years |
> | Computer and office equipment: | 3-5 years |
> | Laboratory equipment: | 5-10 years |
> | Motor vehicles: | 3 years |
>
> Laboratory equipment purchased solely for a particular project is depreciated over the life of that project. Leasehold improvements are depreciated over the lease term concerned.

The two pieces of information needed for any depreciation policy on any type of fixed asset are:

1. what is the rate of depreciation; *and*
2. how is the depreciation calculated.

Pharmagene shows its rate of depreciation as a number of years over which the assets are written off. If anything, these periods are on the short side. Fixtures and fittings can be written off over periods of up to 20 years. Desks, carpets and curtains can easily last that long. And does it really replace every computer, fax machine and photocopier every four years on average?

Motor cars have an average life of eight years, though four years is widely used for depreciation (in line with the Inland Revenue capital allowance) as companies tend to keep cars for shorter periods than individuals. Commercial vehicles have a longer life with a range of about a year for a demolition truck to indefinite for a funeral hearse.

The shorter the period for depreciation, the more depreciation is charged each year, and the lower are the profits. Over time, this will even out as any overstated depreciation on new assets is balanced by understated depreciation (or even zero appreciation) on old assets still in use.

Understated depreciation policies, as for Pharmagene, are an indicator that the accounts have been prepared prudently.

The rate of depreciation is described as either a period or a percentage. So the same policy could be described as 'five years' or '20%'.

The method of depreciation should also be stated. By far the commonest is the 'straight line method'. This simply charges the same amount of depreciation each year until the asset has been written down to zero. The straight line method is so called because if you plotted a graph of the asset's value (y-axis) against years (x-axis) it would be a straight line looking like this:

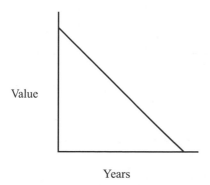

Value

Years

However there are several other methods. The next commonest is the reducing balance method. This applies the same percentage each year, but to the balance after the previous year. This is the method used for calculating some capital allowances for tax purposes. Each year a smaller amount is deducted, so that the asset is never written down to zero while still in use. The percentage rate for a reducing balance method must be higher than for the straight line method.

For example, a fixed asset costs £10,000. Company A depreciates it at 20% a year on the straight line basis. Company B depreciates it at 30% on the reducing balance basis.

	Company A	Company B
Depreciation policy	20% straight line	30% reducing balance
Acquisition cost	£10,000	£10,000
Year 1 depreciation net book value	£2,000 £8,000	£3,000 £7,000
Year 2 depreciation net book value	£2,000 £6,000	£2,100 £4,900
Year 3 depreciation net book value	£2,000 £4,000	£1,470 £3,430
Year 4 depreciation net book value	£2,000 £2,000	£1,029 £2,401
Year 5 depreciation net book value	£2,000 zero	£720 £1,681
Year 6 depreciation net book value	- zero	£504 £1,177
		and so on

In each the figure for 'Year 1 depreciation' (or Year 2 etc) is shown in the profit and loss account, and the 'net book value' shown immediately underneath is included in fixed assets after depreciation in the balance sheet.

The reducing balance method gives higher figures for depreciation and lower asset values in the earlier years, but lower depreciation and higher asset values as the asset gets older.

Other methods of depreciation are sum of the digits, actuarial depreciation, double declining and machine hour. All methods of depreciation seek to spread the cost of a fixed asset over the years of its lifetime. Methods other than straight line are appropriate when an asset does not lose its value evenly over these years. An obvious example is a mine where the material is most easily extracted in the early years. Otherwise there is little real need for depreciation to be calculated other than on a straight line basis. Depreciation is, after all, just an approximation anyway.

The investor should simply ask if the depreciation policy used by a company is credible. Long periods inflate profit (at least in the early years). This can magnify any losses in any later years. Shorter periods understate profit and indicate a responsible attitude to accounting.

Depreciation has no effect at all on the amount of tax paid. When calculating the tax payable, the depreciation must be added back to the fixed asset and a set formula for a capital allowance used as set out in tax law.

Has it recently changed its policy on depreciation?

Any change in a depreciation policy is significant. You must always ask why there has been a change.

There are many proper reasons why depreciation policy changes. For many years, companies depreciated computers over ten or more years, rather than five which is now more realistic.

A shortening of the depreciation period reduces profits; a lengthening of the depreciation period increases profits. However for most businesses, the advantage of doing this lasts only for one year and is largely cancelled out in future years.

Working capital

What is the working capital ratio?

Formulae: Current ratio = Current assets ÷ Current liabilities
Acid test = [Current assets − Stock] ÷ Current liabilities

There are two ratios commonly used for the working capital ratio. The current ratio indicates solvency. The acid test indicates liquidity.

Current assets are traditionally listed according to their liquidity. This means the ease with which the asset can be turned into cash. The most liquid current asset is therefore cash itself. The list, starting with the most liquid, is:

- cash
- prepayments (now usually included with debtors)
- debtors
- stock

The first three are, or will become, cash by the passing of time, whereas stock requires a sale to become cash (usually by becoming part of debtors first).

Current liabilities are now more commonly described as 'creditors falling due within one year'. They include bills awaiting payment by the company, VAT and other taxes which have yet to be paid to the government, wages which have been earned but not yet paid, short-term borrowings from the bank, and any other amount for which the company has incurred a liability which it has not yet paid but must pay within the next year.

Figures for current assets, stock and current liabilities should be readily disclosed on the face of the balance sheet.

The **current ratio** should normally be above 1.0, and preferably much higher. But, as always, it is necessary to consider the ratio in the context of the business and other figures. In general, the more cash-positive a business is, the lower the current ratio can safely be. You should consider the nature of a business, when it pays and receives its cash for a job, and the size of the business, as larger businesses can negotiate better terms for paying and receiving.

At one extreme, a highly cash-positive business is a supermarket. Goods are sold promptly after being bought and paid for in cash at the time. The suppliers are probably paid well after the goods have been sold. The other extreme is a small construction company, which may be paid by its customers months or even years after the materials have been bought. The accounts may explain how the business cashflow works. For example, Electric World sells educational software which is subscription-based, so profits are behind cashflow, exacerbating its losses.

The most cash-positive company of all was Green Shield Stamps which existed in the 1960s. A store bought stamps which it gave to shoppers who stuck them into a book over weeks or months. They then collected books which were redeemed for goods.

The extent to which a business is cash-positive is also relevant when considering debt, as cash-positive businesses can usually reduce debt more quickly. Wincanton had gearing of up to 388% but could generate cash to reduce that quickly.

The **acid test** is more a measure of solvency than liquidity. It is broadly the same measure but excludes stock, which is the least liquid asset. This is a particularly important measure if there is any doubt about the saleability of the product.

At one extreme, oil companies have a readily saleable product, almost as good as cash itself. The same applies to many mining companies; gold is as good as cash (possibly better).

The other extreme is where the product has market vulnerability. This includes most items related to fashion and technology. Fashion here includes not just clothes and pop music, but anything which is celebrity-endorsed. Toys and accessories which are spun off from television programmes remain saleable only while that programme remains in fashion.

These ratios are of most importance when considering small companies in a fiercely competitive market making specialised products.

Salaries

How much are the directors being paid, and how are they being paid? This question is addressed in Section 2.8.

Tax

How much tax has the company paid?

Tax is shown as a separate figure on the profit and loss account towards the bottom.

In the UK, companies pay corporation tax at one of various rates depending on whether they are a big or small company. In this context, 'big' and 'small' refer solely to the size of the profit.

Tax is charged on **adjusted profit**. This is the net profit before tax, as stated in the accounts, which is adjusted according to rules in tax law. The commonest adjustment relates to depreciation of fixed assets. This is not deductible and so much be added back to net profit, increasing the amount of taxable profit. Instead the business may be able to claim a capital allowance for fixed asset expenditure which is deducted from profits. Often the capital allowance is greater than the amount of depreciation it replaces, which means that the taxable profit is less than the actual profit. It also means that in later years, the capital allowance will have reduced the written down value to less than depreciation will have reduced the net book value, meaning that in those later years taxable profit will be greater than actual profit. Where a company routinely replaces fixed assets, as normally happens with vehicles and machinery, this effect will reduce as the capital allowances on new plant will tend to compensate for the lack of capital allowance on older assets.

There are some items of expenditure which a business may properly deduct in its profit and loss account, but which are not tax-deductible. These items are also added back, increasing the taxable profit. Such items include:

*   personal expenses (but not staff expenses) of the owners;
*   general reserves and provisions, such as for doubtful debts;
*   entertainment;
*   payment of other taxes;
*   fines;
*   reimbursement of employees' commuting expenses;
*   losses on non-trading activities;
*   sums recoverable by insurance;
*   contingent liabilities which are not justified by normal accounting; and
*   criminal payments (such as bribes and protection money).

For any company with adjusted profit of at least £1.5 million, the rate of corporation tax is 30%. So it can be illuminating to multiply the net profit before tax by 30% and compare it with the actual tax figure.

If the actual tax figure is *more* than 30% of stated profit, this means that:

- it has incurred many disallowed items; *or*
- it is spending little on new fixed assets.

Or it could be doing both. The former may be detectable by looking at expenses. However, in practice, the ten items of disallowable expenses listed above (and there are a few more) are unlikely to be big enough to make much impact on the profit and loss account. It is more likely to be the latter, which can easily be seen from the balance sheet.

If the actual tax figure is *less* than 30% of stated profits, this means that:

- the company is investing in fixed assets.

There are some other reasons why the tax figures may be different. Sometimes a change in tax law or accounting standards can trigger a change. So can the correction or adjustment of the figure stated for a prior year. However if such a change is significant, this will be indicated in the notes to the accounts. We are looking at what can be detected directly from the figures after considering what we have been explicitly told.

Expanding and healthy companies usually have an actual tax charge below 30% of net profit before tax, but care must be taken in understanding these figures.

Consider the 2001 accounts of Thornton's, the chocolate makers. The net profit before tax is £6.085 million. Thirty percent of this is £1.826 million, but the actual tax shown is £1.465 million, which appears to be less, and healthy.

But note 11 to the accounts explains that the tax for the current year is £1.909 million, which is more than 30%. This figure has been reduced by £0.444 million adjustment in respect of a previous tax year. Therefore the current year's tax is more than 30% which would indicate a reduction in fixed assets. Sure enough, the balance sheet shows a reduction in fixed assets from £104 million to £96 million.

This is not devastating news, but it indicates a company which is struggling a bit, as clearly indicated in the various written reports before the accounts.

Sometimes a company may report tax as an *addition* to profit rather than as a normal deduction. Consider the 2001 accounts of specialist paper maker James Cropper plc. The accounts show a net loss on ordinary activities of £779,000. The tax figure underneath shows tax as £121,000 which *reduces* the loss after tax to £658,000. You should always observe whether the figures have brackets round them; brackets indicate a reduction in profit. Note 9 to the accounts explains that it arises from a £318,000 tax rebate from the previous year, which made a profit, from which about £200,000 must be subtracted in respect of a change in calculating deferred tax from adopting a new accounting standard.

How much deferred tax is there, and what does this indicate?

Deferred tax is the difference between:

- the tax ultimately payable on the profits earned in the year; and
- the actual amount of tax payable in the year.

Deferred tax is a long-term creditor in that it represents money payable to the Inland Revenue more than one year after the balance sheet date.

The previous question explained that actual profit and taxable profit may differ for two reasons:

- permanent differences, such as the profit and loss account including non-tax-deductible items; and

- timing differences, such as the difference between capital allowances and depreciation.

Deferred tax is only concerned with timing differences. The permanent differences do not affect the amount of tax payable in any year. If the company has paid £100,000 in fines, this is not allowable for tax in the current year, nor in any future year. It does not create any future tax liability; a non-tax-deductible expense simply increases the current tax liability.

Timing differences now relate almost entirely to the difference between depreciation and capital allowances. There are over 14 different capital allowances, some with special provisions for small businesses or in other special circumstances. Sometimes the capital allowance can be 100%, which means that the whole cost may be deducted against taxable profit in the year of acquisition (as applies to research & development, and to buildings in enterprise zones). Sometimes there is a first year allowance which allows the business to deduct a larger amount from its taxable profits in the year of acquisition. The government has extensively used the capital allowance provisions to promote business investment in particular areas it wishes to promote, such as encouraging expenditure on information technology and relocation to Northern Ireland.

If the capital allowance in one year is more than the equivalent depreciation, the company has in effect saved some tax that year, though it will have to pay that tax in a future year. Deferred tax is simply the amount of tax on that saving.

The two commonest rates of capital allowance are:

- 25% reducing balance method, on plant and machinery; and
- 4% straight line method, on industrial buildings.

There are many other rates of capital allowance, including for some assets which come within the scope of those mentioned above.

Suppose a company depreciates £100,000 worth of plant on the straight line basis over five years. Tax law says that the maximum capital allowance is 25% on the reducing balance basis. The difference between depreciation and capital allowance can be shown below:

Year	Capital allowance	Depreciation	Difference	Cumulative difference
1	£25,000	£20,000	£5,000	£5,000
2	£18,750	£20,000	(£1,250)	£3,750
3	£14,062	£20,000	(£5,938)	(£2,188)
4	£10,547	£20,000	(£9,453)	(£11,641)
5	£7,910	£20,000	(£12,090)	(£23,731)
6	£5,932	nil	£5,932	(£17,799)
7	£4,449	nil	£4,449	(£13,350)
8	£3,338	nil	£3,338	(£10,012)
9	£2,503	nil	£2,503	(£7,509)
10 onwards	£7,509	nil	£7,509	nil

Look at the column marked 'Difference'. It shows how much the capital allowance has exceeded the charge for depreciation in that year. If the figure is in brackets, it shows how much the capital allowance is less than the depreciation charge. For this typical profile, you note that there are three stages:

- the first year when capital allowance exceeds depreciation;
- the second stage when capital allowance is less than depreciation; and
- the final stage when depreciation has finished but capital allowances continue.

The effect in year 1 is known as **accelerated capital allowance**. The effect in years 2 onwards is known as reversing deferred taxation.

If the asset was thrown away in year 10, the whole balance of £7,509 would be allowed in year 10 as a balancing allowance. If the asset continued in use after year 10, it would continue generating capital allowances, each of them three-quarters the size of that for the previous year until the asset was disposed of or the written down value went below £1 (which would take about 40 years).

Over the whole lifetime of the asset, the amounts allowed for capital allowance and depreciation are exactly the same, namely the £100,000 acquisition cost of the fixed asset. The differences relate solely to how this £100,000 is apportioned to the years in which this fixed asset was owned.

The figure for deferred tax is, broadly, the figure indicated as 'Difference' in the above column multiplied by 30%. So the deferred tax arising from this asset in year 1 is £1,500. This is because the capital allowance means that the taxable profit for that year may be reduced by £25,000 whereas the actual profit stated in the accounts is reduced by only £20,000. The £1,500 represents the 30% tax on the profit made in year 1 but where the tax is payable in a future year.

In year 2, the deferred tax is 30% of £1,250, which equals £375, but this time the deferred tax is an addition to the tax charge. This is because the taxable profit for year 2 is £1,250 less than the actual profit (subject to any other adjustments).

Depreciation policy affects the amount of deferred tax, but does not affect the amount of taxation.

Suppose in our example, the company decided to depreciate the asset over ten years, which is how long the asset has actually lasted in our example. The annual depreciation charge would be £10,000, so it would not be until year 5 that the capital allowance was less than the depreciation charge.

Suppose the asset was depreciated over three years. The annual depreciation charge would be £33,333, so there would be no first stage when capital allowance exceeded depreciation, and the third stage would start in year 4.

In some cases, the asset may have attracted a 100% capital allowance in year 1, meaning that there was no capital allowance from year 2 onwards. This would attract a massive liability for deferred tax in year 1, which would gradually reduce from year 2 onwards.

So deferred tax represents the value by which depreciation so far exceeds capital allowances. For Thornton's in 2001, the deferred tax is a net figure of £157,000. If we divide this by 0.3 (representing 30% tax), this indicates £523,000 worth of fixed assets which have been given capital allowances but which have yet to be depreciated in the accounts.

Unfortunately life is a bit more complicated than this. Deferred tax can change because of a change in tax law, tax rates or accounting standards. This is exactly what happened in 2001 when Financial Reporting Standard FRS 19 on deferred tax replaced statement of standard accounting practice SSAP 15.

In practice, deferred tax tends to cancel itself out when companies replace assets. Using the example above, assets acquired from year 2 onwards will create a deferred tax liability which starts to reverse from year 3. Thus in any year there will be new acquisitions creating a deferred tax liability and older assets reversing it.

SSAP 15 allowed companies to reduce the amount of deferred tax shown in the accounts to the amount of tax it expected eventually to pay Inland Revenue. So the effect of future acquisitions in reversing the charge for deferred tax could be used to anticipate profits. FRS 19 takes a much less compromising line and requires the whole deferred tax to be shown in the accounts without any allowance for the rolling effect described above. Many companies therefore suffered a significant increase in deferred tax in their 2001 accounts. This is nothing to worry about, though the amount of the increase itself is an indication of how far the directors intended to replace assets.

As deferred tax is added to the tax charge in the company's accounts, it does not affect the figures for net profit, retained profit or earnings per share.

To the investor, deferred tax can be significant in that:

* a charge for deferred tax which is large relative to working capital could indicate a possible problem when the tax becomes payable;
* the size of the deferred tax indicates how far the directors have been prudent in their depreciation policy; and
* a negative deferred tax could indicate that the company is scaling back on replacing fixed assets.

Remember that deferred tax reflects differences between depreciation policy and tax policy, so that points 2 and 3 above may not apply when the company has benefited from a particularly generous capital allowance policy. This should be stated clearly in the notes to the accounts.

Deferred tax as an asset

Deferred tax can be an asset rather than a liability. This commonly arises when a company has incurred losses which can be offset against future profits if it ever earns any. This is not indicated on the face of the accounts, but in a note.

Such notes are commonly found in young companies which have yet to earn profits. An example of such a statement appears in the 2002 accounts of Pursuit Dynamics plc:

> The Group has an unrecognised deferred tax asset totalling £760,000 made up of losses and advance capital allowances of £1,231,000 (asset) and £471,000 (liability), respectively (2001: £400,000). This potential asset has not been recognised due to uncertainty as to when it will be recoverable.

This means that the Group can offset at least £760,000 of its tax liability when it starts to make profits and pay tax. This is a hidden asset.

However, this example also illustrates the fundamental principle that all the ratios and other methods in this book are intended to provide information which must be considered with other information. For Pursuit Dynamics, your investment decision should be based simply on whether you believe the company will be successful in producing and marketing its revolutionary steam pump engine. If it is, your investment could multiply. If it fails, your investment could fall to zero. In such a context, the existence of such hidden assets as deferred tax (and research & development, see next section) is unlikely to affect your decision.

Research & development

How much has been spent on research & development?

Larger companies must disclose how much they have spent on research & development. Smaller companies need not disclose how much they have spent, but may choose to do so. Research & development is only relevant for companies in certain fields, such as technology and pharmaceuticals.

The accounting treatment for research & development is set out in statement of standard accounting practice SSAP 13, which was issued in 1977 and has been amended only once (in 1989) since.

SSAP 13 distinguishes research & development into three elements:

- pure research – such as mixing chemicals together to see what happens;
- applied research – finding two that go bang, and trying to make the bang bigger;
- development – a project to produce bird scarers from the two chemicals that make the biggest bang.

The first two must be written off as expenses in the profit and loss account in the year that the work was undertaken. The development cost *may* be capitalised if certain strict conditions are met.

Capitalisation means that the company does not regard the expenditure on development costs as gone for ever, but sees them as a fixed asset of know-how which can be used to develop a profit-earning product. This was the very issue which prompted accounting standards to be issued in the first place when Rolls-Royce unexpectedly went bust in 1971 because it capitalised research expenditure. The sad story is told in Part IV on page 185.

These days, the concern to investors is not likely to be whether capitalised development costs represent a real asset but the opposite – how far written off research & development should be regarded as an asset.

For example, Oxford Glycosciences plc accounts for 2000 show a net loss of £16,814,000 before taxation. However the notes to the accounts say that it spent £22,233,000 on research & development, which was quite properly written off in the profit and loss account. Indeed research & development represents 77% of the business's entire operating costs.

Whether that research & development was worth doing is a matter of judgment in how competent you think the management is. But let us assume that the management knows what it is doing. That £22 million has gained knowledge which has the potential to be turned into drugs to relieve human disease, such as

Vevesca to relieve Gaucher's disease. You are unlikely to be able to make much of a judgment on this matter, even with specialist pharmaceutical knowledge. But what matters is that the company has, in effect, got a hidden asset of £22 million (plus several million more from previous years) which could generate future profits in the same way that £22 million worth of buildings and plant could.

You cannot tell whether the research & development will realise profit, but if you have confidence in the company generally, you can regard research & development expenditure as being the equivalent of a fixed asset.

Does it make a profit?

Relevant to
All fundamental investors

Underlying worry
'Its sales may be growing, and its costs may be under control, but is the industry so competitive that no-one can make a profit?'

Profit margins

What are the gross and net profit margins?

Formulae: Gross margin = Gross profit ÷ Sales
            Net margin = Net profit ÷ Sales

These formulae provide the most basic analysis of the profit and loss account.

Of these two, the net margin is by far the more important. It is from net profit that dividends are paid. A company is not a good investment if it has a huge mark-up on its sales which it then spends on uncontrolled overheads.

Traditionally the profit and loss account may be summarised as:

Turnover is	Sales
minus	Costs
equals	Gross profit
minus	Expenses
equals	Net profit

Consider a shop. The amount which goes into the till represents sales. The cost of buying the goods (properly known as 'cost of sales') is how much the shop paid to buy the goods from the wholesaler. The expenses are all the overheads, such as electricity, advertising, staff, rates, cleaning, till rolls and the such like.

If the company is a manufacturer, the costs represent the materials and labour to make the goods, usually with a proportion of relevant overheads.

For some businesses, particularly in service sectors such as banks, it is not easy to distinguish between costs and expenses, so the two are often lumped together and only a net profit quoted.

No profit and loss account comprises just five figures. Yet most profit and loss accounts should include those five figures, though probably with longer descriptions. Also, many of the five figures will be broken down into their constituent parts as explained below. Remember that for our ratios, we only need three of the five figures: turnover, gross profit and net profit. We need not be concerned about the figures for costs and expenses, at least not yet.

- *Turnover* is usually analysed between continuing operations and discontinued operations. The figure we want is the total. For these ratios, we are not interested in the breakdown between continuing and discontinued operations.

- *Cost of sales* is usually indicated as a single figure, though sometimes there is a breakdown.

- *Gross profit* should be a highlighted figure, probably printed in bold type.

- *Expenses* will rarely appear as a single figure. There will be general headings such as 'administrative expenses' which are subtracted to give 'operating profit'. Then there are various figures relating to investments and interest payable. However we are not interested in the total of expenses for these ratios.

- *Net profit* is variously called 'net profit before tax' or sometimes just 'profit before tax'. That is the figure we want. In practice, operating profit is in effect the same as net profit.

The figure for net profit before tax is usually followed by more figures, such as tax and (predictably) 'net profit after tax'. There may also be a figure for minority interests. We are not concerned with these figures.

The two ratios simply divide the turnover by either gross profit or net profit. If the company is making a profit, the figure is above 1.0. It is possible for the gross margin to be above 1.0 and the net margin below 1.0, or it is possible for both to be below 1.0.

Margins are the simplest indicators of a business's health. By themselves the margins tell you little. A high margin is not necessarily good as it could mean that the company is overcharging for its products and could be vulnerable to new competition. Margins are most relevant when compared, either with similar companies or with margins for the same company in different years.

How do margins compare with previous years?

Margins are considerably affected by the nature of the business. Stores have low margins because of the high volume of their sales. Service companies have high margins (particularly gross margins) because their costs are low.

Increased profit margins are usually the consequence of one or more of these three factors:

1. more sales;
2. higher prices; or
3. reduced costs.

All of these are good news for the investor, provided that the development is sustainable. For example, higher prices should not be at the expense of reduced sales.

An increased profit margin will not tell you which of these is the reason, but an investor is not usually that concerned. To some extent any increased margin must involve management of all three factors. If prices are increased but sales fall as a consquence, or if prices rise but so do costs, the margins will not increase.

A healthy business is usually one where the margins are stable or slightly increasing each year. Declining margins usually indicate a problem. Even a slow decline indicates a problem, as it means that the company cannot keep its costs under control.

Sometimes you get specific comments about margins, such as EasyJet increasing net profit margin from 9% to 10% by selling more seats at full price.

How do they compare with equivalent companies?

There are two ways of making a comparison. The first is the simpler but less accurate. It uses a table of profit margins produced by a statistical source. The other is to obtain accounts for equivalent companies and calculate the figures for those also.

Some gross profit margins for smaller businesses produced by the old Central Statistical Office include the following:

Wholesale		Retail	
building materials	22.1%	alcohol, sweets, tobacco	16.9%
clothes, footwear	23.0%	all types	29.7%
consumer items, various	21.0%	cars	11.1%
food, drink:	20.1%	clothing, footwear	41.7%
industrial machinery	30.0%	food	23.4%
industrial material	16.2%	hire, repair	87.6%
leasing	54.2%	household goods	34.6%
petrol	15.1%	mixed retail	34.0%
		non-food	34.4%
		petrol	11.3%

Making comparisons is not as easy as it seems. Consider the 2003 accounts for the UK's three leading supermarket companies. The figures extracted from the accounts (including the notes to the accounts) are set out below:

Company	Turnover £m	Gross profit £m	Operating profit £m
Tesco	26,107	1,997	1,448
Sainsbury's	17,430	1,391	674
Morrison	4,289	1,106	262

This gives the following figures for margins:

Company	Gross margin	Net margin
Tesco	7.6%	5.7%
Sainsbury's	8.0%	3.9%
Morrison	25.8%	6.1%

Gross margins indicate that Morrison is significantly out of line with its two much larger rivals, though the figure is in line with the 23.4% for smaller food retailers given in the table above. A large measure of this is probably in the different definition of what they regard as a cost of sale. Nevertheless it is true that smaller supermarkets have a larger gross margin, usually by selling less but at higher prices than smaller stores. This does not necessarily translate into higher net margins as the smaller stores have proportionately higher overheads. So we can see that Tesco and Morrison both have a *net* margin around 6%.

> Gross margin is usually an indication of policy, whereas the net margin is an indication of efficiency.

How can I tell if margins are under pressure?

Partly by sensitivity analysis, and partly by considering other factors.

Consider the margins indicated by Tesco's accounts for 2003. We are saying that £10 spent in the store generates 76p of gross profit and 57p in net profit.

Suppose Tesco decides to have a price war with Sainsbury's and cuts its prices by 2%. The costs and expenses are the same, so each of the figures above is reduced by 20p, which means that every £9.80 spent in the store generates 56p of gross profit and 37p in net profit.

This means that the gross margin falls from 7.6% to 5.7%, and net profit falls from 5.7% to 3.8%.

In terms of the reduction in amount of profit, a 2% drop in price leads to a 26% drop in gross profit, and a 35% drop in net profit. (This is calculated by dividing 20p by 76p and 57p respectively). This is why a price war is sometimes regarded as retail suicide.

However the opposite also applies. Suppose Tesco increases its prices by 2%. This means that £10.20 spent in the store generates 96p gross profit and 77p net profit. The gross and net profit margins increase to 9.4% and 7.5% respectively. So a 2% increase in prices leads to a 26% increase in gross profit and a 35% increase in net profit.

However, there is an obvious fallacy in all this. As prices reduce, the store can expect to sell more. As prices increase, the store can expect to sell less. The art of pricing goods is to find the point where the reduced margin is compensated by the increased quantity. This can be calculated by applying differential calculus to the formula:

$$y = ax^2 + bx + c$$

where x is price, y is profit, and a, b and c are constants determined by interpolation from actual results as shown by an ogive-shaped graph. I could explain more, but I would suggest that you don't go there – just assume that some clever boffin at headquarters already has.

We have established that profit is hugely sensitive to price. Assuming that prices are already at the optimum to maximise profits, any adjustment to price will affect margins.

This is where we leave mathematics and consider other factors. How far will buyers be prepared to pay more if prices go up, because of a poor harvest of a particular item for example? How much do we expect the competitors to put pressure on prices, bearing in mind that they will have similar high sensitivity? And so on.

There is no mathematical formula to calculate the second half of this question, but there are questions which can be answered.

Gross profit

How is it achieving its increased/decreased profit?

If a company sells widgets, there are three ways it can increase its profits:

- sell more widgets;
- put up the price;
- cut costs.

A company can do any combination of these things.

You can find out what a company has done by both analysing the accounts and reading the reports, and not just the former, as the example below will illustrate.

What a company has done can be determined most easily by the five-year summary which all listed companies must include in their annual report. Keeping with Tesco, we find this information in the five-year summary:

Yr ended Feb.	1999 £m	2000 £m	2001 £m	2002 £m	2003 £m
Turnover (ex VAT)	17,158	18,796	20,988	23,653	26,337
Operating profit	965	1,043	1,174	1,332	1,509

From this we can calculate that operating profit in succeeding years is:

1999	2000	2001	2002	2003
5.6%	5.5%	5.6%	5.6%	5.7%

In other words, turnover has grown by 53.5% between 1999 and 2003, but the operating profit has remained around the same. In other words, the increase in profit is generated almost entirely by increasing sales.

However Tesco indulges us with more figures in the five-year summary. Considering just their UK operations, the five-year summary gives us these figures:

Yr ended Feb.	1999	2000	2001	2002	2003
Turnover (£m)	15,835	16,958	18,372	20,052	21,615
Operating (£m)	919	993	1,100	1,213	1,297
No. of stores	639	659	692	729	1,982
Sales area (000 sq ft)	15,975	16,895	17,965	18,822	21,829

From this we can calculate more figures. We can determine that the operating profit just in the UK is:

1999	2000	2001	2002	2003
5.8%	5.9%	6.0%	6.0%	6.0%

From this we can see that the UK is slightly more profitable than the company's overseas operations, which is normal. Also that the UK accounts for 82% of turnover in 2003, and that most of the UK profit growth has come from increased sales.

We can calculate the profit per UK store:

1999	2000	2001	2002	2003
£1.4m	£1.5m	£1.6m	£1.7m	£0.7m.

In succeeding years, the profit per store slowly increased until 2003 when it suddenly plummeted to less than half. It is easy to see that the reason is that number of stores more than doubled while turnover and profits did not.

The chief executive's report explains that the company acquired hundreds more stores when it took over T & S Stores, "a leading convenience retailer" whose branches we may assume are much smaller than a normal Tesco store.

We can also calculate turnover per square foot. In fact, we don't have to as Tesco has already done it for us. The figures are:

1999	2000	2001	2002	2003
£21.05	£21.43	£22.01	£22.33	£22.16

This figure is not growing but static, indicating that growth is coming from increased size rather than increased margins. The consistent picture is of a company with static prices, static costs and static overheads, but becoming more profitable simply by selling more.

And this is where Tesco becomes an interesting example of why fundamental analysis alone is insufficient, because the chief executive's report tells us a different story.

> "We are now into our second £bn of price cuts following further price investment this year. This represents an 11% price drop in real terms ..."

This statement is rather vague, because we do not have the time-frame in which prices fell by 11%. The expression "in real terms" means after allowing for inflation. If this is running around 2%, this would mean a price cut of 9% in one year, or 7% over two years.

But our early price sensitivity said that even a 2% cut in prices would lead to a 35% drop in net profit. Every £10 generates only 57p in net profit. An 11% price cut would mean that each figure declines by £1.10, so every £8.90 spent in the shop generates a loss of 53p. But we know that the store has managed to maintain its profit margins.

The answer comes a little later in the report:

> "Our Step Change programme has delivered over £230 million of efficiency savings which we pass on to our customers."

The report continues to explain where these efficiency savings have been made. In other words, the company has maintained profit margins by both cutting prices and cutting costs. Note that this is not obvious from the accounts. It can only be found out by reading the reports as well, as stated at the beginning of this section.

What scope is there for increasing profit?

If we stay with Tesco, what scope is there for increasing its profits? In an answer to an earlier question, we identified the three traditional ways that a widget maker may increase his profits: increasing price, selling more, and reducing costs.

These three options are always available for any business, but we need to unpack the 'sell more' option for Tesco. It is already the country's largest food retailer. The population of the UK is fairly static and there is no great scope for us all to eat much more, so the choices for 'sell more' are:

- expand the range of products;
- increase market share by beating competitors;
- buy up competitors;
- persuade customers to buy more expensive products;
- move into other countries.

This provides a simple checklist to compare against statements in the chief executive's report (or similar). Let us do so:

Expand the range of products ✔

"This year we have introduced over 5,000 new food products...."

"Half our new space in the UK this year has been for non-food."

Increase market share by beating competitors ✔

"This, along with improved capability, has seen our non-food market share grow to 5%. This year we have achieved a 16% share of chart music sales...."

Buy up competitors ✔

"We acquired T & S Stores, a leading convenience retailer". [It goes on to say that it wants to buy Safeway.]

Persuade customers to buy more expensive products ✔

"...increased our Finest brand to nearly 1,100 products...."

Move into other countries ✔

"We purchased the HIT chain of hypermarkets in Poland this year."

Tesco's chief executive has identified opportunities in each of the five 'sell more' options. There are other parts of the report that could also be quoted under the five headings.

It is not necessary for all five options to be identified in this way. Normally fewer than all five would be identified, but you should be concerned if none is identified by a mature company.

Merely identifying an opportunity does not mean that the company will meet it. For that, you need to consider the company's track record.

What matters for investors considering investing in Tesco is that the company has identified its profit growth plans, and can achieve profit growth however much Sainsbury's flourishes.

And I bet you never realised that one in six music CDs was bought at Tesco. The store is also fast becoming the country's leading supplier of DVD players.

What is its return on capital employed?

Formula: ROCE = Profit before interest and tax x 100 ÷ Net capital employed

Return on capital employed (ROCE) is one of the main financial measures of how well a company is performing.

ROCE looks at the total return generated by the company without bothering about whether this takes the form of dividend or retained profit. Ultimately both belong to shareholders and should result in a direct financial benefit. Retained profit should pass to the shareholder in the form of future dividends and higher price when the share is sold.

As ROCE is widely used for comparison between companies it is essential that the two elements are precisely defined to ensure that you are comparing like with like. Profit before interest and tax is probably shown separately on the face of the profit and loss account. If not, it can easily be calculated by adding interest payable to the figure for net profit before tax.

Net capital employed (NCE) is the capital of the business provided by shareholders and long-term creditors such as bond holders and debenture holders. The figure is most easily calculated from the balance sheet by adding up all the balance sheet assets (this is the figure at which the balance sheet "balances") and subtracting current liabilities. There are other ways to arrive at this figure.

Probably the commonest variation in the formula is to take the average NCE for the year by adding the NCE from the accounts to the equivalent figure from last year and dividing by two. This has the logic in that the return has been earned throughout the year and therefore an averaged figure more closely relates to the return. It has the disadvantage in that investment decisions are based on the present and future rather than the past. If the NCE is averaged, the ratio is strictly the return on average capital employed (ROACE). However sometimes this ratio is called ROCE, so be careful that you are using the same formula in any comparison.

Unlike almost all other ratios, ROCE is capable of simple interpretation. A high ROCE is good; a low ROCE is bad. A low ROCE is often an indication of poor management. If the ROCE is less than you get from National Savings, you should avoid the company. Any reasonably managed company should achieve a ROCE of at least 10%.

A high ROCE does not always mean that a company is a good investment. A high ROCE is reflected in the share price which may make it a poor investment. The company may be well managed but that does not make it a good investment if the share is overpriced.

Sometimes ROCE is compared with the cost of capital. This is explained more in Section 2.6 when discussing gearing. The reason for such a comparison is that if the ROCE does not sufficiently exceed the cost of capital, the company is in effect consuming its capital base, which will ultimately damage shareholder value. In practice, a sufficiently intelligent look at ROCE on its own is usually sufficient.

> Unlike almost all other ratios, ROCE is capable of simple interpretation. A high ROCE is good; a low ROCE is bad.

There are further measures such as return on equity which measure the net profit attributable to shareholders against shareholders' equity. In practice, such measures are unlikely to tell you anything not disclosed by considering ROCE and gearing. People-based businesses, such as consultancies, can report a high return on equity which conceals the company's volatility.

Whatever ratios are used to measure returns, their main purpose is to compare with companies in similar activities, and to compare with other forms of investment. It is essential that you compare ratios calculated in the same way.

What is EBITDA?

Formula:　　EBITDA = Pre-tax profit + Interest + Depreciation

EBITDA stands for earnings before interest, tax, depreciation and amortisation. Sometimes depreciation and amortisation are not excluded, when the abbreviation becomes EBIT.

The term EBITDA is as flowery as it is meaningless. It is calculated by adding back to net profit, the figures for interest, depreciation and amortisation. Tax is not added back as that is not subtracted to calculate net profit in the first place, and amortisation is rarely added back as it is rarely there in companies for which EBITDA is quoted.

In UK accounts, the term amortisation is the 'depreciation' on purchased goodwill, such as when a business is taken over. EBITDA is typically quoted for young start-up companies which are hocked up to their eyebrows. Amortisation of goodwill is itself a meaningless figure representing an expense that has not been incurred of using an asset that has never been acquired. So adding back amortisation is more easily justified than adding back interest and depreciation. However EBITDA companies are usually struggling to cope with running their own businesses without looking for other businesses to take over. Also they struggle to pay their milk bill, and do not have the cash to take over other businesses.

This measure was introduced during the heady boom period of the 1990s to justify inflated prices of certain non-profit-generating shares. Its aim was to show that the underlying operations were profitable even if the whole business was not. EBITDA is meaningless as you cannot invest in underlying operations, but only in complete businesses. It is like saying that you are living within your income if you ignore your HP repayments and credit card bills.

> EBITDA is meaningless as you cannot invest in underlying operations, but only in complete businesses.

Any company which says it has a positive EBITDA is almost certainly making a net loss, as it would otherwise declare the net profit. The most charitable observation about EBITDA is that it could be seen as a milestone on the journey to profitability.

Quoting EBITDA does not mean that a company is a bad investment (though it should raise suspicions). But you should consider its investment potential on the basis of net losses and cash burn. EBITDA is often served with other exotic ratios, all lavishly garnished so that you cannot taste the real flavour.

Before leaving the subject, it is worth mentioning the most exotic of the measures, known as 'mindshare'. This was used to justify the ludicrous high values put on dotcom companies in the 1990s, when three whizz-kids with a computer and an idea were worth billions. The theory was that a market was to be created and this company was positioning itself to bag a large share of that market. It is like buying an interest in Jack's Beanstalk, and with a similar credibility. Investing in a mindshare company will give you the same return on capital as investing in a crate of whisky, but will be much less enjoyable.

If you are tempted to invest in a company because you have become excited at its EBITDA or mindshare, make yourself a cup of Ovaltine and lie down in a dark room. If you still feel the same when you wake up, put your money in National Savings, cancel your subscription to *The Financial Times*, and buy *The Beano* instead.

How much cash does it have?

Relevant to
All fundamental investors

Underlying worry
'This isn't one of those companies that makes profits but then goes bust because it runs out of cash, is it?'

Cash generation and consumption

Is having lots of cash good or bad?

It can be either. A large pile of cash provides protection and allows a company to do what it wishes, such as buying up suitable targets. However if not used effectively, the cash will simply generate a small amount of interest, which is always at a rate much lower than a successful trading company should otherwise generate. Taking the historic benchmark of 12% overall return for shares, consider a company which is doing better than average with an overall return of 16%. Half its net assets of £10 million are in the form of cash earning 4% interest. Its overall return is:

Amount	Earning	Yields
£5m cash	4%	£200,000
£5m other assets	16%	£800,000
£10m total assets	10%	£1,000,000

See how the cash pile has dragged down the company's performance. You must make your own judgment on how much performance you are willing to sacrifice for security.

Sometimes cash piles do not excite investors because of how they were acquired. Biocompatibles surprised investors when it sold its main business, generating a huge cash pile which did not initially impress the market.

Borrowing money gears up the company. Gearing is explained in Section 2.6.

Does the company generate or consume cash?

This is where the cash flow statement comes into its own.

The two main financial statements are the balance sheet and profit and loss account. The cash flow statement is an additional statement which expresses information from these two financial statements in a different form.

> **Cashflow statements have one great advantage - they are incontrovertible fact, free of opinion.**

The fundamental purpose of any business is to generate cash. It is cash which rewards shareholders and funds growth. It is cash which ensures that bills get paid and the business does not become insolvent.

In most cases, a business generates cash by making a profit, but that is not always the case. British Rail, the Post Office and several other publicly-owned bodies made losses year after year, but kept going because they kept receiving subsidies to maintain their cash. Public transport companies receive government and local authority subsidies. Some businesses may make a profit, but do not get paid, or cannot fund the work to completion so that they can get paid. So cash is king.

Cash flow statements have one great advantage over profit and loss accounts and balance sheets – they are incontrovertible fact, free of opinion. When preparing the other financial statements, the company must decide how much its factory is worth. £10 million? £15 million? There is no exact value. And over what period should it be depreciated? 40 years? 50 years? There is no exact answer. The company has a fair guess, and this is the basis for figures in the balance sheet and profit and loss account for fixed assets and depreciation.

However cash flow simply looks at what cash flows into the business and what cash flows out of the business. And that is fact. A revaluation of the factory, or a change of depreciation policy does not involve any cash changing hands, so it is ignored in the cash flow statement.

Cash flow statements are now regulated by Financial Reporting Standard FRS 1, introduced in 1991. Originally it included 'cash equivalents' with cash. This classed deposits with more than three months to maturity as investments and not a cash equivalent. Corporate treasurers claimed that this negated the purpose of FRS 1 which was to indicate the company's liquidity. In 1997, the concept of cash equivalents was dropped, and cash flow statements now refer purely to cash including currency, bank accounts and readily accessible deposits. Cash which is converted to or from financial instruments is now shown as a separate item in the statement, allowing the investor to see clearly how it affects liquidity. There is further explanation on cash flow statements in Part IV on page 182.

Let's consider the cash flow statement for Crown Sports plc in 2002. Taking the main headings, the statement shows the following:

	£'000
Net cash flow from operating activities	5,224
Returns on investment and servicing of finance	(3,211)
Taxation	(255)
Capital expenditure and financial investment	11,377
Acquisitions and disposals	(625)
Financing	(14,797)
Decrease in cash	(2,287)

In the statement, unbracketed numbers refer to inflows – cash coming into the company. Bracketed numbers refer to outflows – cash going out of the company.

From the above we can see clearly that its normal trade brought in over £5 million in cash. However more than double that figure was brought in under 'capital expenditure and financial investment'.

Trading and the net sale of investments brought in £16.6 million (£11.4 million + £5.2 million), but against that we have £14.8 million going out merely to finance the company's borrowings. The full cash flow statement shows that comprises £14.2 million to service bank loans, and £0.6 million for finance leases. If we include the £3.2 million figure for servicing of finance, we can see that the company's trading and sale of investments does not generate enough cash to pay for the cost of its borrowings. At the end of the year, it had £2.3 million less cash. It also has £14.5 million less investments.

This would appear to indicate that the company is a hopeless case. However financial analysis must always be considered in context. At the time of this cash flow, it had £51.1 million net assets, so even an unmitigated cash burn of £2.3 million per year would not exhaust the assets for another 22 years.

If we move on to the interim accounts for the six months to June 2003, the chairman says:

"The results for Crown Sports for the first six months of 2003 reflect a group which is entirely different in structure from the corresponding period in 2002. In line with the previously announced strategy, the disposals of the non-core businesses have been completed and the group is now entirely focussed on health and fitness."

This is a typical statement from the chairman of a company in deep trouble. You can take a positive view and see that the management is taking steps to get its act together, and the company has the financial strength to survive. Alternatively, you can take the negative view and ask why it became un-focussed and indulged in non-core activities in the first place.

Crown Sports sold Crown Golf, The Winning Line and Crown Content during 2003, so it could concentrate on Dragon's Health Clubs. Yet at the start of 2004, it sold its branch in Leamington Spa because it "does not fit within the current location profile for the Dragons Group". It also happened to raise £1.3 million in much needed cash. Is the company on the way up or the way out? The jury has yet to decide.

Does the company reinvest?

A company must reinvest some profit each year to fund its ability to make profits in future years.

The simplest way to check whether it is doing this is to look at the cash flow statement. There should be a section marked 'capital expenditure and financial investment' with a sub-heading of 'purchases less disposal of fixed assets' or something similar. This should be against a figure in brackets (indicating an outflow of cash).

WS Atkins plc produced an annual report with the slogan 'Intergrated solutions for tomorrow's world', so we can expect them to be reinvesting. In the 2001 accounts, the cash flow statement shows £11.006 million of purchases less disposals of fixed assets.

A similar figure can be found from the notes to the accounts, cross-referenced from the balance sheet. For Atkins, this shows acquisitions of £17.867 million and disposals of £7.370 million. This gives £10.497 million, with the missing £0.509 million presumably explained by such factors as depreciation, exchange differences and disposal costs. It is easier to take the figure from the cash flow statement.

The figure of £11 million on its own means little; it must be compared to something. There are four obvious comparators:

- depreciation;
- fixed assets after depreciation;
- fixed assets before depreciation; and
- disposals.

Depreciation is shown in the consolidated profit and loss account as £11.513 million. That is how much the directors estimate their fixed assets have lost value. They have replaced it with a little under that amount, indicating a very small reduction in fixed assets.

The second comparison is with fixed assets. This shows a total of £34.9 million. So the acquisition represents almost one third of the value of all fixed assets, which paints a different picture.

In terms of original value before depreciation, the asset value at the beginning of the financial year is £92 million, so the acquisitions represent less than one eighth of fixed assets by original value. A caveat should be made here that some of the assets may be very old so that their original value in current terms would be more.

A final comparison could be simply made between additions and disposals. If we look at tangible assets for the company, we see that additions were £17.867 million against disposals of £8.371 million. This gives a healthy ratio of 2.1.

The adequacy of asset replacement can look different according to which of the four measures you choose, which is why more than one is useful. However, for WS Atkins, there is clearly a healthy asset replacement programme.

Paying suppliers

How long does the company take to pay its creditors?

Formula: Creditor period = [Trade creditors x 365] ÷ Cost of sales

This figure gives the average number of days a company takes to pay its suppliers. You do not need to calculate this figure as English law now requires the company to state both the figure and its policy for paying creditors in its report and accounts.

The policy is usually an anodyne statement such as "it is the company's policy to pay all undisputed creditors within the terms agreed". This neatly avoids the fact that the company may have pressured the creditor to agree unfavourable terms (for which supermarkets are notorious) and that any invoice may easily be disputed.

As with most formulae, this ratio is best understood in the context of the business and other ratios. Many businesses, such as construction, agree long creditor periods.

The other ratio in which the creditor period should be considered is the debtor ratio, as explained below.

Getting paid by customers

How long does the company take to get paid by its customers?

Formula: Debtor period = [Trade debtors x 365] ÷ Sales

The debtor period is the average time it takes for a customer to pay the company's invoice. In some businesses, such as banks and supermarkets, this figure will be of little value as the customers generally pay immediately.

In all companies, this figure must be understood in the context of the business. A good comparison is with other companies in the same business.

Is the number of debtor days increasing or decreasing?

In the normal course of events, an investor would expect the number of debtor days to remain fairly constant from one year to the next. Therefore any variation of more than, say, five days could be significant.

A large change may be due to a change of policy. The company may have decided to write off some historic debts, or to change the definition of trade debtors or sales. You should look for a statement to this effect.

Increasing debtor days could indicate lax credit control, particularly if the number of debtor days is higher than for equivalent businesses. This indicates poor management generally. It could also point to future financial problems. The chances of a debt turning bad (i.e. never being paid) increase as the debt gets older. As many debtors routinely pay without any credit control anyway, an increasing number of days is disproportionately significant.

Decreasing debtor days may indicate better management such as stricter enforcement of trade terms.

How significant is the number of debtor days?

This ratio has some significance for all businesses, as they all buy and sell. However the significance of this ratio reduces for businesses which:

• generate much of their product value internally;
• are engaged in long-term work;
• work largely for the government;
• are in the retail sector.

What is the ratio of debtors to sales?

This ratio is sometimes encountered. It measures the value of debtors against annual sales to see what percentage of annual sales are outstanding at the year end.

If you multiply this figure by 365, you will find that it equals the number of debtor days. The comments about debtor days apply equally to the debtor-to-sales ratio.

Is its market value supported by assets?

Relevant to
Value investors, those interested in a 'margin of safety'

Underlying worry
'If the company closed down tomorrow, how much would it be worth based on instant realisation of its assets?'

Market value

How much is the company worth?

Formula: Market value = Issued shares x Share price

Market value is simply how much the stock market thinks a company is worth. A public company must have capital of at least £50,000. To be listed on the London Stock Exchange, a company must be worth at least £700,000, though most are worth many many times that figure.

Issued shares means the number of shares which are held by shareholders. The shareholders themselves decide the number of 'authorised shares'. That is the maximum number which the directors may issue. The number of issued shares cannot exceed the number of authorised shares, but is often less.

If a company buys its own shares, those shares are cancelled, and the number of issued shares is reduced. From 1 December 2003, a company may buy back shares without cancelling them. These are known as Treasury shares. Their value may not exceed 10% of the issued share capital. Such shares may be sold as new shares without needing to be freshly issued. For accounting purposes, Treasury shares are treated as though they do not exist. So if a company has 20 million authorised shares of which 15 million shares were issued at the beginning of the year, but 1 million have been bought back for cancellation, and 1 million have been bought back and held as Treasury shares, the company has 13 million issued shares for our purposes.

You will find this number buried in the notes to the accounts. Look at the balance sheet for "shares". This will have a number by it which refers to the appropriate note. You should use the figure for the end of the year. Note, that you do not use the number used to calculate earnings per share. This number is the *average* number of shares issued during the year. You must use the actual number at a specific point of time.

The **share price** is simply the figure quoted by the stock market for that share. This is an average of the buying and selling prices. It is readily available from newspapers and from websites. Many companies give their share price on their own websites. Make sure you find the price for the ordinary shares, and not A-shares, debentures, loan stocks, warrants, bonds, partly paid shares, options or derivative products.

This share price is the result of many factors, of which an opinion of the company is just one. The price is also affected by views of the general economy. Share prices are also determined under the normal rules of supply and demand. A stock which is in demand, perhaps because it has been tipped in a Sunday newspaper, may well see its price rise on Monday.

The market value simply multiplies the Issued Shares by Share Price. There is the obvious point that the two numbers must relate to the same point in time.

This job is done for you in Monday's editions of *The Financial Times*. The market value of each company is listed already calculated. This is fine for those companies which are listed in the newspaper. You must do your own calculation for companies which are not, or look on one of the many websites which calculate market values of quoted companies on a daily basis.

The market value tells you the overall worth of the business, as seen by the market. As the number of shares is unarguable fact, the only subjective element of this figure is the share value.

By itself, this number means little to the investor. After all, it hardly matters whether you hold shares in a company worth £10 billion rather than £5 billion. Its importance to investors lies more in two indirect ways:

1.   As an element in other measures (such as price-to-book value, and in comparison with sales and profit); *and*

2.   In determining its benchmark status in indices.

Benchmark status needs an explanation. The largest 100 UK companies (as measured by market capitalisation) make up the FTSE 100 index. Every quarter this list is reviewed. Numbers 1 to 90 stay in the list, while numbers 111 down are excluded. Between 91 and 110 some discretion is exercised as to whether the company stays in.

The next 250 companies make up the FTSE 250 index (note this is not the largest 250 companies). Together the FTSE 100 and FTSE 250 companies make the FTSE 350. These are followed by the Small Cap index. In practice, the index is usually stated for you. In most listings FTSE 100 index companies are indicated in bold type, for example.

Companies are keen to be in the highest possible index. This not only confers prestige, but can:

- make it easier for the company to borrow money;
- enable the company to borrow at a lower rate;
- encourage more investors to buy their shares, thus pushing up the price even more. For example tracking funds will want their shares.

For the investor, a higher index means:

- it is easier to sell the shares;
- the 'spread' (difference between buying and selling price) is smaller.

However even inclusion in FTSE 100 index does not guarantee unchanging continuity. This index started in February 1984 and was therefore 20 years old in 2004. Of the original 100 companies:

- only 41 remain in the index;
- 36 have been taken over;
- 14 have been relegated to the FT 250 (which measures companies from 101 to 350 in size);
- 3 have fallen to the FT Small Cap index (outside the top 350);
- 4 have been broken up;
- 2 have gone bust.

Of the 41 companies still in the index, only 23 are regarded as still the same company. The others have changed by acquiring significant new businesses. Just 21 of the original 41 still use the same name.

At individual share level

This measure can be looked at more simply if you know the net asset value per share. This figure is given in many publications. Below and overleaf is a selection of ratios of share price to net asset value per share taken from *Investors Chronicle* of 6 February 2004. For comparison, the P/E ratio is also given.

Many obvious conclusions can immediately be drawn. Don't touch anything to do with football, for example. The two cash shells are trading around 1.0, as would be expected. Drug companies trade well above their asset value, reflecting the hidden assets of their research & development. Software companies do well in such a table simply because their assets are so low.

You also note that there is little correlation between the asset value ratio and P/E ratio, demonstrating that you get quite different conclusions depending on whether you are primarily concerned with asset-backing or profit-earning.

A dash in the P/E column indicates that the company is not making a profit. It is no surprise that the bottom six companies are loss-making, but it may seem surprising that six of the top eight companies also are. The market clearly believes that these companies will do great things.

The runaway top is Domino's Pizza whose sales have doubled in four years to 2004, and whose share price has risen sixfold in the same period. But can it continue? Its growth comes from opening new stores at a rate approaching one

Ratio	Share price	NAV	P/E ratio	Company name	Nature of business
9.00	216p	24p	25	Domino's Pizza	Pizza delivery
7.50	60p	8p	-	Vernalis	Drug development
6.34	260p	41p	-	Neutec Pharma	Drug development
6.00	12p	2p	-	I-Document Systems	Planning software
6.21	2627p	423p	27	AstraZeneca	Pharmaceutical
5.67	17p	3p	-	Clipper Ventures	Yacht race organiser
5.25	21p	4p	-	Patsystems	Derivatives software
5.20	26p	5p	-	ML Labs	Drug development
5.11	174p	34p	19	Whittard of Chelsea	Tea and coffee seller
5.09	448p	88p	24	Air Partner	Aircraft charter
5.07	66p	13p	44	Caffe Nero	Coffee shop
4.00	4p	1p	-	Osmetech	Diagnostics
3.83	11.5p	3p	40	Celstone	Phone mast disguise
3.66	333p	91p	16	Invox	Phone competitions
3.16	455p	144p	103	Filtronic	Wireless technology
3.00	0.9p	0.3p	-	Bakery Services	In-store bakery
2.88	458p	159p	23	Aero Inventory	Aircraft parts
2.71	1399p	517p	23	Rio Tinto	Mining
2.68	158p	59p	-	Interior Services	Office facilities
2.38	14.25p	6p	1450	Protec	Security monitoring
2.23	150p	67p	17	Aggreko	Power supplier
2.11	268p	127p	38	XP Power	Power supplier
2.04	49p	24p	17	James R Knowles	Constr. consultancy
2.02	394p	195p	13	Chemring	Decoys and flares
2.00	453p	226p	11	NWF	Mini-conglomerate
1.88	115p	61p	14	Centurion Energy	Oil and gas producer
1.67	55p	33p	48	Fairbriar	Construction mgt.
1.59	196p	123p	6	Country & Metropolitan	House builder
1.57	193p	123p	-	Manganese Bronze	Taxi maker
1.50	336p	224p	7	Crest Nicholson	House builder
1.48	413p	280p	-	Amvescap	Fund manager
1.44	34.5p	24p	12	Eleco	Building products
1.43	288p	201p	10	Lookers	Car dealer
1.26	398p	315p	13	Scottish & Newcastle	Brewer
1.18	45p	38p	25	Acquisitor	Investment
1.16	65p	56p	-	Westmount Energy	Oil exploration
1.11	304p	275p	10	Carr's Milling Ind.	Animal feed
1.08	205p	189p	9	Thorpe FW	Industrial lighting
1.06	725p	683p	16	Wadworth	Brewer
1.06	33p	31p	-	Baltimore Technologies	Shell company
0.90	27p	30p	-	Boustead	Shell company
0.74	37.5p	51p	-	Integrated Dental	Dental care
0.55	51p	92p	-	NBA Quantum	Claims resolution
0.55	40.5p	73p	-	Newmarket Investments	Football promoter
0.37	123p	334p	-	Preston North End	Football club

a week. By the beginning of 2004 it had 318 stores and believes it can cope with 500. Assuming it can find the sites, that is enough for four more years of growth. The market likes it because it is a simple business with a proven core strategy. Whether that can really justify 800% goodwill is most questionable.

At the other end, Integrated Dental is considered to be worth less than it owns, as the market has no confidence in that financial disaster. Its share price has fallen from 150p when launched in 2002 to 37.5p two years later. The problem is simply that it failed to find enough dentists. Such a company would ordinarily be ripe for a takeover, but the fact that 30% of shares are owned by its founder makes that unlikely. As with all disasters, the company has a credible story of how it will improve. If you believe it, this is an excellent investment for you.

Enterprise value

Formula: Enterprise value = Market value + Total debt − Total cash

Enterprise value is a modification of market value. This is a useful alternative figure when interest received and paid is less important. To determine the enterprise value, it is first necessary to look up or calculate the market value as explained above.

For these purposes 'Total debt' includes all long-term and short-term debt instruments issued by the company and any subsidiaries. These include bank loans, debentures, preference shares, overdrafts, and all other forms of loans. This figure is usually the total of two figures in the balance sheet representing short-term and long-term debt respectively. Debt here is what the company owes, so it appears in the balance sheet under creditors or current liabilities. Long-term loans will usually appear near to share capital. There may be more than one form.

'Total cash' means the amount the company has in the bank and other assets which are very similar in nature to cash. These can include foreign currencies and gold. It does not include anything where a transaction must take place for it to be turned into cash. So goods in stock and shares held in other companies are not included. Debtors (money owed *to* the company) are not usually included as part of total cash, even though there is an argument that they should be to match the creditors.

Some of the figures needed to determine total debt and total cash may need to be extracted from the notes to the accounts rather than from the face of the accounts.

Like market capitalisation, enterprise value means little on its own. Its main value is in comparing companies more easily. At its simplest, enterprise value is the market capitalisation regardless of how the company is financed.

For all the numbers and ratios which use market capitalisation, you may substitute enterprise value where you regard the financing arrangements as irrelevant, or where the financing arrangements are so different that simple comparison of market value is of limited value.

Fixed assets

What value is given to fixed assets?

What is the price to book value?

Formula: Price to book = Share price ÷ Shareholders' funds per share

The share price is simply the current value of the share, as obtained from a financial newspaper or website.

The 'Shareholders' funds per share' usually involves another calculation. Shareholders' funds are sometimes also known as shareholders' equity, net tangible assets or net assets. It is basically the value of the business (excluding minority interest and goodwill). This is divided by the number of issued shares.

It should be noted that there are sometimes other bases used to calculate the price to book value. These other bases include or exclude different elements in shareholders' funds. In making any comparison, it is essential that the definitions used are the same.

This figure compares the share price with the assets which support the share. Normally the figure should be above 1.0. The extent by which the price to book exceeds 1.0 represents what the market expects of the company. For example a price to book of 1.5 could mean that a share price is £1.50 against assets per share of £1.00. The additional 50p is considered to be the value of the business as a trading entity. It is the simplest ratio which demonstrates the basic principle of valuing a business that:

> value of a business = net assets + goodwill

A high or low ratio by itself does not indicate whether a share is or is not a good investment. The ratio needs to be interpreted. In particular, you need to consider whether the extent by which the ratio exceeds 1.0 is justified.

It is possible for a ratio to be below 1.0. This means that the market has a poor opinion of the company. It means that, even though the company has assets of (say) £10 million, the market only values it at £8 million. An obvious observation is why does such a company not simply sell its assets and gain £2 million. The answer is that the asset value of £10 million is based on what is known as the 'going concern' basis. This is an accounting assumption that a business will continue to trade for the foreseeable future. Most assets are worth much less if sold rather than used.

A company with a ratio below 1.0 is not necessarily a poor investment. As with all investments, you are looking for businesses which you believe will do better than the market expects. If the market expects a business to perform terribly and you expect it to perform only fairly badly, that is a good investment.

Another point to remember is that price to book is most reliable when the company has plenty of tangible assets, such as property, machinery, stock and cash. If the company value is largely represented by intangible assets, such as purchased goodwill and brand names, the price to book ratio becomes unreliable.

The price to book indicates how well a market expects a business to perform. You need to compare that with your opinion of how you expect it to perform.

How much of the value given to fixed assets is realisable?

In most circumstances, an investor need not ask this question at all.

A company acquires a fixed asset to use in its business to generate profits. It does not buy a factory, lathe, lorry, computer or desk to sell, but to use. The economic value of an asset in a going concern is usually significantly higher than its realisable value in a forced sale, such as when the business goes bust. Second-hand equipment normally sells for much less than its new equivalent – look at car prices in the local newspapers and local showrooms, for example. Also, many assets will have been personally designed or adapted for the particular business.

Realisable value of fixed assets is usually only important if the business is likely to go bust, in which case there are many more fundamental questions an investor needs to ask, assuming the investor is even considering such an investment.

In other circumstances, realisable value may be relevant in terms of whether a business has enough assets as security to borrow funds. However, even here the issue is one of whether the business is likely to go bust. A healthy business should be able to borrow funds without having to pledge all its fixed assets. And a properly run business should already know where and how it can raise future funding.

Asset-stripping

There is one other circumstance when realisable asset value is relevant to an investor, and that is in determining its likelihood of being taken over. A company with undervalued fixed asssets is most vulnerable. Even today, book values can be less than saleable value. In 2001, for instance, Madisons Coffee sold 27 outlets for £2.3 million which were on its books for £1.3 million.

An extreme form of 'undervalued target as takeover target' is asset-stripping. The venture capitalists who indulged in asset-stripping in the 1960s would typically find a sleepy engineering company whose balance sheet might look like this:

	£m
fixed assets	2
current assets	10
current liabilities	4
net assets	6

They would establish that the fixed assets include £10,000 for the main factory at the price paid for it in 1923, but which is now worth £10 million. The venture capitalists offer £8 million to the shareholders and directors, who can't believe their luck – according to the books their company is only worth £6 million. The business is closed, and the factory site sold by the new owners for £10 million as a housing development. Other assets are sold for £9 million and the liabilities paid, with perhaps £1 million for expenses. The £8 million expenditure has become a £14 million cash windfall, which is good news for the venture capitalists and their own shareholders.

So asset-stripping sounds like a win-win situation. Unfortunately not so. The workers are made redundant, customers lose a supplier, and the nation loses productivity and, possibly, technical expertise. This last element is often ignored, as wealth is ultimately simply the capitalisation of productivity, so the loss of a healthy business is very damaging to the national economy.

The worst excesses of asset-stripping have in effect been outlawed since the 1970s by better accounting standards, particularly in terms of property valuation. However some asset-stripping still occurs occasionally.

In March 2002, blue-collar workers at Australian building company Holland's went on strike when its new owners decided to lay off the blue-collar workers in an asset-stripping exercise.

In Russia, asset-stripping is one of several reasons why its leading company Gazprom is seen as such a poor investment. Gazprom owns 25% of the world's known natural gas reserves. Gazprom provides 20% of Russia's entire export income. In terms of natural resources, it has more oil deposits than the whole of Saudi Arabia, and is ten times the size of Exxon, the world's largest quoted oil and gas company. Yet Gazprom is capitalised at only $25 billion. There are many reasons here (including incompetence, corruption and daft Russian laws). One reason is the alleged asset-stripping by Rem Vyakhirev, the chief executive until fired by President Putin in 2001. If Gazprom and similar East European countries manage to rid themselves of such shackles, they will provide a rich source of new investment opportunities.

To some extent, almost every takeover and merger contains an element of asset-stripping, as the rationale usually includes merging head office functions, laying off duplicate staff and selling off no longer needed premises.

Does it matter if a company has hardly any fixed assets?

Yes. A company with plenty of fixed assets, particularly tangible assets, is said to be **asset-backed**. Historically such companies have tended to survive hard times much better than unbacked companies.

Although the existence of lots of fixed assets is not so important in terms of realisable value or security for borrowings, it is important for the continuation of a business.

Compare a marketing consultancy with an engineering works. What are their real assets which earn the profit? In both cases, primarily the staff. For a marketing consultancy, the assets are the staff and some ideas and some contacts. If the staff leave, most of the company leaves with them. It is easy for a new business to start up, possibly led by a disgruntled ex-employee, and to poach staff and clients. Restrictive covenants can obstruct some of this, but cannot stop it completely.

Now consider the engineering company. Its primary asset, the staff, can also leave, but where can they go? A new business would have to invest large amounts in premises and plant. Such a business is unlikely to be able to raise the funds needed to get going on the basis of poaching someone else's business.

A lack of fixed assets indicates a possible lack of stability.

Are fixed assets being replaced?

Fixed assets are consumed through use and the passing of time. That is what makes them fixed assets. If the business is to continue, fixed assets must be replaced. There is an exception for land, and possibly for buildings also as they can be maintained for centuries. Other fixed assets, such as machinery, vehicles and computers must be replaced.

It is usually sufficient simply to compare the figure for depreciation with the cost of acquisitions for each category of replaceable fixed asset. Some of these figures will be buried in the notes to the accounts. If a company has 100 cars which are written off over five years, you might expect the company to acquire an average 20 cars each year.

There are some ratios which can be used. One is to divide fixed asset acquisitions by depreciation for each category of replaceable fixed asset. Even in large organisations with many fixed assets, replacement will rarely be that smooth from year to year. The company with 100 cars may have acquired 50 in one go, and thus have to replace most of that 50 in the same year. For that reason, it is common for this ratio to be calculated for a three-year period.

Sometimes a fixed asset is sold. This is shown as disposal proceeds in the notes to the accounts. This figure is ignored in calculating any ratio.

The ratio of fixed asset expenditure to depreciation is healthy if it averages between 1 and 2. If it is below 1, the company is slowly reducing its fixed assets. That is not necessarily bad. Computers in particular can often be replaced for much less.

What are intangible assets?

Intangible assets are fixed assets without physical form. Examples include goodwill and all forms of intellectual property, namely copyright, patents and trade marks. It also includes scientific know-how, franchise rights, product development, licences and brand names.

The accounting problem with intangibles is, how do you value them? Clearly a brand name has considerable value, though it can be difficult valuing it. Sometimes the intangible asset is so nebulous in nature, it is difficult to see exactly what can be valued.

UK Financial Reporting Standard FRS 10 makes 'separability' the main condition to including an intangible asset.

In some cases, separability is easy. For example, a company buys a seven-year licence to make Whizzo Cakes. It is easy to determine the value and term of the licence. The point about separability is that the intangible becomes sellable, and therefore a discrete item.

The next condition is control. This may be exercised by:

- statutory rights, such as copyright and patent;
- contractual rights, such as franchises and licences; or
- secrecy, such as know-how.

The value of a workforce and customer base cannot be valued as an intangible.

Goodwill

For goodwill and many other types of asset, the rule is that an acquired intangible may be separately valued but an internally generated intangible may not. For example, imagine a successful trading company with the balance sheet shown opposite, and suppose this company makes an annual profit of £5 million.

If such a company were taken over, the acquiring company may be willing to pay perhaps £64 million. The extra £20 million reflects the fact that it is not just buying buildings, equipment stock and cash which will need staffing, systems

	£m
Fixed assets	<u>20</u>
Current assets:	
stock	15
debtors	12
cash	<u>10</u>
	<u>37</u>
Total assets	57
Current liabilities	<u>13</u>
Net assets	**44**
Represented by:	
Ordinary shares	5
Retained profit	39
Capital employed	**44**

and marketing. It is buying a business which is already up and running with a reputation, trained staff and making a profit from the first day it is acquired.

This is what is known as goodwill. It has nothing to do with how people or businesses feel about each other, though the two meanings have the same origin. From 1571, the word 'goodwill' was used to denote the right granted by a trader in allowing another to be recognised as his successor to whom every success was wished.

In our example, the acquiring company has paid out £64 million. In the acquirer's accounts, he will add the various assets and liabilities to his own, and the other £20 million will be shown as a new fixed asset of £20 million 'goodwill'.

The acquired company has suddenly increased in value by £20 million even though it is worth just the same on its day of acquisition as on the day before. What an investor must understand is that the acquired company *was already worth £64 million*. In other words, its assets were understated by £20 million. The value of anything is simply the price someone will pay for it, whether it is consumer goods, property, shares or entire businesses.

However accounting standards are strict that a company must not show this goodwill in its accounts. It is easy to see why, as it is in effect asking a company to say how wonderful it is. There is no way that any objective value can be put on internally generated goodwill until someone makes an offer to buy it.

Companies grow in two ways: organically and acquisitively. The former is when a company grows within itself; the latter when it acquires other companies. In the latter case, the company will include goodwill while in the former it will not, even though the companies will have the same value. This means that companies which have grown organically can be undervalued compared with equivalent companies which have grown acquisitively.

To make a comparison between the two types of company, the simplest way to compare their net assets is simply to deduct goodwill wherever it occurs. This means that both companies will be undervalued, but they will be directly comparable.

Amortising goodwill

Acquired goodwill does not sit in the balance sheet for ever, but must be amortised over its life. Amortisation is exactly the same as depreciation except that it refers to intangible assets rather than tangible ones. If you really want to be pedantic about amortization, you can spell it with a Z.

Amortisation is calculated in the same way as depreciation – by writing off a bit each year of its economic life until you reach zero or dispose of it. The amount written off is shown in the profit and loss account as amortisation.

The problem is how to determine how long the goodwill of an acquired business will last. At least with a lorry or lathe, you can have some idea of how long it will be before the asset falls to pieces. Financial Reporting Standard FRS 10 gives three choices:

* up to 20 years;
* more than 20 years;
* indefinite.

The definition of the useful economic life of acquired goodwill is that it lasts while the value of the acquired business exceeds the net value of its identifiable assets. Suppose the value of the business fell from £64 million to £54 million, and the value of net assets fell from £44 million to £38 million. The value of the goodwill would have reduced from £20 million to £16 million.

This is not quite as subjective as it sounds, as goodwill is often calculated as a multiple of profit. In our example, the multiple is 4. If profit of the acquired business dropped from £5 million to £4 million, and that drop was seen as likely to continue, that could indicate a reduction in the value of the acquired goodwill. However this is a very simplistic explanation of how such a value would be determined.

In the absence of any evidence to the contrary, there is a rebuttable presumption that goodwill does not exceed 20 years. A rebuttable presumption is something accountants and auditors assume to be true in the absence of any evidence to the contrary.

A company cannot just automatically adopt 20 years, nor (at the other extreme) write off all acquired goodwill in the year of acquisition. It must make some effort to estimate useful life. Where goodwill is amortised over less than 20 years, the company must conduct a 'first year review' after one year, to see if its written down value of the acquired goodwill is still realistic. Thereafter the goodwill continues to be written down unless there is evidence that the value of the goodwill has become impaired, when it must be written down to the impaired value.

A company may amortise goodwill for more than 20 years or may decide not to amortise goodwill at all if it can demonstrate that the goodwill has this longer or indefinite life. If it does make such a decision, the goodwill must be subject to an annual impairment test to see if the value of the goodwill is still realistic. There have been objections to this provision on the basis that, as acquired goodwill is slowly replaced by created goodwill, the long amortisation or non-amortisation of acquired goodwill is, in effect, allowing internally created goodwill to be capitalised in the balance sheet. Nevertheless this procedure is permitted.

Sometimes one company will acquire another at a price which is less than its net asset value. The difference is known as **negative goodwill.** This is still shown as an asset although with a negative value. If there is positive goodwill, the two figures are netted off.

An example of a goodwill policy is taken from the 2001 accounts of glass maker Pilkington.

> The goodwill arising on the acquisitions in the year, principally arising from the acquisition of a further 20% holding in Pilkington North America Inc. and Pilkington Polska Sp z.o.o. is being amortised on a straight line basis over 20 years. The goodwill arising on the additional shareholding in Shanghai Yaohua Pilkington Glass Co Limited is being amortised over 10 years. The negative goodwill arising on the acquisition of Shanghai Yaohua Pilkington Autoglass Co. Limited is being amortised over 10 years. These amortisation periods are the periods over which the directors estimate that the values of the underlying businesses acquired are expected to match the value of the underlying assets.

A company may adjust its figure for goodwill, up or down, whenever it believes that is necessary to reflect its fair value. Guidance on this is given in Financial Reporting Standard FRS 11. A company cannot adjust its acquired goodwill to a figure greater than was paid for it.

Whatever policy is adopted for amortisation of goodwill must be stated in the accounts, in exactly the same way as the policy for depreciation must be stated. The two are often given together.

Brand names

Cadbury Schweppes is a company with an impressive collection of household names in confectionery and soft drinks. Its policy on brand names is:

> Intangibles represent significant brands acquired since 1985 valued at historical cost. No amortisation is charged as the annual results reflect significant expenditure in support of these brands and the carrying values are reviewed on an annual basis for any impairment in value. Acquired brand values are calculated based on the Group's valuation methodology, which is based on an internal valuation of discounted cash flows.

This note to the 2003 accounts goes on to explain that the company has capitalised goodwill acquired from 1998. It is written off over 20 years. Goodwill acquired before 1998 was immediately written off and has not been written back since. The goodwill from acquiring Seven Up and Dr Pepper is not amortised as the company believes "these investments are considered to have an indefinite durability". In other words, it expects us to continue drinking Seven Up and Dr Pepper indefinitely.

Cadbury Schweppes' accounts for 2003 show a massive £3.9 billion worth of intangibles and goodwill on the balance sheet, of which £2.6 billion is intangibles, presumed to be brand names. The total capital employed, as shown on the balance sheet, is £3.3 billion. So the brand names represent 78% of the company's entire value.

Put another way, if the brand names were removed from the balance sheet, the company would be worth only £700,000. If acquired goodwill were also removed, it would not be worth anything.

It should be noted that Cadbury Schweppes' accounts are inconsistent. They place no value on the obvious high value for such long-established brand names as Cadbury's Dairy Milk, yet for Seven Up they are maintaining a brand name value beyond its acquisition cost, which means in effect that the company is capitalising advertising. For Cadbury's Dairy Milk, the company is understating value; for Seven Up it is overstating value (at least in strict accounting terms). If the company sells more Cadbury's Dairy Milk than Seven Up, the overall effect is to understate asset values. However greater consistency in the accounting would be appreciated.

Cadbury Schweppes has total assets of £5.3 billion, but heavy liabilities of £2.0 billion.

The company showed a net profit of £548 million, of which £210 million was paid to shareholders as dividends and £338 million retained by the company. The net profit represents an acceptable 10.3% of its turnover of £5.3 billion.

Cadbury Schweppes is a solid, established company which has a strong position in a stable market. It is a classic investment choice in the Warren Buffet school of investment. However investors should realise that the value of the company's asset backing is in little more than the names of its products.

When was property last valued?

You don't know, and probably don't need to.

However some understanding of property valuation can be needed in understanding accounts.

Fixed assets normally wear out. This is reflected by depreciation, as explained in Section 2.2. There is an exception for land and buildings, which often gain value rather than lose value. The accounting treatment is contained in Financial Reporting Standard FRS 15, which replaced statement of standard accounting practice SSAP 12 in 2000.

Accordingly, property is given special accounting treatment, different from all other forms of fixed asset. Separate figures must be determined for the value of:

- land; and
- buildings.

So a figure for freehold property must be split between the value of the building and the value of the land it stands on. Both must be periodically revalued. Buildings must be depreciated over their useful life. Land is not depreciated.

This may be expressed in tabular form:

Type of fixed asset	Revalued?	Depreciated?
Land	Yes	No
Buildings	Yes	Yes
Other assets	No	Yes

The general rule is that land and buildings must have:

- a full valuation every five years;
- an interim valuation on the third year after a professional valuation; and
- valuations in other years only if there has been a material change.

There are some situations when this routine need not be followed. For example, a company with many premises may revalue its premises on a five-year rolling programme.

There are also some special provisions about investment properties. A 'material change' is something which affects the user's perception of the accounts.

A valuation can put the valuation down as well as up. Sometimes properties fall in value, as many home owners discovered in 1991. The changes in values are reflected in the statement of total recognised gains and losses, which is further explained in Section 2.10.

You can compare gain on revaluation of properties with their balance sheet value, and compare it to the index of property prices generally.

In the 2000 accounts of Royal Bank of Scotland, the statement of total recognised gains and losses shows a £24 million gain from revaluing premises. The notes to the balance sheet show that the company ended the year with £1,768 million worth of freehold premises. This represents a gain of 1.4%. The note explains that the company revalues premises on a five-year rolling programme, which is exactly what you would expect for any major retailer. But 1.4% is a very low figure, considering that property prices were generally soaring that year.

However, the answer is contained in the same note, which explains that the group gained £1.6 billion worth of freehold premises on the acquisition of a subsidiary, namely National Westminster Bank. The value of its freehold premises a year earlier was £523 million, mostly in Scotland, on which £24 million starts to represent a more realistic 4.6%.

Before you get carried away with property valuations, you should realise that the various detailed Financial Reporting Standards are designed to ensure that property is properly valued. There may be a little hidden value in property not fully revalued, but that is likely to be reflected in the share price anyway.

What significance is the figure for minority interest?

A company (the holding company, or parent company) may own all or some of another company's shares. This is broadly accounted in three different ways depending on the percentage of the other company's shares owned:

Amount owned	*Accounting treatment*
up to 20%	investment
over 20% to 50%	associate company
over 50%	subsidiary

This is a summary of the provisions of what is now Financial Reporting Standard FRS 9 published in November 1997, though it largely continues what was the standard under statement of standard accounting practice SSAP 1. There are situations where shareholdings may be treated differently, such as when the control implied by the accounting treatment is not present.

An **investment** simply means that the amount invested is shown with fixed assets, and the dividends received are added to operating income. So if company H owns 20% of the shares of company X, it will add nothing to its separate figures for assets, liabilities and profits. The consolidated accounts of H are not affected by the profit earned by X, only by the amount of dividend it declares.

For an **associate company**, the holding company takes a percentage of the associate's assets, liabilities and profits and adds them to its own. So if company

H owns 40% of the shares of company Y, it will add 40% of the fixed assets, current assets, liabilities and profits to its own figures. The London Stock Exchange regards a 30% holding as a controlling holding.

For a **subsidiary**, the holding company adds the whole of the assets, liabilities and profits of the subsidiary to its own figures. If the holding company owns less than 100% of the shares, it subtracts from this figure a figure of minority interest representing the shares it does not own. So if company H owns 75% of company Z, it will add 100% of the figures for assets, liabilities and profits to its own, and then subtract a figure to reflect the 25% it does not known. This figure is known as minority interest.

It is important to understand these three relationships. A holding company has little if any control over an investment, other than to vote at the annual general meeting. For an associate company, the holding company has significant influence, but not control. If company H wishes to impose its will on company Y, it can cast 40% of the votes on its own, and only needs one sixth of the remaining shareholders to agree with it to succeed. For a subsidiary, the company has control. If it owns 75% of the shares in company Z, it can do whatever it likes as the other 25% can never out-vote H.

The main change introduced by Companies Act 1989 was that reference became to control rather than shareholding. In many cases, this amounts to the same thing. However there are many situations where control does not follow shareholding. An overseas subsidiary may be subject to such overseas law that the parent company cannot exercise any real control. There may be systems of non-voting shares or golden shares that also remove real control.

Where percentage of control is not the same as shareholding, it is likely to downgrade the category of accounting treatment, rather than upgrade it. So a 75% holding may not make company Z a subsidiary but an associate company. So there will be no minority interests. Conversely, a 20% holding may allow company H to exercise control over company X, particularly if the other 80% of shares are held by passive investors. In such cases, company X will be consolidated with company H. The minority interest is really a majority interest, but the term 'minority interest' is still used. All this will be explained in the notes to the accounts.

This is a sweeping summary of the much more detailed provisions in FRS 9, but it provides all that needs to be understood by an investor, except in the most unusual circumstances.

Minority interest is defined in Companies Act 1985 as "the amount of capital and reserves attributable to shares in subsidiary undertakings included in the consolidation held by or on behalf of persons other than the parent company and its subsidiary undertakings."

A minority interest therefore only arises when a holding company has subsidiaries which it does not wholly own. Minority interest is calculated solely by the net assets of the subsidiary, ignoring goodwill.

There can be adjustments to minority interest when a company buys or sells shares. For example companies F, G, H own 30%, 30% and 40% respectively of company W. Company H buys G's holdings. This increases H's holding in W from 40% to 70%, turning an associate company into a subsidiary. This means that H will now go from including 40% of W's assets, liabilities and profits, to including 100% of those assets, liabilities and profits. It will add 60% of W's assets even though it has only acquired 30% of W's shares. The other 30% is shown as a minority interest.

The basis of calculating minority interest in the UK is set out in Financial Reporting Standard FRS 2. International accounting standard IAS 22 allows a slightly greater flexibility.

The minority interest is not particularly significant for shareholders. It should be understood solely because it is there in the accounts, and can be relevant in understanding other matters.

Current Assets

What is the value of net assets?

Formula: Net assets = Fixed assets + Current assets – Liabilities

Net assets simply means what the company is worth, excluding its value from being able to trade.

Fixed assets are valued less depreciation charged to date. Current assets are added, and all liabilities (not just current liabilities) are subtracted.

It is important to understand that assets are valued according to their value to the business. One of the fundamental accounting concepts is the going concern concept. (Accounting concepts are explained in Part IV.) This states that the business will continue for the foreseeable future. The alternative is the forced sale basis, which assumes that the business will soon go bust.

Suppose a hotel chain has spent £1 million on signs saying 'Bloggs Hotels'. These signs are of value while the hotels continue to trade. If they go bust, the signs are probably worthless. You must never assume that the value of net assets is what the company could sell its property for. In most cases, the forced sale value of assets is much less than the going concern value.

There are many specific provisions regarding how companies value their assets. Land and property must be periodically revalued, and details published in the annual accounts.

Trading stock is valued at the lower of cost and net realisable value. This means that stock is usually valued at the amount the company paid to buy it, make it or grow it, even if the product now costs more to acquire. However a lower value must be used if that is the maximum you could realise.

For example, suppose you have a large stock of yearbooks which are fast going out of date. They cost £100,000 to produce and would normally sell for £200,000. However they can only be sold now for £50,000. The net realisable value of this stock is £50,000.

Another example is a company which has made electrical appliances which cost £100,000 to make and would normally sell for £200,000 except that the law on electrical product safety has changed making the product unsaleable. The product can either be dumped or converted to comply with the new regulations for £70,000, when the stock could be sold for £150,000. The net realisable value of this stock is £80,000.

The figure for debtors includes amounts which customers are obliged to repay. However some customers will not pay, so the figure is reduced by a figure for bad debts and doubtful debts to what the business expects actually to receive.

What premium or discount is the share price to asset value?

Formula: Premium or Discount = [Market capitalisation – Net assets] ÷ Net assets

Normally, the value of a business is the value of its assets plus a sum representing the value that the business is up and running, and making a profit.

A prerequisite of this ratio is that the assets are properly valued in accordance with accounting standards. A different valuation policy can make a large difference to the company's reported figures, so the same valuation policies should be followed by all companies being compared.

The amount by which the market capitalisation exceeds the net assets indicates how confident the market is that the company will perform well. This, in turn, is a function of two factors:

• the rate of profit expected; and
• the likelihood of achieving that profitability.

So if a company has a million shares, a market capitalisation of £3 million and net assets of £2 million, its premium is 50%.

Sometimes, the shares sell at a discount to net assets. For reasons not fully understood, investment trusts tend to sell at a discount. This means that a company with net assets of £2 million may have a market capitalisation of £1.5 million. The discount is 25%. A discount means that the market expects the company to lose value.

An obvious question to ask is why, if a company has net assets of £2 million but the market thinks it is only worth £1.5 million, does not someone buy it for £1.5million, sell the assets and make himself £500,000 easy profit? Quite apart from the fact that such buying would quickly push up the share price, the main reason is the basis of asset valuation on a going basis concern, rather than a forced sale which would realise a much lower figure.

A company with a discount to net asset value is not necessarily a poor investment. If you believe that the company will perform less badly than the market expects, it could prove to be a good investment.

The factors regarding premium or discount to net asset value are similar to those which apply to price to book values mentioned earlier in this chapter. The two ratios largely measure the same factors.

Premium and discount ratios are most commonly used for asset-backed companies, such as investment trusts and property companies. As the assets are regularly valued, the net asset value is more accurate than for most companies. Also these businesses send to have similar trading styles and demands than in other sectors. This makes such companies more comparable, and this ratio therefore becomes more useful.

As ever, it is essential to compare the figures with those for the sector. St Mowden Properties' premium of 52% to NAV does not sound very impressive, until you realise that property companies trade at an average *discount* of 19%.

How much cash does the company have?

Ultimately cash is what matters to a company. Its assets, creditors, stock, capital, workforce and goodwill are all designed to generate cash.

Sometimes companies are criticised for putting "profit before people". This is a meangingless expression, as a company is established to make a profit just as a car is built to carry people. A company serves people by making a profit. This is used to employ its workforce, meet the needs of customers, provide business for suppliers, generate financial growth for pension funds, and pay tax towards the common good. None of this stops a company from pursuing other socially desirable goals, such as environmental protection, support for charities and fair working practices. But these are ancillary to the main socially desirable goal of generating cash.

A company must disclose how much cash it owns, but there is no legal definition of cash. Financial Reporting Standard FRS 1 gives a definition of cash for the purpose of cash flow statements. This broadly includes all bank accounts where funds can be withdrawn at not more than 24 hours or one working day. It thus excludes short-term deposits.

The FRS 1 definition of cash is commonly referred to as 'cash in hand'. The expression 'cash at bank and in hand' usually includes short-term deposits.

However even this is not a constant rule. Boots and Hanson both use the expression 'cash at bank and in hand', but Boots excludes short-term deposits while Hanson includes them.

A lack of cash is a problem. However much a company is worth in fixed assets and other current assets, and however much work it has in hand, if it has no cash, it cannot pay its bills, wages, tax and other demands.

The 2002 accounts for Systems Integrated Research plc (now known as SiRViS iT plc) show zero for cash at bank and in hand. The company makes educational software. It appears it has not got a brass farthing to its name and cannot pay the milkman. However there is a statement that Berg & Berg Enterprises Inc., its major shareholder, has lent it £483,000 to keep it going. The accounts show that the company's net assets are £1.071 million. This is quite common for small companies. In this case Berg & Berg is the investment vehicle for C. E. Berg, the chairman.

A statement that a shareholder has tipped more money into the company is one of the many examples of second-hand information available to investors. You can be sure that the shareholder has done his homework in providing such a loan. That does not mean that the shareholder was right. Atlantic Caspian Resources plc kept receiving shareholder loans from JAV Ltd to drill for oil in Kazakhstan. After repeated drilling from 1996, it failed to find any oil in commercial quantities and declared itself insolvent in November 2003.

How liquid are the current assets?

The three main current assets in order of liquidity are:

*   cash;
*   debtors; and
*   stock.

Liquidity means the ease with which the asset becomes cash, therefore cash itself is the most liquid of all assets. Debtors is the next liquid, as all a company has to do is wait for the company to pay. It may have to chase the customer and some customers may not pay at all. But in general, debtors will turn to cash merely by the passing of time. Stock must be sold, and then becomes a debtor. It is still a current asset, but it is less liquid than debtors or cash.

As each of three types must be shown separately on the balance sheet, it is a simple matter to see how liquid the company is. What this means in practice to the investor is determined by various ratios mentioned in other sections.

In most cases, an investor need not consider the figures for current assets any further. However there are some specific issues where the figures can merit closer scrutiny. The issue of how to define cash was addressed in the previous question.

With regards to debtors, there are some points to note.

Company law requires that debts are split between current debts and long-term debts, where the latter are repayable after more than one year. This is defined as the date on when payment is due, rather than when it is expected. Long-term debts must be disclosed separately if material. A debt payable in more than a year's time is really a loan. Banks and finance companies have long-term debts as that is their business. You should enquire why a non-finance company has any significant long-term debts.

A more significant problem is when current assets are transferred to fixed assets. Simple examples are when a garage decides to keep a car for its own use, or a plant manufacturer retains some of its own plant. In such cases, the change is not significant.

When the current asset is property, the matter is different. In its 1991 accounts Trafalgar House transferred investment properties from current assets to fixed assets. The consequential write-down was taken to the revaluation reserve rather than the profit and loss account. The Financial Reporting Review Panel intervened and the write-down was shown to the profit and loss account in the comparative figures for the 1992 accounts.

What provision has been made for bad and doubtful debts?

The figure for debtors must be after subtracting any amounts for bad or doubtful debts.

Legally, the accounts must show debtors after deductions for bad debts and doubtful debts, but these figures need not be disclosed separately.

- A **bad debt** is a debt which the company believes will not be paid and therefore has written off in its accounts. It is always specific to a particular customer, usually when the customer has become insolvent.

- A **doubtful debt** is a debt which the company has good reason to doubt will be paid. The debt is not written off, but a provision is made to allow for the possibility of non-payment. This is not necessarily customer-specific, as a doubtful debt provision may, for example, be 1% of all debts in the light of experience.

Bad debts and doubtful debts both reduce the disclosed figure for debts. But for doubtful debts, this is compensated by the same amount being added to provisions.

There is one curiosity in accounting regarding bad debts. Suppose a company buys something for £7 and sells it for £10 to a customer who never pays. This will be shown in the accounts as:

turnover	£10
less cost of sales	(£7)
gross profit	£3
less bad debt	(£10)
net loss	(£7)

The net loss figure is obviously correct. Selling £7 worth of stock to someone who does not pay for it is no different from having it stolen or throwing it away. The curiosity is that we show £3 gross profit. This is accounting convenience. Unless there are significant bad debts, it is unlikely to affect the accounts significantly.

You will only know about bad debts or doubtful debts if the company chooses to tell you, perhaps to explain some appalling results. If they do, remember that the operating profit is overstated. Disclosure of bad debts is normally made only by financial sector companies like banks. For example in 2004, mortgage lender Kensington reported that its bad debt provision has reduced from 0.6% of mortgage assets to 0.5%. HBOS's bad debt provision on advances is 0.81%; Barclays' is 0.73%.

You must always understand the business when considering any figures. London Scottish Bank reported 17% bad debt provision in 2004, but you must understand that this bank specialises in buying distressed debt. In other words, the debts are pretty bad when the bank acquires them.

How can I tell if the stock is fairly valued?

In most cases, you cannot and do not need to.

Stock valuation only becomes an issue in particular circumstances, explained in the answer to the next question.

What is the company's stock turn?

Formula: Sales ÷ Stock

Stock turn indicates how long stock stays in the company before being sold. In reality it also indicates a measure of gross profit, as the sale figure includes gross profit but the stock figure does not. This figure cannot be calculated for service companies.

In general, the higher this figure, the better. This indicates that the company is shifting its stock efficiently. It is therefore maximising profit and showing good management.

Sometimes this figure is expressed as 'stock days'. This is simply 365 divided by the figure for stock turn. It indicates how many days the stock sits on the shelf before being sold (after allowing for gross profit). For stock days, the lower the number, the better.

As with almost every ratio, the figure makes most sense when compared with equivalent figures for the industry.

Stock turn is a useful measure for businesses which manufacture products as well as those which simply sell them, such as retailers.

Unlike almost every other figure in the balance sheet and profit and loss account, the figure for stock is not calculated from the accounting records, but is calculated by physically counting the number of items in stock, and valuing them. If a business can find another £100,000 worth of stock, that increases both its year's profit and its value as a business by £100,000. For that reason, stock counting and stock valuation should be closely monitored by the auditors. This is a common area for business fraud.

It is well-known that businesses often seek to inflate their stock figures by almost any means. One private company sought to persuade its auditors that it owned large quantities of salad oil. The auditors insisted on seeing the oil, measured the vats, checked that the vats went to the bottom and took a sample to test that it was salad oil. Duly satisfied, the auditors agreed the figure. Only later, did they discover that the oil was floating on water.

Manufacturers include work-in-progress in their figure for stock. Sometimes manufacturers are tempted to inflate the stock figure by a generous valuation of work-in-progress. Any business may be tempted to inflate its stock to increase its profit and overall value. Stock which in truth is obsolete may be included, and any stock may be overvalued.

> A similar or slightly reducing stock turn should indicate a healthy and well-managed company.

Stock turn is one area where this will show up. If a company has inflated its stock value it will suffer by having a poor stock turn, so a significantly lower stock turn than the industry average could indicate dishonesty.

Stock turn is most comparable between retailers in the same area. Food suppliers have low stock turn periods while building suppliers have high stock turns.

Perhaps more important than the stock turn for a company is how this is changing from year to year. A similar or slightly reducing stock turn should indicate a healthy and well-managed company (at least as far as shifting stock is concerned).

What is the burn rate?

Formula: Burn rate = Cash ÷ Monthly operating expenses

A burn rate is only appropriate for a new company which has yet to make a profit. It is a useful substitute for all those ratios which such a company cannot provide, such as P/E ratio and dividend yield.

It should be appreciated that all start-up companies are high risk. If you are averse to risk, you should not be bothering with burn rates as you should not have invested in such a company in the first place.

A company getting going incurs start-up expenses which are funded from the initial investments, usually a mixture of share sales and borrowings. It must live on that until it earns sufficient profit to become self-financing.

The burn rate is the number of months the company can survive at the present rate before it must become self-sufficient.

In calculating this figure, it is important to use the correct figures. Cash means money that the business can put its hands on immediately. It may include readily saleable investments such as gilts, but not investments in other companies.

Monthly operating expenses means those items which represent cash outflows. In practice this is the total of operating expenses listed between gross profit and net profit, for which you can subtract the figures for depreciation and amortisation of goodwill. These two items are accounting adjustments which do not represent cash outflows for the period. They represent an element of money which has already been spent but where that expenditure has been deferred from that previous period.

The directors' report should include comments about how the burn rate is going. No director is likely to say that they will run out of money before earning profits (and would almost certainly be committing a criminal offence if he did). However it is not unknown for directors to have an over-optimistic view of the matter. So some healthy cynicism is appropriate.

The start-up process is in two stages. The first stage is when the company generates no revenue at all. The second stage is when it starts to generate revenue but insufficient to support the business yet.

In the normal course of events, you would expect a company to generate increasing amounts of income until they are sufficient to support the business. Once a company has passed the first stage, it is possible that a burn rate equal to 36 months could mean that the company could actually survive for four years, as its small but increasing revenue over the four years could cover another 12 months of expenditure. So burn rate should always be considered in the context of whether revenue is being earned.

If a company starts to run out of money before becoming sufficiently profitable to support itself, the company may try to raise more funds to keep going. This is always bad news for investors for two reasons. First, the company may not be successful. Lenders are suspicious of companies that keep coming back for more funding rather than those which obtain sufficient funds from the start. Second, any new funding will be on terms beneficial to the new lenders not to existing shareholders.

You must be particularly careful about burn rate. For most other accounting ratios, if things turn out badly, your investment will perform less well than you had hoped. If the burn rate proves excessive, the company will go bust and you will lose your entire investment.

Burn rates are often quoted every six months. You should monitor these closely to see if they remain constant or reduce slightly. Any significant increase probably means you should get out quickly, even at the expense of making a big loss. Losing half your money is better than losing it all.

What is cashflow?

A basic accounting concept is the matching concept, also known as the accruals concept. This states that income and expenditure must be matched in the period in which the income is earned and the expenditure incurred. Only by doing so is it possible to calculate the amount of profit earned for that period.

An obvious example of what this means applies when considering fixed assets. A company buys a lathe for £10,000 which it intends to use for ten years. Suppose its other expenses are £4,000 a year and its income is £8,000. We could prepare accounts entirely on the cash basis. This shows that for year 1 it made a loss:

income	£8,000
cost of lathe	(£10,000)
other expenses	(£4,000)
net loss	(£6,000)

And for each of years 2 to 10, the accounts would show:

income	£8,000
expenses	(£4,000)
net profit	£4,000

So we would report a £6,000 loss in year 1 and then a £4,000 profit in each of years 2 to 10.

It is obvious that this is ridiculous as the facts are unchanged from year to year. So we use the matching concept under which we regard the lathe as a fixed asset and to charge £1,000 in each year's accounts. This charge is known as depreciation. It represents the amount of a fixed asset which has been 'consumed' in the period by getting old and wearing out.

So accruals basis would show for each of the 10 years:

income	£8,000
depreciation	(£1,000)
other expenses	(£4,000)
net profit	£3,000

This gives a more accurate representation of the profit earned. It should be noted that the total profit earned over the ten-year period is exactly the same. The accruals basis shows ten years each with £3,000 profit. This is £30,000 over the ten-year period. The cash basis shows nine years of £4,000 profit, which equals £36,000. When we subtract the £6,000 "loss" in the first year, we come back to £30,000 profit over the ten-year period.

The point to all this is that the matching concept only affects how much profit is reported in a particular accounting period. Over the whole life of the business, the accruals basis and cash basis will show the same total figure for profit. The difference is said to be a timing difference.

While the accruals basis measures profit more accurately than the cash basis, it gives no indication of where the cash comes from or goes. This is determined by the cash flow statement. This appears in the annual accounts as a separate financial statement. It must comply with the provisions of Financial Reporting Standard FRS 1 (explained in Part IV).

The cash flow statement ignores bookkeeping adjustments which do not involve the movement of cash. So cashflow ignores depreciation, amortisation of goodwill, accruals and prepayments of creditors and debtors, capitalised interest, and minority interest. Unless money has changed hands, a transaction does not appear in the cashflow statement. The difference between the inflows and outflows is the net cashflow. This figure represents the net amount of cash which has flowed into the business or out of it.

The value of a cashflow statement to investors (or anyone else) is hotly disputed. The statement for a company like BP indicates that much of its cash inflow goes out again as shareholder dividends, paid four times a year. That indicates that BP is a good cash cow for investors wanting income, particularly as it is a stable and established company. It is less attractive for someone looking for a growth stock.

In precarious businesses, the cash flow statement can indicate whether the company is likely to survive.

In a large business where fixed assets are routinely replaced, the differences between net cashflow and net profit tend to cancel themselves out anyway.

Net cashflow is sometimes used as part of other ratios. Discounted cashflow is explained below. Otherwise, investors probably need not worry too much about cashflow. You are investing for the profit the business makes, and that is what you need to monitor year on year.

What is the discounted cashflow?

Formula: Discounted cashflow = Sum of cashflows for each year

Over the lifetime of a business, net cashflows will equal net profits. The differences relate to time. However inflation means that money loses value over time, so, while timing differences do not affect how much money a business receives, it can affect how much that money is worth.

When inflation is low, and when fixed assets are routinely replaced, such timing differences are not significant. However in times of higher inflation or over long periods, the change could be significant. Discounted cashflow (DCF) is a means by which this can be resolved.

Discounted cashflow multiplies the inflows and outflows by factors representing inflation for the relevant period. The adjusted amounts are totalled to give the net present value (NPV) of the future cashflow.

It should be noted that there are several measures of inflation. The commonest are:

* RPI: retail prices index
* RPIX: retail prices index without mortgages;
* HICP: Harmonised Index of Consumer Prices.

There are many other indices relevant to specific products. All measures of inflation relate to how prices increase in amount not to how money decreases in value, so inflation rates must be converted to a grossed up factor. So 5% inflation becomes the factor 100/105, which equals 0.952. For a two-year period, the factor is 0.952 multiplied by 100/105, which equals 0.907.

Suppose we are considering cashflows of £1,000 in five consecutive years when the rate of inflation is 5%. The DCF calculation is as follows:

Year	Cashflow	DCF factor	Discounted cashflow
1	£1,000	1.0	£1,000
2	£1,000	0.952	£952
3	£1,000	0.907	£907
4	£1,000	0.864	£864
5	£1,000	0.823	£823
	£5,000		£4,546

This means that, although we will have received £5,000 at the end of the 5-year period, it is only worth £4,546 at current value. Even with a low inflation rate and a short period, our investment has lost almost 10% of its value.

DCF has many applications beyond considering companies for investment. For example, it is the only means by which a fair comparison can be made when comparing investments with different payment patterns. DCF is a monkey wrench. It is a tool you will not need often, but when you do, you cannot manage without it.

What is the internal rate of return?

Formula: [cannot be calculated]

The internal rate of return (IRR) is the total annual percentage rate of return on any investment (not just shares). It is widely used when there is more than one source of return. In shares, this will include the return and the dividend.

In algebra, IRR may be expressed in the form:

$$y = ar^n + br^n$$

where y is the total return, r is the IRR, n is the number of years, and a and b are the factors contributing to the return. Mathematicians have yet to work out how to recast that formula in the form:

$$r = ?$$

This means that the formula cannot be solved using elementary algebra, but it can be solved by other means, such as iteration. This involves guessing a figure for r, substituting it in the original formula, and then trying a higher or lower figure, and repeating the process until the correct answer is found. This sounds very hit-and-miss, but can be a quick process in which as few as five guesses can lead to a correct answer. It is also easily solved by computer. The iterative process can also be speeded up using compound interest tables.

There is an online calculator available from the US company DataDynamica International Inc. on www.jamesko.com/irr.asp. The website includes instructions. You simply enter the inflows (with a minus sign) and outflows for successive years and hit the return key. The answer appears within seconds. To take a simple example, an investment of £100,000 in year 1 produces an income of £30,000 in each of years 2 to 5 and is then worth nothing. This gives an overall return of £20,000. Using the online calculator, we find the internal rate of return is 7.7138%.

This can be checked thus:

Start balance	Cashflow	Balance	Interest	Final balance
£100,000	-	£100,000	£7,714	£107,714
£107,714	(£30,000)	£77,714	£5,995	£83,709
£83,709	(£30,000)	£53,709	£4,143	£57,852
£57,852	(£30,000)	£27,852	£2,148	£30,000
£30,000	(£30,000)	nil	nil	nil

Although companies use internal rate of return to evaluate their own spending and investment decisions, this information is not usually available to the investor. Internal rate of return is useful to the investor for comparing how the return on a particular investment (not just shares) compares. In the example above, you would need to find an investment with an annual return above 7.7138% to better the return from the investment outlined there.

Is it using debt wisely?

Relevant to:
All investors

Underlying worry
'Is the company financing growth with debt it cannot afford to service?'

The level and type of debt

How much debt does the company have?

This figure is shown on the face of the balance sheet as 'Creditors falling due after more than one year', or similar words.

As with all financial information, interpretation is at least as important as raw data. As an example, on the following page we quote the balance sheet (with some figures totalled) from the 2003 accounts of the troubled welding and metal cutting company Charter plc.

Its balance sheet paints an extraordinary picture. If you look at the last three figures, you see that the company is worth £13 million, of which non-shareholders own £18.5 million, leaving minus £5.5 million for shareholders! These non-shareholders are the other parties who own shares in the company's subsidiaries.

The total figure for debt is £255.9 million. Incidentally, this figure does not appear on the original balance sheet, which simply lists the constituents without a total figure. This is a massive amount of debt against a share capital of £1.9 million. Later in this section, we explain that gearing of 200% or more is high. This company has a gearing ratio of 13,468%. (Strictly speaking this is wrong, as gearing is normally calculated as debt to total shareholders' funds, which here is a negative figure, giving a meaningless gearing ratio. Also, the actual borrowings, against other forms of provisions and liability total £226.2 million.)

Charter plc is a profitable company. In the year to 31 December 2002, its turnover was £900.5 million and its profit £12.0 million. It is not its trading that need concern an investor, but whether it can continue to exist under this massive weight of debt. Will it collapse like Marconi (see page 18)? If it does, the trade will probably be continued under new owners, but you will lose out as an investor.

	£m	£m
Fixed assets		175.8
Current assets	370.3	
Creditors: falling due within one year	(182.6)	
Short-term borrowings	(94.6)	
	(277.2)	
Net current assets		93.1
Total assets less current liabilities		268.9
Creditors: amounts falling due after more than one year:		
Other long term creditors	(1.0)	
Long term borrowings	(131.6)	
Provisions for liabilities and charges	(123.3)	
		(255.9)
		13.0
Capitals and reserves:		
Called up share capital		1.9
Share premium account		5.9
Profit and loss account		(13.3)
Shareholders' funds: equity interests		(5.5)
Minority interests: equity interests		18.5
		13.0

How secure is the debt funding?

The first step is to look at what the company says about the **going concern basis**. This may appear in the notes to the accounts or operating review. The going concern basis is one of the fundamental accounting concepts.

This is what Charter plc says, omitting a few irrelevant bits. The italic and bold formatting are mine and do not appear in Charter's original accounts.

In the year to 31 December 2002, the group met its day-to-day working capital requirements through a £127 million syndicated *revolving credit facility*. In addition, it has in issue US private placement loans totalling £128.2 million and, as at 31 December 2002, net debt stood at £194.0 million.

Charter is discussing with its lending banks the renewal of its syndicated revolving credit facility which is due to expire on 31 July 2003. At present some £91 million of the facility is drawn, leaving a balance of £36 million undrawn and available. Whilst the terms of the renewal have yet to be agreed with the banks, the company will need to reduce its debt significantly during the course of the next 12 months and plans to do this through *planned asset disposals*. The directors believe that disposals can be made both within a timeframe and at prices that will prove acceptable and ensure that the group is able to meet its obligations on an ongoing basis.

The company has been informed by the agent bank that the outstanding issues should be capable of being satisfactorily resolved prior to expiry of the current facilities, but after receipt of an accountant's report commissioned by the banks. There can be *no guarantee that the renewal negotiations will be satisfactorily concluded*. However, in the light of the information currently available to them, the directors consider it appropriate to prepare the accounts on a going concern basis. Should the banks not support the company in this respect, adjustments would be necessary to records additional liabilities and to write down assets to their recoverable amount. Furthermore, additional provisions might need to be made in the group's and company's balance sheets in respect of liabilities which are currently contingent. It is not practicable to quantify these possible adjustments.

Certain holders of the group's US private placement loan notes have informed the company that they consider that a *default* has arisen under the loan notes as a result of the *accounting irregularities* which were acknowledged by the company on 27 January 2003 at one of the air and gas handling units in North America. The directors' view, based on their knowledge of the situation and on advice by the company's legal advisers, is that no default has occurred and the note holders have been advised accordingly. Of the total loan notes of $206.3 million, $72.3 million are due for *scheduled repayment in March 2004* and the directors envisage that the terms of the renewal of the company's banking facility will take account of the need to repay those notes in 2004. In the event that the company's and its advisers' views are proven to be incorrect and the note holders elect to accelerate the notes, then the full amount of notes outstanding would become repayable immediately.

Rarely will an investor read such a depressing statement. You must remember that the only alternative to a going concern is usually insolvency. This company is openly admitting that it may go bust.

In assessing this likelihood, you should always remember that directors are perennial optimists. Every storm is represented as a light shower and every straw as a guardrail.

In the above statement, I have highlighted phrases which should start alarm bells ringing, and shown below what such statements may mean.

---

revolving credit facility

The company is basically living on a bank facility. There is no long-term commitment by the lenders to the company, as you would have in other forms of debt instrument, such as debentures, preference shares or loan notes.

planned asset disposals

The company is having to sell the family silver to keep going. Then it will have to sell the kitchen table, fridge and kitchen sink. It is selling its ability to make future profits. This is sheer desperation.

no guarantee that the renewal negotiations will be satisfactorily concluded

This statement means that the company is at the mercy of the banks, who are themselves commercial bodies answerable to shareholders. Banks are merciless to troubled customers and err on the side of caution. They are more likely to wind up a saveable company than save a hopeless company. The next section is a well-written summary of what happens if a company ceases to be a going concern.

default

Most insolvencies are triggered when a company defaults on a repayment. Even if the lender spares the company, this will usually be at the price of some penalty, perhaps in a higher rate of interest.

accounting irregularities

It is rare to find a company admitting accounting irregularities so openly. It is unfortunate that we are not told more.

scheduled repayment in March 2004

The company has an immediate problem. Not only is it running out of money, it is running out of time.

When you read a going concern statement such as this one, it is not necessary to look at the accounts to find details of the borrowings, but we will do so for the sake of completion.

Short-term borrowing	£m	
Loan notes	1.9	
Bank loans and overdrafts – secured	0.3	
Bank loans and overdrafts – unsecured	92.1	
Obligations under finance leases	0.3	
	94.6	94.6
Long-term borrowing		
6.78% 2004 loan notes of US $72.3million	45.0	
7.24% 2005 loan notes of US $6.0 million	3.7	
7.33% 2005 loan notes of US $5.0 million	3.1	
6.88% 2007 loan notes of US $85.0 million	52.8	
6.96% 2009 loan notes of US $35.0 million	21.7	
Loans – unsecured	0.8	
Obligations under finance leases	4.5	
	131.6	131.6
Total borrowings		226.2

A further table helpfully explains that £46.8 million of these borrowings are repayable between one and two years after the balance sheet date. This means that the company must pay £94.6 million in the next year, and £46.8 million in the year after. This is a tough call.

You may also note that much of the long-term borrowing is in dollars, exposing the company to currency risk.

The fact that some loans are described as unsecured indicates that the others are probably secured, which would be normal. Secured loans means that the lender can seize assets ahead of other creditors (though UK law now provides that some funds must be set aside for unsecured creditors). Seizing assets would hasten the insolvency of the company.

None of this means that Charter plc is necessarily a bad investment. Remember that the principle of a good investment is that you expect the company to perform better than the market does. So what did the market expect? These accounts were published on 22 May 2003. The shares were trading at or below 38p for three weeks before. When these accounts were published, the shares immediately leapt to 42p and continued to rise.

So the market expected the company to recover. The accounts were commendably honest and well-received. The issue for you to decide is whether you believe the market is over-optimistic or under-optimistic. You could build on your knowledge from the accounts, by studying this market and reading press comments on the company, among other sources.

A little more time has passed since those accounts were published. We now know that the market was under-optimistic and Charter would have been a good investment after all – at least for the next year.

By November 2003, shares had more than doubled to over £1. At the beginning of February 2004 they rose to over £1.50. This is still well below the £9.50 the shares were worth in 1996, but represents a 300% improvement in less than one year. The company issued a set of announcements about disposals of property, with explanations of where it would rehouse. It was not selling the kitchen sink after all.

The surge in February 2004 was when it won its case brought by note holders alleging default. At the same time, it announced that it had raised £40 million from asset disposals and reduced its debt from £193 million in June 2003 to £140 million by December 2003.

Paying off debt

How much is the company paying in interest on its debt?

The interest rate should be shown in the list of borrowings, usually as a note to the accounts cross-referenced against long-term creditors in the balance sheet. In the example of Charter plc used above, we can see that the rates of interest varied between 6.78% and 7.33%.

In considering the rate of interest, you should remember that even large businesses must borrow above the base rate. You should also remember that, even though UK interest rates in 2003 reached a 40-year low, they were still significantly higher than interest rates in the US, Europe and Japan, our main trading competitors.

An example of an explanation on interest rates is given in the 2000 accounts for Pearson plc (which owns *The Financial Times* and Penguin books).

> Net interest rose by £10m to £157m, with average net debt remaining largely constant. This increase in interest cost followed a general rise in interest rates during the year. A weighted three month LIBOR rate, reflecting the group's borrowings in US dollars, euros and sterling, rose by 110 basis points, or 1.1%. The effect of these rises on the group was mitigated by its existing portfolio of interest rate swaps, which converted over half of its variable rate commercial paper and bank debt to a fixed rate basis. As a result, the group's net interest rate payable averaged approximately 6.9%, rising 0.5% from the previous year.

You need not trouble yourself understanding interest rate swaps. It is sufficient that you appreciate they are a form of insurance so that if interest rates move adversely, the company receives a measure of protection.

This clear statement explains that interest is 6.9%. Interest rates rose by 1.1 percentage points, but because the company had taken precautions, its payable interest rate rose by only 0.5 points.

When is its debt repayable?

Like the interest rate, this should be disclosed in the notes to the accounts, usually in the description of the form of debt, such as '2010 debenture'. Where a range of dates is shown, this indicates that the debt is repayable at any time between those dates, usually at the company's choice.

The question of when debt is repayable is only of concern to an investor if the company has a large repayment imminent. However any concerns about this are likely to have been addressed already in the going concern statement, as explained above.

Is it earning enough profit on its borrowings to cover its debt?

This can be seen clearly from the profit and loss account which records both interest payable and net profit. However any concerns are likely to have been addressed in the going concern statement.

Is the amount which the company has to pay linked to its credit rating?

There is no way of knowing this from the published accounts unless the company chooses to tell you. There is no legal obligation for a company to do so.

The world's two leading ratings agencies are Moody's and Standard & Poor's. They have different systems of expressing their ratings, using letters. This is based on their analysts' judgement on the creditworthiness of the company. Ratings is itself a $2.5 billion a year business. The views of ratings agencies are widely respected and routinely reported in the financial press.

Sometimes the interest rate is linked to the credit rating given by one of these agencies, so if an agency downgrades the company, the interest rate rises or the loan becomes repayable sooner. This is a much more common practice in the US than in the UK.

In 1975, the US Securities Exchange Commission (SEC) appointed four agencies as a nationally recognised cartel. The other agencies were Dominion

Bond and Finch. By June 2003, SEC were concerned about the activities of the agencies. The two concerns are:

*   the agencies failed to spot the deficiencies at Enron and WorldCom, among other scandals; and

*   issuers of securities pay agencies for their ratings, leading to suggestions that they are not independent.

The Bank of England issued similar warnings in June 2003.

A downgrading of Enron's credit rating led to $4 billion worth of debt becoming payable, helping to trigger its collapse.

A 2003 survey by *Financial Satellite Review* has identified 22 major US and European companies who have contracts where the interest rate is linked to credit rating.

What will happen if the company cannot pay its debt?

It either goes bust or the creditors take over. Either way, the investor loses out massively.

Even when a company gets into difficulties, existing shareholders can expect to lose out heavily in favour of the new investors who bail out the company.

Eurotunnel is a good example of this. The project of a tunnel under the Channel linking England and France was conceived as far back as 1715. The modern project was agreed in 1986. In 1987, the company raised £770 million on the Stock Exchange and estimated construction costs at £4.9 billion. It soon became clear that the money would run out before the tunnel was completed, so investors were asked for another £556 million. The tunnel opened in 1994, one year late. In 1995, it is revealed that the cost had risen to £12 billion. The group's debt was £9 billion. Interest payments were £2 million a day. Its 1996 loss of £925 million is one of the largest ever reported. Shareholders found another £858 million. In 1997, the company was forced to convert much debt into shares, to the protests of French shareholders. The company started making an operating profit in 1998 and a net profit in 1999. But by then the share price was 71p, against £3.50 twelve years earlier. No dividends have been paid, nor are any expected before 2006 at the earliest.

What is the interest cover?

Formula: Interest cover = [Pre-tax profit + Net interest paid] ÷ Net interest paid

Interest cover indicates how well the company's finances are managed. Interest cover is sometimes called income gearing.

Interest cover measures how many times the net profit could pay the interest charge. This measure clearly only applies to companies which have borrowings.

The usual way of expressing interest cover is to add pre-tax profit and the net interest paid, and divide the total by the net interest paid. Mathematically, you can arrive at the same number by dividing the pre-tax profit by net interest, and adding 1 to the answer.

Net interest paid is the amount paid by the company on overdrafts and other bank debts, and on various types of bonds. Any interest received, such as from deposits or short-term investments, is usually subtracted.

Sometimes companies capitalise part of their interest payments. This happens when they borrow money to finance a capital project, such as new premises. If it costs £1 million to build a new store, for which the company has borrowed the money and must pay £100,000 interest, it is reasonable for the company to say that the store has cost it £1,100,000. Capitalised interest is removed from the profit and loss account and is added to fixed assets in the balance sheet. As with all comparisons, it is important that an investor compares like with like. An investor must be careful to ensure that any figures for interest charge consistently either include or exclude capitalised interest.

In practice, it is sensible to use the figure for non-capitalised interest, as capitalised interest really represents expenditure on fixed assets for which other measures provide sufficient oversight. Also, the accounts may not readily disclose the figure for capitalised interest, whereas uncapitalised interest is always disclosed.

Interest cover is a measure of more interest to lenders than investors. However investors should not ignore it for several reasons.

Any figure below, say, 5.0 starts to indicate that an established company is heavily indebted. The company may argue that the borrowing is to fund future growth. That is irrelevant to the investor. If the interest cover is too low, the company could struggle to pay its debts, forcing it to make a fire sale of assets at low prices or even become insolvent. Companies exist to make profits, some of which they retain to fund expansion. It is usually prudent for companies to borrow some money to augment retained profits for expansion, but borrowing which is too high to be unsustainable is bad news for investors regardless of the purpose of the borrowing.

An exception may be made for new businesses where most of the borrowing is from the directors. Such companies may have very low interest cover but be safe. A director is unlikely to foreclose on his own company and risk losing his own investment.

Low interest cover indicates that a business is vulnerable to interest rate increases. The base rate has been at or below 4% since November 2001, which has generated some complacency about debt costs to both consumers and businesses. It should be remembered that interest rates were above 10% from 1988 to 1992 and could go that high, or higher, again. When interest rates start to move, they can move quickly. It took only two years between 1977 and 1979 for interest rates almost to treble from 6% to 17% (a record high).

In considering such vulnerability to interest rate increases, you need to form your own view on how you expect interest rates to move. You may also wish to hedge your bets so that investments in rate-averse businesses are balanced by rate-friendly businesses, such as banks. Remember also that interest rates can affect businesses in other ways. Turnover of businesses in luxury markets is particularly vulnerable to interest rate rises as customers tend to economise on luxuries when their spending is hit.

Low interest cover indicates a possible vulnerability to competition. If a company with a high interest cover notes that its main competitor has low interest cover, it could be tempted to start an aggressive price war knowing that this will hurt the competitor more than itself, possibly even killing off the competitor. Such considerations are discussed in the next section on gearing.

Many bond issues include provisions for penalties if the interest cover falls below a set figure. This is a double whammy as it exacerbates the problem. It means that a company which is struggling to pay its debt is then hit by more debt. If bond issues are a significant factor in the debt of a low-cover company, an investor should look at the terms of the bond issue in the notes to the accounts.

What about buying back shares?

Traditionally a company could not buy shares in itself because that would amount to a reduction in capital, which required the consent of the courts under traditional company law. This was decided in the court case *Trevor v Whitworth* back in 1887. This law was changed in 1981, when companies were allowed to buy their own shares subject to some conditions.

The effect of a company buying its shares is almost always to improve the value of the remaining shares. It is a way of passing some of a company's cash to its shareholders without triggering an immediate tax charge.

An example of a statement about a share buyback is found in 2003 interim accounts from beer brewers Fuller Smith and Turner plc.

> In the first six months of this year, we have bought back 75,000 £1 'A' ordinary shares and 2,531,000 unquoted 10p 'B' ordinary shares. The average price paid was £5.48 (per £1 share equivalent). Although higher than the average price paid in previous years, this is still a significant discount to our net assets per share. The cumulative buybacks to date have increased normalised earnings per share and net assets per share by 12% and 3% respectively.

Other ways of returning cash may not be simple. In March 2002, Marks & Spencer decided to return £2 billion to shareholders. This is how their scheme worked:

- for every 21 shares held, the shareholder was allotted 17 new shares and 21 B shares;
- the B shares could be immediately redeemed for 70p in cash;
- if not redeemed, they would attract a dividend equal to 75% of the six-month LIBOR interest rate;
- B shares could be redeemed for 70p at six-monthly intervals every March or September.

What this boils down to is that shareholders received £11.90 cash for every 21 shares held, equivalent to a 57p dividend. However the shareholder could choose when to take the dividend, allowing large shareholders to maximise the tax advantage.

What is the gearing ratio, and how does it matter?

Formula: Gearing = [Total borrowings – Cash] ÷ Shareholders' funds

Gearing is the ratio of borrowings to shareholders' funds. In the US, gearing is more commonly known as 'leverage'.

As explained, the capital of a company is ultimately of only two sources: debt and equity. Debt is where the company borrows money which it usually must repay with interest regardless of how much profit it makes. Equity is in the form of shares, selling itself, where the dividend is related to the profit it makes and decides to distribute.

Gearing, as its name suggests, means that the benefit to shareholders is magnified when the company does well, but that the detriment to shareholders is similarly magnified when the company does badly.

Gearing is usually classified as:

- low: less than 100%
- medium: 100-200%
- high: above 200%

Sometimes companies have a stated policy on gearing. For example, van hire company Northgate has a policy of gearing up to 250%. Its 2003 accounts show gearing at 223%.

The effect of gearing can be shown by a simple example of three companies A, B and C which are respectively low-geared, medium-geared and high-geared. Each company has £100,000 capital in the form of shares and borrowings. We consider what happens in three years when they make a small, medium and large profit.

Company structure	A low-geared	B medium-geared	C high-geared
Shares	£80,000	£50,000	£20,000
5% debentures	£20,000	£50,000	£80,000
Total capital	£100,000	£100,000	£100,000
Small profit			
Net profit	£3,000	£3,000	£3,000
Interest on debentures	£1,000	£2,500	£4,000
Balance for shareholders	£2,000	£500	(£1,000)
Earnings per share	2.5p	1p	(-5p)
Medium profit			
Medium profit	£5,000	£5,000	£5,000
interest on debentures	£1,000	£2,500	£4,000
Balance for shareholders	£4,000	£2,500	£1,000
Earnings per share	5p	5p	5p
Large profit			
Large profit	£20,000	£20,000	£20,000
Interest on debentures	£1,000	£2,500	£4,000
Balance for shareholders	£19,000	£17,500	£16,000
Earnings per share	23.75p	35p	80p

These earnings per share in these examples can be tabulated thus:

	A low-geared	B medium-geared	C high-geared
Small profit	2.5p	1p	(5p)
Medium profit	5p	5p	5p
Large profit	23.75p	35p	80p

The example shows how a highly-geared company generates a much larger EPS for shareholders when profits are good, but generates a much smaller EPS (or turns a profit into a loss, as in our example) when profits are small.

If a company makes a loss, gearing exaggerates the loss. If, in our example, the companies made a loss of £5,000, the loss per share would respectively be (7.5p), (15p) and (45p).

Gearing is an aspect of financial accounts which you either understand or do not. All the above is either completely clear to you or is a total mystery. If the latter, go through the example again very slowly, and calculate figures for yourself making up different amounts of profit. One day, the light will come on.

What is the gearing balance point?

Formula: Gearing balance point = Net profit after tax ÷ Total capital

Assuming that you understand the concept of gearing, the example above illustrates another often-overlooked aspect – that there is a point where EPS is *not* affected by gearing. In our example, EPS is exactly the same when the companies make a medium profit regardless of the gearing. In the absence of a generally recognised term, we will call this level of profit the 'gearing balance point'.

You can calculate this point by using algebra. However there is a simpler way of understanding this. The interest rate on the debentures is 5%. The balance point occurred when the profit was £5,000 on £100,000 capital, which is also 5%. In other words, both shareholders and debenture holders received a 5% return on their investment. As the profit margin was at exactly the same rate as that payable on the debentures, the EPS will be 5p (i.e. 5%) regardless of what the ratio is between debt and equity at the gearing balance point.

This principle of the balance point can be extended even when there are several different forms of debt instrument with different rates. It does not even matter what form the debt instrument takes. It is still possible to calculate the gearing balance point, as the example below shows:

Type of debt instrument	Amount of instrument	Interest rate
preference shares	£200,000	4%
bank loan	£100,000	5%
loan note	£100,000	2%
total	£400,000	

You simply calculate the total amounts of interest payable and express that as a percentage of the total for debt instruments:

Type of debt instrument	Calculation	Interest
preference shares	£200,000 x 4%	£8,000
bank loan	£100,000 x 5%	£5,000
loan note	£100,000 x 2%	£2,000
total		£15,000

In this example, £15,000 represents 3.75% of £400,000, so 3.75% is the gearing balance point.

In practice, the interest calculations will already be calculated for you in the profit and loss account account (or in the notes to the accounts). The only calculation you will need to do is to add up the total amount of the instruments.

What all this means is that if the percentage of profits exceeded the gearing balance point, the gearing works in your favour. If the profits are below the gearing balance point, gearing works against you.

For these purposes, 'profit' is net profit after tax. Note that this is different from many other measures where we use net profit *before* tax. This is because interest on debentures is deductible from taxable profits, whereas dividends on shares is paid from taxed profits. So tax must be excluded from both elements of the comparison otherwise we are not comparing like with like.

Having calculated the percentage of the gearing balance point. It is necessary to compare this with the percentage represented by net profit after tax. This figure can be read straight off the profit and loss account. The total capital must be calculated by adding up all the various forms of debt instrument and adding them to the share capital plus retained profit (which also belongs to shareholders).

If you believe that the company will generate profits above the gearing balance point, gearing works in your favour. This does not mean that the company is necessarily a good investment, as all this ignores the value of the shares. It is simply a tool to help you in making that decision.

One final comment is that the term 'gearing balance point' is not widely understood. It is a term made up for this book to explain an aspect of gearing, which *is* widely understood. Gearing balance point is similar to the well-understood concept on return on capital employed (ROCE).

What does gearing mean for investors?

A book could be written on this answer.

However there are some generally understood basic principles of gearing.

1. Stable companies can support higher gearing

A stable company with a reliable cashflow can support higher gearing much more easily than a volatile company with erratic or unreliable cashflows.

Supermarkets, banks and insurance companies are obvious examples of businesses which can support higher gearing. Computer software companies and advertising agencies are companies which are less likely to be able to do so.

2. Gearing may be overstated

Gearing compares borrowings to shareholders' funds. The latter includes retained profit, which, in turn, is partly based on the valuation given to fixed assets and current assets. If these assets have been undervalued, the retained profit is understated, which means that the shareholders' funds are understated, and the gearing is overstated.

In Section 2.5, we considered the valuation of assets. If you concluded that assets are undervalued, you must also conclude that the gearing is overstated.

Conversely if the assets are overvalued, you must also conclude that the gearing is understated, but in this case you must also conclude that the finance director and auditors are hopeless.

If the gearing is overstated, you simply revise your opinions by assuming lower percentages than are derived from calculations. This is bad news for growing companies but good news for declining companies. However the bad news for growing companies must be offset against the knowledge that the company is worth more than it thinks it is.

The effect of undervalued assets and overstated gearing will pass to the shareholders eventually, even though the value of assets may never be corrected on the balance sheet.

3. Gearing is influenced by interest rates

Most forms of debt instrument have a finite life. There are some exceptions as preference shares and loan notes can assume the form of indefinite capital. Most others expire after a few years, as will usually be shown on the balance sheet as part of the description of the debt instrument.

As debt instruments expire, they are usually replaced. The new instruments are usually fixed, not at the current interest rates, but at a rate which reflects what the parties expect interest rates to be over the term of the instrument. Between 2000 and 2003, the general trend and sentiment was for interest rates to reduce. At the start of 2004, the expectation was for small increases. Note that what actually happens to interest rates does not affect the rate of capital instruments. The interest rate agreed will be based on expectations of future rates.

Just as gearing influences your opinion about your return from future profits, so your view on interest rates should influence your opinion about gearing.

In general, rising interest rates adversely affect highly-geared companies.

4. Gearing is also about perception

Gearing has more than a financial influence. Highly-geared companies tend to be seen as high-risk and vulnerable. This is a perception which may not be underpinned by the financial reality.

As a consequence, highly-geared companies' shares may be undervalued, particularly in difficult economic times. As undervalued shares, they represent a better investment opportunity than otherwise.

Another view

There is another common view among investors that investors should ignore gearing completely. If a company is making a profit and keeps its cost of capital under control, there is no need to worry about gearing at all.

Certainly, if you follow the arguments in the previous few pages, you will notice that advantages and disadvantages can sometimes cancel each other out. So there will be occasions when gearing is irrelevant.

Understanding accounts is not just about calculating dozens of ratios and following pre-digested guidance on the answers. Understanding accounts is also about knowing which ratios are particularly important to the company under review.

You may quite properly decide that gearing is irrelevant in a particular case, but you should understand why you have come to that conclusion.

Are there any hidden nasties?

Relevant to
All investors

Underlying worry
'The company may look in good health, but are there special factors which affect the picture?'

The level of liabilities

What is the ratio of liabilities to costs and expenses?

Formula: Liabilities ratio = Liabilities ÷ Costs and expenses

In this section, we move from reasons to invest into reasons *not to* invest. We are looking for possible problems. These are not easy to find, and not easy to evaluate when they are found. However there are some tools for the job. The biggest nasty is pensions, which therefore takes up much of this chapter.

However, the first simple test is to see whether the spending is under control.

Liabilities is the total figure taken from the balance sheet. Costs and expenses are taken from the profit and loss account. This latter figure may not be shown separately, but is the difference between gross profit and operating profit.

As an example, consider the 2002 accounts of the drugs company Pharmagene. The creditors are shown in the balance sheet at £2,766,000. The total operating expenses are £11,658,000, shown on the face of the profit and loss account. They turn £1,466,000 gross profit into a £10,192,000 loss.

This gives a liabilities ratio of 2,766 ÷ 11,658 = 0.24.

This figure measures how much of the annual costs and expenses are outstanding at the year-end. In this case, the answer is just under a quarter, representing about three months' expenditure. It can be seen that this formula is similar to the creditor period in Section 2.4. The main difference in presentation is that the latter formula multiplies the answer by 365 to convert it to a number of days.

However the liabilities ratio considers all costs and expenses, including depreciation, and all liabilities, not just trade creditors. It is a measure of coping rather than policy.

As a rule of thumb, a figure around 0.2 is fairly healthy. As the figure starts to go much above this, there could be problems. But, as ever, such figures must always be interpreted in accordance with the particular circumstances of the business and the information given in the written reports.

Contingent liabilities

A contingency is something that may never happen. In accounting terms, it is an asset or liability which arose before the balance sheet date but cannot be quantified until a date in the future.

An obvious example is a court case started before the balance sheet date but not due to be heard until after the accounts are signed. If the company is suing someone for damages, the company could win a large sum. If the company is being sued, it could become liable for a large sum.

Other examples of contingencies include disputed tax, insurance claims, guarantees, warranty claims, redundancy costs and restructuring.

Another example arises from the assignment of a commercial lease. If the next leaseholder defaults before the lease term expires, the first leaseholder could be held liable even though he has vacated the premises. An example of such a contingent liability is found in the notes to the 2001 accounts for Theratase plc

> On 18 October 1999 the Company assigned its leasehold property at Sandy to a third party. In the event of default by the third party in the future the Company has a contingent liability in respect of rental obligations amounting to £125,000 per year for a further 18 years.

The accounting treatment for contingencies is now governed by Financial Reporting Standard FRS 12. Contingent assets and contingent liabilities cannot be netted off to a single figure; they must be shown separately.

The accounting requirement is that neither contingent assets nor contingent liabilities are included in the balance sheet, profit and loss account or other financial statement. They are disclosed as notes to the accounts. A contingent liability must be disclosed unless the likelihood of an obligation is remote. A contingent asset is only disclosed when its likelihood is probable. Note that a contingent liability is more readily disclosed than a contingent asset.

In most cases, the certainty increases with the passing of time. As a court case progresses, it may become more obvious which way the verdict is likely to go and how much will be paid. Claims and counter-claims may be dropped, and ancillary matters settled. It is thus possible for something to become a contingency long after the original event.

Some contingent assets are 'bunce' – unexpected income. The publisher Faber & Faber, founded in 1929 and still run by the Faber family, was kept going from

1982 by the royalties payable from Andrew Lloyd-Webber's musical Cats which ran for 18 years in the West End and was based on T S Elliot's book.

Measuring contingencies requires forecasting skills. The Met Office accounts for 2001/02 show two contingencies:

- £600,000 unsecured loan facility; and
- £28.1 million staff relocation cost.

A contingency should concern the investor if large relative to profits, and if you consider it likely. In practice, it is rare for a contingency to be that significant.

Tax

Are there any tax nasties?

The accounting for tax is explained in Section 2.2. Any disputed tax is a contingency, as explained above. Deferred tax cannot be a 'tax nasty' as it is purely an accounting item to be agreed with auditors, and is not a liability to be agreed with tax authorities.

There is always a possibility that some new tax ruling could unexpectedly hit a business. In practice, this is more likely to be a contingent asset as a company succeeds in making a claim for tax relief. There have been several instances of companies winning VAT windfalls by successfully challenging Customs.

Marks & Spencer has repeatedly challenged Customs on everything from credit card charges to tea cakes, and with some success. The five companies which won third generation telephone licences are claiming £3.35 billion from Customs as overpaid VAT.

Even when a tax ruling does adversely affect a business, it will affect businesses in the same situation equally and will usually be a one-off event anyway. A different situation applies if the tax authorities discover tax evasion, but that is a fundamentally different problem addressed in Section 2.10.

In short, you are unlikely to be concerned about tax nasties.

Pension liabilities

What pension provisions does the company have for its workforce?

This is currently the biggest nasty likely to be in any company accounts.

Pensions is an area where many eyes glaze over as investors believe the matter is too complicated to understand and move on. Pensions is not particularly complex to understand, nor is it something which investors should ignore. It is important to understand what is meant when different types of pension scheme are described in the accounts as they can have a huge impact on a company's accounts.

A pension is simply an arrangement whereby workers put aside money during their working life to provide an income in retirement. There are three main sources of pension:

- the government
- the individual
- the employer

An individual may receive pensions from more than one source.

Government pension schemes include the basic state retirement pension funded by national insurance contributions during your working life. This can be supplemented by additional pension, also funded by national insurance unless the employee is 'contracted-out'. The three types of additional government pension and the years of national insurance contribution to which they relate are:

- state second pension (from 2002)
- State Earnings Related Pension Scheme or SERPS (1978 to 2002)
- graduated pension (1961 to 1975)

All these schemes have their own rules which are outside the scope of this book. (However, they are within the scope of *Gee's Payroll Factbook* published by Sweet & Maxwell, and written by the same author who would be delighted if you bought a copy.)

Individual schemes are either private pensions (from 1988) or retirement annuities (previously).

We are primarily concerned with employer schemes. No employer is obliged to run a pension scheme (other than stakeholder schemes). A pension scheme is a benefit in kind which is negotiated between employer and employee in the same way that they must negotiate other benefits such as company car and medical insurance. If a company does agree to provide a pension scheme, the company must comply with a vast amount of regulation. Pension schemes still enjoy some tax benefits, though these were reduced in 1997.

Stakeholder pensions must be provided by an employer of five or more people. However this involves little more than choosing a pension provider and being prepared to deduct contributions from wages. One year after their introduction, four-fifths of stakeholder schemes have no members.

The pension fund is a pot of money usually funded by contributions from both the employer and employee. Sometimes contributions come from just the employer, in which case the scheme is said to be 'non-contributory'. The Church of England runs a non-contributory scheme for its clergy. The amount an employee must contribute from his wages is usually fixed as a percentage of earnings, typically around 5%. The pension pot is invested, which generates further funds.

The pension fund is held by a trust run by trustees. They enjoy some independence from both the employer and employee, though both will be represented on the trust board. It must be understood that the money in the pension fund does not belong to either the employer or employees. It does not appear in the company's accounts as it does not belong to the company. It belongs to the trustees who must apply it for the benefit of the beneficiaries who are present and past employees.

When Robert Maxwell died in 1991, it was discovered that he had raided his employees' pension funds from Mirror Corporation and other companies to prop up his collapsing business empire. An investigation led to the Pensions Act 1995 which tightened up pension regulation to prevent such fraud happening again.

Company pension schemes operate under one of two sets of rules depending on whether they are:

*   money purchase schemes (also known as 'defined contribution'); or
*   final salary schemes (also known as 'defined benefit')

Money purchase schemes allow the employer and employee to contibute throughout the employee's working life, building up a pot which does not belong to the employee but gives him certain rights in retirement. The employee decides when to 'retire' (which is not always when he stops work) between the ages of 50 and 75. He can have up to one quarter of the fund in a tax-free lump sum, and the rest is used to buy an annuity. This is where a lump sum is converted to a series of annual payments until the pensioner's death. The amount of annuity depends on the life expectancy of the pensioner at retirement and on current investment rates.

For example, a money purchase scheme builds up a pot of £100,000 for Bill Bloggs who retires at 65. He chooses to have £25,000 tax-free, leaving £75,000 to buy an annuity. At the rates then current, at current rates he may receive £80 a year for every £1,000 left, giving him a pension of £6,000 a year. (Alternatively, he could have chosen to take no lump sum and received a pension of £8,000 a year). There are other alternatives to him, such as having his pension indexed or allowing his widow to continue receiving a pension on his death.

If he dies after six years of retirement, he would have received £25,000 lump sum plus £36,000 in pension, meaning that he only received back £61,000 against £100,000 in the pot. The £39,000 balance is lost to him and his inheritors, as the pension fund never belonged to him. Conversely, if he dies after 30 years of retirement, he would have received £25,000 in lump sum plus £180,000 in pension, and would have received £205,000 in total against a fund of £100,000. In effect, those who die young subsidise those who die old.

All personal pension schemes and some company pension schemes are money purchase schemes. Some company schemes allow employees to make additional voluntary contributions (AVCs). These in effect are mini money purchase pension schemes.

Final salary or defined benefit schemes approach the issue of pensions the other way round. A money-purchase scheme asks how much have we got in the pot, and how much pension will it provide. A final salary scheme starts by asking how much pension do we provide and then asks how much will it cost.

A final salary scheme gives its members a right to receive a pension calculated by reference to 'final salary' (as defined in the scheme rules). Legally a scheme may pay up to two-thirds of final salary as a pension. It may pay up to 1.5 times final salary as a tax-free lump sum, but this reduces the annual pension.

The pension scheme must have sufficient funds to be sure to be able to meet this defined future liability. This is done by considering the sex and age profile of the workforce, when they are likely to retire, how long they are likely to live, and what return can be earned by the fund. This dry computation is done by specialists called actuaries, leading to the old joke that an actuary is someone who finds accountancy too exciting.

This figure computed by an actuary is compared to the amount actually in the fund to see if it is adequate. The amount contributed by employees is fixed in their contracts of employment, so any shortfall can only come from employers. It should be remembered that these pension funds can become huge, sometimes even being worth more than the employer company itself. Even a small percentage shortfall can be a huge liability to the company which is obliged to make up the difference.

The converse is that, if a pension fund contains more than the actuary computes, the scheme is overfunded. This is known as a pension surplus. The employer may then enjoy a contributions holiday. The employees continue making their contributions under their contracts of employment, but the employer pays nothing. Such surpluses were common during the boom periods of the 1980s, leading to some companies trying to 'reclaim' some of these surpluses.

Employees clearly prefer final salary schemes as they know in advance exactly how much they will receive in retirement. Also employers tend to make much higher contributions to final salary schemes than they do to money purchase schemes. The trade union Unison found that employers contributed an average 10% to final salary schemes against 5% for money purchase schemes. Another survey found that some employees could receive up to five times as much pension under a final salary scheme than they would from a money purchase scheme to which they paid the same contributions. All public sector schemes are final salary schemes. This applies to those who work for the government, local government, health service, police etc. This open-ended commitment is funded by the government from taxation. Private sector employees are now fortunate if they can find a final salary scheme.

An investor must understand the descriptions of pension schemes in the accounts, or notes to the accounts. Money purchase schemes present no problem to investors. The company contributes a defined amount of money to a scheme which buys what it can.

An investor should only be concerned about company pension schemes which are final salary schemes.

All this information should be clearly set out in a note to the accounts.

Against the disadvantage of final salary company schemes, an investor may wish to consider how far such a provision enhances employee morale and thus increases productivity. Research by Christopher Cornwell from the University of Georgia, USA in 2000 suggested that such a scheme can raise productivity in large manufacturing companies by up to 6%. In the UK, pay and benefits have less motivational impact than in the USA. Also, you should remember that any improvement in productivity is worth nothing if the company goes bust.

All the above assumes that there is a pension fund to meet the pension liability. Such a scheme is called 'funded'. It is still, just, possible for a company to agree a pension without a fund at all. This is called an unfunded scheme. The company simply pays the pensions as an additional payroll. This was common in old paternalist companies which wanted to honour a loyal servant. The amount was often small. Unfunded schemes are rarely found today. If an employer wishes to provide an additional unfunded pension, perhaps as part of a termination agreement, it is more likely to buy an annuity than incur an open-ended expense which generates no further economic benefit to the company. If you do encounter a company with an unfunded pension commitment, you should consider whether a company has properly accounted for such an open commitment. You should also consider whether the directors are sane.

Is there a risk of a huge liability to maintain the pension fund?

Yes, if the company runs a final salary pension scheme. The government is considering a raft of changes to pension law, but these are unlikely to have much effect on pensions from the investors' perspective.

From 1997, final salary pension schemes have been under considerable pressure for three different reasons:

- the first Budget of the new government in 1997 removed the right of pension funds to claim back the tax on dividends, in effect imposing an unexpected tax charge on them of about £5 billion a year. This increased pension costs by 18%;

- the stock market fell by over 40% between 1999 and 2002, leading to huge reductions in pension fund values. Boots withdrew from shares to put all its money in government securities, though few other schemes followed this example. Even in 2003, 78% of pension funds were invested in shares;

- a new accounting standard, Financial Reporting Standard FRS 17, required pension shortfalls to be taken immediately to the profit and loss account rather than be spread over several years as previously allowed. The implications of FRS 17 are discussed further below.

An extreme example was Kalamazoo, the software company. The company's pension scheme became so underfunded that it bankrupted the company, which previously had enjoyed a contributions holiday. The value of the pension fund was worth £80 million against a mere £6.6 million value for Kalamazoo itself. The company still needed to find another £600,000 for the pension fund from its £295,000 cash. A pension fund can only pay out the funds it has, so the workers did not do much better. Ex-Kalamazoo workers yet to retire have lost about half their pension.

Another catastrophe was specialist steel makers, ASW Holdings. The company went bust and was unable to fund pension shortfalls. Current pension law requires that a pension fund must pay current pensioners before future pensioners, so some employees found they had contributed for 40 years and would now receive nothing, not even a refund of their contributions. Similar stories can be told about the pension schemes for United Engineering Forgings (UEF), Melville Dundas, Dexion, Ravenhead Glass, Blyth & Blyth, Samuel Jones, Salvage Association, Pervian White Dove, Lister Yarns, and an estimated 200 other companies. These concerns have repeatedly been raised in Parliament and have led to public demonstrations. Caparo had a strike over the closure of its pension fund.

From the workers' point of view, all these problems have been compounded by annuity rates falling by 20% or more over the ten years to 2001 because of revised calculations on life expectancy.

It should be appreciated that loss of confidence in pensions leads to a loss of investment by pension funds and greater social problems to be afforded by government, both of which contribute to a deteriorating investment climate.

Reports in the early years of the 21st century make depressing reading. Opposite is a selection of some headline conclusions from 2002 and 2003:

Pensions contributions - headlines

- Alexander Forbes Financial Services says that UK companies must double their existing £13.75 billion a year contribution to £27 billion to avert the final salary time bomb;

- accountants KPMG show that 44% of British workers have no pension fund at all. Among those under 30, two-thirds now do not bother with a pension. Only 5% of workers have put aside 10% or more for their pensions, which is the amount now estimated as necessary for a comfortable retirement;

- the trade union Unison found that 44% of final salary schemes are closed to new members;

- Mercer Human Resource Consulting found that the number of large companies with an open final salary scheme fell from 64% to 40% during 2002;

- actuaries Lane Clark & Peacock shows that some companies are still using unrealistic investment expectations of return as high as 9% in valuing pension schemes;

- Russell Mellon CAP show that pension funds showed an overall loss of 6.7% in the year to 30 June 2003 despite a good return in the second quarter of 2003. In the 12 months to March 2003, pension funds lost 23.7%;

- Lane Clarke & Peacock said the stock market must rise by at least 50% for final salary schemes to fill the estimated £55bn gap in funding. In January 2004, new government requirements on reporting pension shortfalls were expected to show that the gap is about £13bn higher;

- a separate survey showed that pension sales in the first six months of 2003 were 32% less than a year earlier, indicating that people are simply losing faith in pensions.

- UBSL said the 100 largest pension schemes in the UK have a deficit of £72 billion; CFSB put the figure at £77 billion. Schemes operated by the 100 FTSE companies lost £68 billion during 2002 because of falling equity markets. Small companies face pension fund deficits of 133% of operating profits;

- investment bank Dresdner Kleinwort Wasserstein (DKW) said that the average pension fund assumes assets will grow by 7.5% a year. In recent years, they have been falling by over 10%. On that basis the funding gap could grow to £171 billion. Actuarial assumptions are coming down, but are not yet down to realistic levels.

Similarly, there has been no shortage of stories of how it is affecting companies. Here is a selection of headline stories from 2003:

- BT will increase the £200 million it pays into its pension fund, which is believed now to have a deficit of over £2 billion, though some predict it could be as high as £9 billion under the FRS 17 valuation method. This shortfall is the equivalent of about seven years' profits. BT has already agreed to provide another £1 billion over five years. It has now agreed also to pay in another £1.5 billion over the next 15 years. The scheme has 370,000 members making it one of the country's largest. The scheme is closed to new entrants;

- GlaxoSmithKline announced that it had paid £320 million into its pension fund in an attempt to reduce a shortfall of £1.3bn;

- Associated British Foods is taking £9 million worth of charges to its pension fund.

- BAE Systems faced a strike over plans to scale back retirement benefits to help close a £2.16 billion gap in the pension fund. It has already closed its scheme to new entrants and increased contributions by two percentage points for existing members. The company is making a similar increase. The trade union is angry that BAE took a contribution holiday in the booming 1990s.

However even the worst pension nasties can be recovered. In the USA (which has been affected similarly to the UK), in 2003 General Motors recovered a $19.3 billion pension deficit by issuing bills in the debt market, selling a subsidiary and from trading profits.

Associated British Ports decided to close its pension fund to new entrants despite having a surplus and enjoying a pension fund holiday.

So what is FRS 17 and how does it affect accounts?

FRS 17 has had such a huge impact on reported accounts, that it must be understood in some detail by investors. (Accounting standards are explained in Part IV.)

Financial Reporting Standard FRS 17 is an accounting standard introduced in November 2000 to be effective for accounting periods ending after 21 June 2003 (21 June 2004 for smaller companies). As with all UK accounting standards, earlier adoption is encouraged. FRS 17's main change is that it requires the whole amount of a shortfall in a final salary pension fund to be shown as a liability in the statement of total recognised gains and losses. The previous statement of standard accounting practice SSAP 24 allowed a shortfall to be spread over several years. SSAP 24 was introduced in 1988, when there was a major shake-up of pension law. Both SSAP 24 and FRS 17 took many difficult years to be developed. SSAP 24 was soon found to be lacking in that it was so subjective in practice that the figures made understanding and analysing accounts difficult, if not impossible.

The timing of FRS 17 could hardly have been worse. When the standard was written, the stock market was booming after 11 years of rises, so the change would not have made much difference for most companies. When it came into force the stock market had fallen for three years, creating massive losses which now had to be taken immediately against profits, often turning healthy profits into worrying losses.

The Accounting Standards Board obstinately refused to withdraw or postpone FRS 17, so companies were forced to adopt it with the consequential devastation on published profits. Then the ASB relented in allowing the standard to be delayed by one or two years, so it applies for accounting periods which end after 21 June 2005 for all companies.

As explained in Part IV, UK listed companies must adopt international accounting standards from 1 January 2005. The equivalent international accounting standard IAS 19 is much more lenient than FRS 17. It allows companies to spread any shortfall over the estimated average working life of employees. If a company has a pensionable workforce with ages evenly spread from 25 to 65, this average working life is around 20 years, meaning that only 5% of the shortfall needs to be taken to the accounts in any one year, against 100% under FRS 17. Also IAS 19 allows a shortfall of less than 10% to be ignored. The Accounting Standards Board justified its hardline approach by saying that it was seeking to bring IAS 19 into line with FRS 17.

This created the ludicrous situation in which some companies could find that they are required to use three different accounting standards in as many years, all with fundamentally different approaches. This destroys the principle of comparability which is the main reason for having accounting standards in the first place. Some companies could choose which of the three accounting standards on offer to use.

From the investors' point of view it has been argued that FRS 17 makes no difference at all. It is an accounting standard which deals simply with how transactions are *reported* in the accounts. In itself, FRS 17 does not add a penny to the company's costs. If a company must stump up another £10 million for its pension fund, it matters little when this is shown in the accounts.

This represents only partial truth. Timing in accounts is of crucial importance. It is the fundamental accruals concept, which gives rise to depreciation and deferred tax, for example. But of more importance, FRS 17 can significantly reduce the figure which the law allows to be quoted for its profits. This can affect the amount it may distribute as dividends, which by law must only be paid from profits. It can affect the company's ability to borrow money or raise capital. It could oblige the company to make decisions about selling or not buying subsidiaries or plant.

There is another concern about FRS 17. The stock market is volatile. Having fallen by 50% in three years to March 2003, it then gained 25% in the next six months. A typical pension fund will have new demands put upon it over a period of about 40 years. It is unreasonable to expect a company to make a massive reduction one year and a significant increase the next year for a liability that will not arise for another 38 years. FRS 17 can generate huge changes in company profits from one year to the next which can reflect the stock market rather than the company's fortunes, defeating the point of having accounts in the first place.

For an investor, IAS 19 provides a much fairer representative of a company's pension provision than either FRS 17 or SSAP 24.

An example of the impact of FRS 17 can be found in this statement from the 2002 accounts of British American Tobacco, which decided to continue using SSAP 24.

> The impact of FRS 17 would be to increase group pre-tax profit for 2002 by £4 million.
>
> The impact of FRS 17 would reduce reported shareholders' funds at 31 December 2002 by £561 million (2001 £106 million). In 2002, changes were made to the contractual trust agreement that governs the main pension scheme in Germany, such that the scheme is now treated as a funded scheme for purposes of FRS 17 from 1 January 2002. If this had applied in 2001, then the effect of FRS 17 on shareholders's funds would have been reduced from £106 million to £14 million. A key factor in the increased impact of FRS 17 on shareholders's funds is the decline in equity markets during 2002.

Is management good enough?

Relevant to
All investors

Underlying worry
'Are the people at the helm honest, competent, and working in my interests?'

The Combined Code

To understand about the management of companies, you must understand the Combined Code of Corporate Governance, published in 1998, for listed companies. This does not apply to unlisted companies, though many will choose to follow some of its provisions.

The Code grew from previous reports, particularly the Hampel Report of 1998. You should look for a statement that the company complies with the code, or a statement saying where it departs.

The Code is in two parts: Principles and Provisions. Each is split into two sections:

Section 1: Companies	Section 2: Institutional shareholders
A: Directors B: Directors' remuneration C: Relations with shareholders D: Accountability and audit	E: Institutional investors.

There are 14 principles and 45 detailed provisions in the Code. Among the more significant provisions it requires a "senior independent non-executive director" to be identified, and requires companies to "consider how and when" directors' service contracts may be reduced to one year.

At least one third of the main board must comprise non-executive directors, the majority of whom must be independent of management or of any business relationship which could materially affect their judgment. There must be at least three non-executive directors (a common area of non-compliance).

Incumbents

Who is occupying the key positions, how long have they been there, and how long will they stay?

In 1668, the French East India Company was formed. Its chairman had no trouble raising capital even though the company lacked a corporate strategy. It acquired boats to establish strategic interests in Madagascar without first setting up any kind of head office or commercial oversight. Later in 1668, the chairman scrapped this idea for a more ambitious one. Ships set sail, mostly to disaster with many sinking on their maiden voyage or being captured. By 1675, it was clear that the business had no basis of trade and was insolvent.

So how did such a hopeless chairman succeed in so dominating a company? Because he was the absolute monarch, King Louis XIV, with whom arguing corporate policy was not an advisable option.

But that could not happen in modern times, could it?

Three hundred years later, a successful General Motors executive called John de Lorean charmed the world. With dyed hair, surgically-reshaped jaw, and a glamorous model as his third wife, he emerged from the swinging sixties as a charismatic figure. In 1976 the UK government was desperate for any commercial venture for Northern Ireland and agreed to provide capital for the construction of a de Lorean sport car factory. A change of government did not stop the funding which eventually reached £85 million. In 1982, the company collapsed with losses of £23 million. It was discovered that $17.5 million had been paid to a mysterious Swiss company called GPD. De Lorean was imprisoned for a $24 million cocaine deal, though later cleared because of entrapment. The government spent another £20 million between 1985 and 1997 unsuccessfully pursuing the auditors of de Lorean – Arthur Andersen. Eventually, the government dropped the moulds for the car into the sea to ensure that no-one else could build a de Lorean car.

What information should you look for about directors?

The ideal would be:

1. director details appearing towards the end of the report;
2. an identified photograph of each director;
3. what relevant qualifications the director has;
4. how old he is;
5. how long he has been with the company;
6. what his particular responsibilities are;
7. what other positions he holds;
8. what he did before.

Director details at the beginning of the report can indicate that the directors have an inflated sense of their own importance, particularly if given undue prominence and with excessive photographs. Inflated importance often means inflated pay.

National Grid 2001 accounts (chosen at random) score eight out of eight. Here is its report on the group chief executive.

Roger Urwin. Group chief executive.

Appointed as a director of National Grid and of the National Grid Company plc in 1995. Roger Unwin was previously chief executive of London Electricity plc. Prior to this, he held a number of appointments within the Central Electricity Generating Board before joining Midlands Electricity Board as director of engineering. He is a non-executive director of Energis, the Special Utilities Investment Trust PLC and TotalFinaElf Exploration UK plc and is a Fellow of the Royal Academy of Engineering. Aged 55.

In addition to knowing about the directors, it is more important to know about the corporate structure. In particular, you need to see in the report:

1. the structure of various boards;
2. how often the main board meets;
3. the function of each subsidiary board;
4. separation of duty between chairman and chief executive;
5. a majority of non-executive directors on the main board;
6. a system of nominations to the board which involves non-executive directors;
7. a system of routine reappointment of directors by rotation; the Code says at least once every three years.

Here National Grid scores seven out of seven. The board meets eight times a year, has five non-executives out of nine, has a Nominations Board of three non-executive directors, and requires each director to retire and (if desired) seek re-election every three years (which is standard practice).

Sometimes subsidiary boards are referred to as committees, which is of no signifance. The Code says a company must have a Nominations Committee unless the main board is small.

In addition to a Nominations Committee, a company will have an Audit Committee and Remuneration Committee. National Grid has combined them as one subsidiary board, which is fine.

Under the Combined Code, the Audit Committee must comprise at least three directors, all non-executive. This committee keeps under review the scope and results of the audit, its cost-effectiveness, and the auditors' independence and objectivity. Where the auditors provide other services to the company (which they always do), the committee should keep under review the nature and extent of such services with regard to balancing objectivity and value for money. This latter point has proved particularly controversial in recent years as auditors have revealed huge fees for other services from auditors. This raises the question of how independent auditors can be when checking their own work and when dependent on that work for survival. For the investor, none of this really matters as the audit report is of no consequence anyway.

What types of management issue are there?

Many. A few of the more common ones are noted below.

Family appointments

Changes of directors which could be of concern are usually accompanied by plenty of news coverage. For example, the replacement of well-regarded Tony Ball as chief executive of BSkyB with Rupert Murdoch's 30-year-old son James led to fears of mass director resignations. However BSkyB is a company with a clear business model and good profits and cashflow, so could probably survive anyway. And the young Murdoch may yet prove himself worthy to the task.

In-fighting

The merger of Royal Insurance and Sun Alliance to create insurance conglomerate Royal & Sun Alliance. The two managements did not merge well, which meant their eye was taken off the ball. Profitability was reduced, asbestos claims were under-estimated and the company was heavily exposed to the falling stock market.

Family feud

The brewer Shepherd Neame lost vice-chairman Stuart Neame after he said his cousin and chairman Bobby Neame was "past his sell-by date". This did not seem to affect the company's performance.

Patak, the suppliers of Indian food, had a family feud in 2004 when chairman Kirit Pathak was sued by his sisters Anila Shastri and Chitralekha Mehta. They claim that they were cheated out of their shareholdings and are victims of a dishonest mother and Hindu culture, where only sons inherit.

Strategy

Has management articulated a coherent and cohesive strategy?

Every chairman's and directors' statement is a coherent and cohesive strategy. If the chairman and directors cannot think of a good story, their spin doctors can. You must look beyond the words and ask what they mean.

Training services company Adval changed its management in 2003 which says that it will "run the business for profit and cash", which should make you wonder what it was run for before.

The best strategy is one expressed by the company itself, as it gives you two opportunities to assess company performance. First, you can see their vision in what they believe they can do. Second, you can see their competence in terms of how they deliver it.

Barclays Bank set itself a four-year goal of being in the top quartile of banks for shareholder return, which it met. In 2003 it set itself a new four-year goal of remaining there by delivering economic profit growth (whatever that is) of between 10% and 13%.

Directors' salaries

How much are they paid?

For the purposes of reporting their pay, a director is anyone who held that office in the current year or the previous five years.

Remuneration includes sums paid by subsidiaries. In one of the few challenges on this, the Financial Reporting Review Panel required Foreign & Colonial Investment Trust plc to restate directors' remuneration for 1991 because payments from a subsidiary had been excluded.

Company law requires the following details to be disclosed in the accounts for each director:

- total emoluments (including benefits in kind such as company car and medical insurance);
- amount of gains on share options;
- amounts plus value of assets under long-term incentives schemes;
- contributions to pension funds.

Remuneration includes payments for being a director of any subsidiary, and does not distinguish between the office of director and status as employee.

The Code says that directors' remuneration:

- should be sufficient to attract and retain directors, but not more than is necessary;
- must be fixed for each director by a formal and transparent procedure;
- must be subject to a statement of policy published in the annual report;
- must have a significant element linked to performance in a way which aligns directors' interests to shareholders'; and
- must have specific provisions on termination payments, except for misconduct.

As far as profit goes, most shareholders probably care little how directors are paid. If National Grid doubled its £2.7 million payment to directors, it would only dent the annual profit by about one third of one percent. Insofar as shareholders see directors' remuneration as relevant at all, it is more likely to be to ensure that they have the best people who are motivated to act in the shareholders' interests.

In reviewing directors' remuneration, it is important not to be motivated by envy. James Ross earned £120,000 for his part-time job at National Grid, whereas chief executive David Jones earned £665,000. That may be a little more than you earn. It is a little more than an author of investment books earns. But that is not the point.

> Would you pay £1,000 for someone to work for you for one day? No.
> Would you pay someone £1,000 to earn you £2,000? Yes.
> Even if it only took them one day to do it? Yes.
>
> *Now that's the right attitude.*

How does their pay compare with previous years?

As with all figures, the annual accounts give comparative figures for the previous year. Previous accounts allow you to go further back. Significant increases should be compared with company performance, which is the more important question.

Directors' pay is a small part of expenses, so does it matter?

Yes.

It is true that directors' pay is often a small part of the company's expenses. To take Tesco's accounts for 2001, the 17 listed directors had total remuneration of £8.8 million. This presents about three-quarters of one percent of the £1,166 million operating profit.

However the concern is not in whether the amount is too large, but what affect the pay will have on company performance. In some cases, the shareholder should be concerned if the pay is not high enough. Reading accounts will soon give you an idea for the going rate of executives.

There must be an element of reasonable reward but not excessive reward. Excessive reward of directors is unlikely to make much impact on profits, but it does on management. One of the main facts behind the Enron scandal was that the directors depended so much on their massive bonuses, that they massively inflated profit figures.

The Tesco accounts include a long 'report of the directors on remuneration'. It gives a good example of a fair system. An extract is reproduced below:

Long-term share bonuses are awarded annually, based on improvements in earnings per share, achievement of strategic corporate goals and comparative performance against peer companies including total shareholder return. The maximum long-term bonus is 50% of salary. Shares awarded have to be held for a period of four years, conditional upon continuous service with the company. The share equivalent of dividends which would have been paid on the shares is added to the award during the deferral period.

Short-term share bonuses are awarded annually, based on improvements in earnings per share and on the achievement of strategic corporate goals. The maximum short-term bonus payable is 25% of salary which is augmented by up to a further 12.5% of salary if the participants elect for the trustees of the scheme to retain the fully paid ordinary shares awarded for a minimum of two years, conditional upon continuous service with the company. The share equivalent of dividends which would have been paid on the shares is added to the award during the deferral period.

There is more, but the main elements are included in the two paragraphs quoted. In particular, the statement answers the questions:

- are incentives long-term or short-term or both?
- on what is the incentive based?
- if based on a comparison, is the comparator appropriate?
- is the director incentivised to maximise shareholders' funds?
- what is the maximum incentive?
- what conditions are attached to the incentive?

As a quick rule-of-thumb, directors' incentives which are sufficient to double the directors' pay are probably not excessive. Incentives which go beyond that could be excessive. There is an exception if the director receives only nominal pay. In such cases, the comparison should be with a reasonable rate for the job.

So what are fat cats?

There has been much controversy over 'fat cats' – the derogatory term for directors who take large pay despite weak or poor performance by their companies. In 2003, *Accountancy* magazine named the fattest of fat cats in order as:

Fat cat	Thin company
Sir Peter Bonfield	BT
Sir Christopher Gent	Vodafone
John Weston	BAE
Ian Harley	Abbey National
Lord Browne	BP

Sir Peter Bonfield was being paid £3.1 million a year after BT had lost 71% of its value over three years.

In 1997, it was suggested, though not adopted, that there should be limits on the maximum multiple of average pay a director could earn. At the time, it was noted that the BP chief executive was earning 60 times his company's average UK wage against 16 times in 1985. The UK average was then 18, above our major competitors except USA (24 times).

Can anything be done about excess pay?

Yes, but leave it to institutional investors to do. Just understand what is happening.

From 1 August 2002, The Directors' Remuneration Report Regulations 2002 (SI 2002/1986) requires companies to let shareholders vote on directors' pay. The vote is not binding on the company, though a 'no' vote is considered highly embarrassing and so constrains excessive pay without the need for any tougher enforcement mechanism.

The first no vote occurred on 19 May 2003 when shareholders voted against a £15 million 'golden parachute' for Jean-Pierre Garnier, director of pharmaceutical company GlaxoSmithKline if he left for any reason, even for poor performance. Garnier was earning £4 million a year. Investors representing 50.72% of shares voted against. The majority of shareholders, financial institutions, abstained. The company refused to say how many abstained. The meeting was packed with 900 shareholders, some waving placards, following weeks of public attack. The vote was widely reported and discussed in the media.

This new taste of shareholder power was followed up on 21 October 2003, when shareholders forced the resignation of Michael Green as chairman of Carlton TV. The company had just received government clearance to merge with Granada TV to form a £4.6 billion business. The revolt was led by Anthony Bolton of Fidelity, the fund manager. He managed to secure backing from other funds which control 36% of Carlton and 33% of Granada. The board initially backed Green, but eventually caved in to pressure. The other fund managers refused even to meet the directors of Carlton. It is believed that the funds want an investment banker as chairman to fatten the company up for an overseas takeover, which is good news for investors, at least in the short term.

Before this, shareholders could only protest about fat cats. One memorable protest concerned British Gas. Chairman Cedric Brown was awarded a 75% pay rise in 1996 to £475,000 plus a potential performance-related bonus of up to £594,000. A shareholder brought along a 30-stone black pig named Cedric to protest against corporate snouts in the trough.

The total of £1,069,000 which Cedric (the human one) could have earned is worth about £1.3 million in 2004 values. No-one would raise an eyebrow or trotter at such pay today.

How does their pay compare with the company's performance?

The increase in directors' pay should be compared to the increase (if any) in the company's performance. Using Tesco's accounts for 2001 again, the £8.816 million paid to directors in 2001 represents a 14% increase in the £7.739 million paid in 2000. In that year, sales, profit, earnings per share and dividend each rose by between 11% and 12%, so the increase in directors' pay seems reasonable.

Note that the percentage increase in directors' pay will normally be a little higher than the increase in profit, because of the need to incentivise marginal improvements.

How are they paid?

In general, it does not matter to an investor whether directors are paid in cash, benefits, pension rights or cowrie shells.

One exception is share options, which must be understood by shareholders for several reasons. Investors should also be concerned about termination payments.

A share option is a right to buy shares at a future time for a set price. Sometimes the time is a period in which the right may be exercised. For example, an option may allow a director to buy 10,000 shares in 2010 for £1 when the share is currently worth 50p. If in 2010, the share is worth £3, the director can exercise the option and buy £3,000 worth of shares for £1,000, making an instant profit of £2,000. If in 2010, the share is worth 80p, the director would not exercise the option which is worthless.

There are some statutory option schemes which provide generous tax relief (to the directors) if the rules are followed. They all have set time limits for holding and exercising the option.

Directors are given traditional options, which should not be confused with traded options. The latter are a separate type of investment which does not concern the ordinary share investor.

First, the investor should be pleased that directors have share options and concerned if they do not. The existence of share options aligns directors' interests with shareholders' interests in that both want to see the share price rise.

There will be a separate table in the directors' report listing how many options each director has, the exercise price and the date when exercisable. Below are some details from the National Grid 2000 report for group chief executive Roger Urwin.

Options held on 31 March 2001	Exercise price (p)	Date from which exercisable
169,340	280.50	September 2000
91,656	375.75	June 2001
22,098	455.25	June 2002
33,867	531.50	June 2003

In each case, he has seven years in which to exercise his option, so the first options must be exercised by September 2007.

An obvious but forgotten point is that **the table of share options granted to directors gives an excellent insight into what the directors think the share price will be**. The directors will have negotiated the option so that they will be exercisable, so the exercise price for the option we may reasonably conclude is a little below the expected share price.

So what happened to National Grid's share prices on these dates? Below we compare the actual share price on the first trading day of the month with the exercise price.

Month	Share price on 1st	Exercise price	Difference
September 2000	573.00	280.50	+292.50
June 2001	568.50	375.75	+192.75
June 2002	494.50	455.25	+39.25
June 2003	404.00	531.50	-127.50

Had the director exercised his share option in September 2000, he would have made a profit of nearly £3 per share. He could have made a total of £459,319 from exercising that option on the first day.

Clearly, and reasonably, the directors expected the share price to rise, when it actually fell in line with the general decline of share prices. The difference between actual prices and the exercise price steadily reduced until by June 2003, the exercise price was above the actual price. If the share price does not rise by June 2010, that last option is worthless.

Two years later, all the above options are still listed in the accounts, plus options for two more years, indicating that the director has yet to exercise any options.

Share options could affect shareholders in terms of dilution. Suppose you hold 1,000 shares in a company with 100,000 shares and a market capitalisation of £2 million. In effect you own 1% of the company worth £20,000. Suppose the company issues another 10,000 shares to one of its directors. The company is still worth just £2 million and you still own 100,000, but now there are 110,000 shares and your holding has fallen from 1% to 0.91%. Your share of the company has fallen from £20,000 to £18,182.

Suppose those 10,000 shares were issued as a result of an option granted five years ago. For that five years, there is a potential for your relative shareholding, your share of the company, to reduce by that amount. That is dilution.

At 31 March 2001, National Grid had issued 1,559,380 share options. (National Grid did not give this total figure, but only showed totals for each director.) This means that when the options are exercised, another 1,559,380 shares will be in existence. The total number of shares in existence on that day was 1,485,034,204. The share options represent about one tenth of one per cent of the shares in issue, and are unlikely to concern an investor. Put another way, a £1,000 holding would become worth £998.92. The cost of the full dilution is just £1.08. This is calculated as

$$\text{effect of dilution} = \text{holding} \times \frac{\text{number of shares in issue before options}}{\text{number of shares in issue after options}}$$

Shareholders need to have some concern about all types of bonus paid to directors. Share options is just one form of bonus. This should be of sufficient amount to encourage effort but not so large that massaging results at bonus time becomes more important than achieving good results, which is what happened at Enron.

The received wisdom in human resources management is that pay is a hygiene factor not a positive motivator. This means that underpaying people demotivates them but overpaying them does not motivate them more than paying them a fair rate. To some extent that received wisdom is likely to apply less to some senior managers where too much is never enough. However such people are unlikely to be good stewards of your investment.

Who decides how management is paid?

The Remuneration Committee which consists of non-executive directors decides, or should do. The company must publish a remuneration policy as well as details of how much each director has earned.

The National Grid accounts show that there are the five typical elements to directors' remuneration:

- base salary
- annual bonus
- share schemes
- pensions
- non-cash benefits

"Base salaries are reviewed annually taking account of the median market position..." appears in National Grid's policy. A median is an average taken by finding the rate for the mid-point. The median is the form of average commonly used for pay, because of the wide variations. So salaries of: £15,000; £20,000; £25,000; £30,000 and £100,000 pounds have a median average of £25,000, because that is the figure in the middle of the list. It is a more representative middle figure than the arithmetical average of £42,000.

Although such statements as 'following the average' are widely used, this is clearly not so. Imagine five comparable companies whose chief executive pay is:

A	B	C	D	E
£50,000	£60,000	£80,000	£100,000	£200,000

Company A notes that its chief executive is the lowest paid so it takes the average pay of the other four, which is £110,000, and A receives that. (The mean average is used as median becomes meaningless with such a small size.) Now B is the lowest paid, and seeks the average of the other four. The steps are as set out below:

A £	B £	C £	D £	E £
50,000	60,000	80,000	100,000	200,000
110,000	60,000	80,000	100,000	200,000
110,000	125,000	80,000	100,000	200,000
110,000	125,000	133,750	100,000	200,000
110,000	125,000	133,750	142,188	200,000
150,235	125,000	133,750	142,188	200,000
150,235	156,543	133,750	142,188	200,000
150,235	156,543	162,242	142,188	200,000
150,235	156,543	162,242	167,255	200,000
171,500	156,543	162,242	167,255	200,000
171,500	175,249	162,242	167,255	200,000
171,500	175,249	178,501	167,255	200,000
171,500	175,249	178,501	181,313	200,000

This can be repeated indefinitely until all five are earning £200,000. This demonstrates the principle that keeping taking the average of everyone else simply pushes everyone up to the top while not allowing any increase for the man at the top. The often seen statement that a director is simply paid the average rate for someone in his position sound credible but is mathematically impossible.

The annual bonus at National Grid is "up to a maximum of 50% of base salary" for "achievement of demanding financial, personal and quality of service targets". A quarter of the bonus is held in a trust for three years and then paid out in shares according to their pre-tax value. This element is counter-productive as the greater the value of the shares, the fewer the director will receive.

Share options may be granted at up to 150% value of base salary, subject to some conditions. There are also some tax-effective schemes which directors may join.

Pension entitlement is a generous two-thirds final salary after 20 years' service (the legal maximum) to which employees contribute 6% were it not for the fact that National Grid was then enjoying an employee contributions holiday.

Benefits include "competitive benefits such as a fully-expensed car and private medical insurance".

A table tells us that Roger Urwin received:

base salary	£440,000
annual bonus	£212,000
benefits	£13,000
total emoluments	£665,000

The maximum annual bonus at half base salary is £220,000. So Roger Urwin scored 96.4% as a chief executive. He also has a pension which was worth £160,000 by the year-end.

By now, you may feel that we know rather a lot of personal details about Roger Urwin except where he takes his holidays and what he eats for breakfast. That is the price stewards of your investment must pay.

Shareholdings

How many shares does each member of the Board have in the company?

This is shown in a separate table, but just as a number, not a percentage.

Roger Urwin held 144,539 shares at the end of the year, ignoring his options. This represents about 0.1% of all shares held, which is quite fair for a company of this size. Directors of younger and smaller companies will have much larger holdings.

Have they recently bought or sold shares?

It is a criminal offence of insider dealing for a director (or anyone else) to sell or buy shares on the basis of knowledge not generally available to investors.

Although insider dealing has been a criminal offence since 1980, there have been very few prosecutions despite many suspicious transactions just before significant price change. It was not until 1987 that anyone was prosecuted. That doubtful honour went to Geoffrey Collier, head of securities at Morgan Grenfell, who had been working on Robert Maxwell's takeover of engineering firm AE. He instructed a colleague to buy shares for him. The law has been made tougher since then.

To avoid accusations, the Code requires directors not to buy or sell shares in the two months before the interim or final results. This does not stop directors having shares awarded to them under incentive schemes, but does mean that directors may only buy or sell shares for eight months a year. Exceptionally, directors may sell shares in the closed periods to meet a pressing financial commitment.

The accounts tell you how many shares the director held a year previously. A reasonable increase suggests continuing confidence in the company, but always consider such matters by looking at the total held by all directors. One director may have sold for personal reasons, but it is unlikely that all directors will have.

Employment contracts

What else do I need to know about their service agreements?

You need to know the length of the service agreement. The Code says that companies should move to agreements of no more than one year, which is what National Grid has done. Longer periods could mean that is difficult or expensive to remove a director.

Can I expect a reliable income?

Relevant to

All investors, but especially those looking for income.

Underlying worry

'Is the dividend safe?'

Dividend policy

What is the company's stated dividend policy?

There are very few rules on what must be disclosed about dividends. The Companies Act 1985 only requires a single figure for paid and proposed dividends. However it is universal practice to show separate figures for proposed dividends and paid dividends.

There is no requirement for a company to publish a dividend policy, but almost all do. Here is an extract from the BOC's 2002 accounts:

> The company has paid cash dividends on its ordinary shares in every year since 1899. Since 1988, the dividend policy has been to pay two interim dividends, one in February and one in August. The dividends are reported in the accounts in the year in which they are paid... Future dividends of the company will be dependent upon future earnings, the financial position of the company and other factors...

Most companies do not refer to two interim dividends, but to an interim and a final dividend. The dividend policy is usually a cautious statement. Few companies, for example, will promise to maintain or gently increase the dividend, even though that may be their intention. Most directors would rather not explain a break of promise.

P & O's 2002 accounts take an even more robust view:

> Our dividend policy remains unchanged. As we have said before, it reflects our view of the long term prospects for the group and it will not be affected by any short term profit volatility resulting from cyclical businesses.

When companies introduce dividends, they often do so cautiously. Chip designer ARM introduced dividends in 2004. Its yield is just 0.5% and costs £6 million when the company has a cash pile of £160 million.

US companies are much keener on maintaining a dividend policy. Coca-Cola maintains its dividend record regardless. Against that, Microsoft resisted paying dividends for years, saying that its profits were better invested in growing the company. It has now started to pay dividends.

In 1997, US Congress changed tax law in a way which favours capital growth rather than dividends; the maximum tax rates are 20% and 39.1% respectively. The higher dividend rates are because both companies and shareholders are taxed. In the UK, capital gains and dividends are taxed at the same rate, but generous allowances for capital gains tax, such as taper relief and a separate annual allowance, tends to reduce the capital gains tax actually paid. Only shareholders pay tax on dividends in the UK, not the company. Although both the UK and USA tax systems favour capital growth over dividend income, the USA has a greater preference built in.

What level of dividend has the company paid historically?

Company law only requires the dividend figure for the previous year to be stated, but it is common to find dividends quoted for longer periods.

BOC quotes its total dividends for five years:

1998	1999	2000	2001	2002
34.75p	32.7p	35p	37p	38p

As can be seen, its policy is for dividends to gently increase, subject to profits. This is probably the best dividend policy of all – a general upwards direction but without the slavish demand of maintaining or increasing dividends year on year.

Remember that some companies, particularly oil companies, may denominate their dividends in dollars, so the amount in pounds may fluctuate because of exchange rates. BP's dividend in sterling was cut by 0.7% in 2003, but has overall still risen by an average 7% over 20 years.

How can I tell if the dividend policy is sustainable?

For most UK companies, the dividend policy is easily sustainable simply by being undemanding. A policy that says we will pay a dividend which is appropriate to our profits and other circumstances is difficult not to sustain.

Legally a company may only pay dividends from profits. It may not use share capital or its share premium account for this purpose. Since 1980 this has been clarified to mean that dividends may only be paid from cumulative realised profits. This is wider than operating profits, as bank interest and profit from selling subsidiaries or plant may be included. However profits cannot be paid from unrealised profits, such as the increased value of its premises.

There is no requirement that profits must have been earned in the year that the dividend is paid. So companies can squirrel away retained profit from good years to maintain dividends in lean years.

Although it is normal to talk of dividends, the legal term is 'distribution', which is wider in scope. All dividends are distributions, but so are issues of bonus shares, redemption or purchase of own shares, authorised reduction of capital and distributions on winding up.

What is its dividend cover?

Formula: Dividend cover = EPS ÷ Dividend per Share

This measures the number of times the dividend could have been paid from earnings. Another way of looking at it is that the dividend cover indicates how much of the earnings have been paid as dividend. This figure cannot be calculated for companies which pay no dividend or which are not making profits.

Sometimes the company will calculate the dividend cover for you. For listed companies, the dividend cover is printed in Monday's editions of *The Financial Times*.

Strictly speaking, the number of shares is averaged during the year, and the amount of dividend paid may differ from that shown as payable because of timing differences. However these differences are not usually likely to be significant. The figure for dividend cover is an indication for which there is no need for spurious accuracy.

One of the beauties of this formula is that both figures are included in financial highlights. For example, healthcare company Amersham's 2001 highlights say:

	2001	2000
Earnings per share	27.2p	22.5p
Dividend per share	7.1p	6.4p

This gives dividend cover of 3.83 (27.2p ÷ 7.1p) for 2001, and 3.52 (22.5p ÷ 6.4p) for 2000. In each case, the company can cover its dividend between 3 and 4 times from earnings. Alternatively, the dividend represents between one third and one quarter of earnings.

In most cases, a dividend cover of between 3 and 4 is healthy, but there may be situations when a higher or lower figure is appropriate, which is why the narrative reports must always be read after the figures.

A dividend cover of 2 or less, or one which declines each year, is a warning. It could indicate that the company is struggling to maintain dividends in the face of declining earnings.

United Utilities has produced a dividend cover of 1.4, 0.9 and 1,1 in the years 2000, 2001 and 2002. The company has a policy of "progressive dividend policy". This requires it to give almost all of its profits to shareholders, keeping none for itself. From 2001 and 2002, the dividend was increased by 2% from 46.1p to 47p. The narrative report explains how the company intends to manage this ambitious dividend policy.

There is no right or wrong figure for dividend cover. The figure must be understood in the context of the company and in relationship to other figures.

A dividend cover above 10 could indicate that the company is not serious about paying dividends, preferring capital growth.

A stable established company will typically have a lower dividend cover than a small fast-expanding company, which needs to keep more of its profits to fund expansion. It is rare to find a bank with dividend cover above 3.0. Where a company listed on the Alternative Investment Market (AIM) is paying a dividend (and most don't), the dividend cover is usually at least 4.0.

> **Dividend cover is more a measure of policy than performance.**

Dividend cover is more a measure of policy than performance. After a company has paid its bills and tax, the remaining net profit is shared between the company and its shareholders. The directors decide how much of the profit should be given to shareholders, and how much the company should retain for its own use. If the dividend cover is 3, this means that the directors have decided to pass a third of the available profit to shareholders and keep two-thirds for its own use. Dividends are usually decided by the directors about three months into the next financial year. This gives them a fair indication of how the company is performing. A warning sign is if the dividend is maintained but the dividend cover drops.

Dividend cover must be considered in conjunction with other information, of which the most important is dividend cover for previous years. The next most important is dividend yield. A dividend yield of 6% with a dividend cover of 1.5 may not be as attractive as a dividend yield of 5% with a dividend cover of 3.0. A rough indication can be given simply by multiplying the figures. In our example this gives 9 and 15, indicating that the latter could be a better investment. This is because ultimately all the profit belongs to shareholders. The retained profit is the seedcorn to grow future profits and future dividends.

If the dividend cover is particularly high for one year compared with previous years, this may be because the company had a particularly profitable year. This can easily be seen from looking at the profit and loss account. Directors usually like to smoothe the amounts of dividend from one year to the next, and avoid large increases or decreases.

Has it ever skipped a dividend or reduced its dividend?

This information will only be included in the accounts if it relates to the current year. Otherwise this information will only be available from market research or investment analysis. However the effect of a skipped or reduced dividend will already be reflected in the share price to the extent that the market considers it relevant.

BT stopped paying dividends when it got into difficulties around 2000, and then resumed them. Other recent examples of skipped dividends include Beale, to cut costs, and Porvair to fund work on fuel cells.

The 'price' of dividend income

What is its earnings per share?

Formula:　　　EPS = Net Profit ÷ Issued Shares

Earnings per share (EPS) is the only ratio which must be disclosed on the face of the accounts. It is also the only ratio which has its own accounting standard, Financial Reporting Standard FRS 14. This was issued to take effect for accounts issued from 1998 when it replaced statement of standard accounting practice SSAP 3, introduced in February 1972. From 2005, listed companies must comply with international accounting standards, for which EPS is covered by IAS 33. The fact that three accounting standards have been issued for this ratio indicates its importance.

The EPS is sometimes called the 'basic EPS', to distinguish it from diluted EPS and other variations.

At its simplest, EPS tells you how much profit each share has earned that year. If a company makes £4 million profit and has two million shares, the EPS is £2 – simple! If a company has made a loss, an EPS is still calculated to show how much loss each share has suffered.

Unfortunately, it is far from this simple as both elements of the formula – net profit and issued shares – can be interpreted differently. Fortunately FRS 14 lays down the law for us, but an investor should understand how.

'Earnings' are the profit or loss after deducting dividends to shareholders (including those yet to be paid from the profit) and after deducting payments to any other providers of capital, such as preference shareholders. The figure must also be after deduction of exceptional and extraordinary items, tax, and minority interest. The inclusion of extraordinary items in FRS 14 was a welcome improvement on SSAP 3. Before, companies could classify inconvenient losses

135

as extraordinary items and leave them out of the reckoning, thus making their profits look better. This is not possible under FRS 14.

'Issued shares' is the weighted average of the number of ordinary shares during the accounting period. This will usually be a different figure from the number of shares at the end of the year. Unless there have been issues or redemptions of large numbers of shares, this is unlikely to be a significant difference in practice. The average is not adjusted to allow for share splits, consolidations or bonus issues.

Even with these tight definitions, there is plenty of scope for accounting adjustments. Most businesses like to report an EPS which is stable or slightly increasing rather than one which is wildly fluctuating. There are various steps the accountants can take to smooth out fluctuating profits. These mainly concern adjustments to accounting policies and squirrelling away bits of profit in good years to 'provisions' which can be raided in poor years.

By itself, the EPS says nothing. Knowing that the EPS is 5p does not tell you whether the share is performing well. The EPS must be related to another figure, of which the commonest is the share price. This is the widely used P/E ratio.

What is its *diluted* earnings per share?

Formula: EPS = Net Profit ÷ (Issued Shares + Shares which may be issued under options, convertible debt and similar)

A problem with the traditional measure is caused by 'dilution'.

This arises when there are convertible preference shares, share options and similar devices which allow lenders and directors to acquire shares. It is possible for a company with a million shares in issue to have issued other forms of instrument and allowed staff to acquire options which could allow, perhaps, another 200,000 shares to be issued. The company has no further control of when these shares will be issued. Dilution is explained further in Section 2.8.

To deal with this, a second figure is given. This is the 'diluted earnings per share'. This takes the same figure for earnings but divides it by a bigger number of shares, assuming that all the rights to acquire shares have been exercised. The diluted EPS will always be a lower figure than the basic EPS.

The diluted EPS is only relevant when it is significantly less than the basic EPS. It states how much profit has been earned by all the shares which could be issued in the company as currently funded.

The value of diluted EPS needs to be understood. Conversion is always in the future whereas the earnings are now. The longer the gap, the less realistic is this figure. Holders will only convert if the share price is attractive enough to do so. If the share price is much below the conversion price, conversion becomes much less likely and diluted EPS therefore less relevant.

Conversion is more commonly fixed for a period than a date. Diluted EPS is relevant when you are in the conversion period and the share price is above or just below the conversion price. Otherwise diluted EPS is probably of little relevance. The impact of high levels of preference shares to ordinary shares is better considered by looking at gearing, explained in Section 2.6.

Other EPS figures

The company must give the basic EPS and the diluted EPS. However, as with all figures in the accounts, the law only prescribes the minimum information which must be published. Companies are free to publish whatever additional information they like. Companies often publish their own versions of the EPS.

Usually these novel EPS figures adjust the amount for 'earnings', usually by adding some income, or, more commonly, excluding some deductions.

The reader of the account should be very sceptical about considering such figures which have been dreamed up by the company itself, purely to present itself in a favourable light.

What is its P/E ratio?

Formula: P/E = Share Price ÷ EPS

The price/earnings ratio or P/E is, by far, the commonest measure for valuing shares. The number divides the current share price by the earnings per share. This latter figure is itself a ratio, whose calculation is explained above. For quoted shares, the listings found in newspapers will usually give you the latest share price. Only companies currently making a profit have a P/E ratio.

The price is usually the mid-market price at the close of business the previous day. The earnings per share is usually based on the average number of shares in issue during the year that the profit was earned.

At its simplest, the P/E ratio represents the number of years at which the current levels of profit would pay for the shares. Suppose a company has two billion shares in issue, makes £4 billion profit and its shares are trading at £6. The EPS is £2, so the P/E is 3.0.

The main advantage of P/E is that it makes comparison between different companies very simple. It allows for their different sizes, and allows them to be compared with other companies, all companies in a particular sector, and with the market as a whole.

It is the most common indicator of how well investors think that company will fare.

Ultimately all profit earned by a company is returned to shareholders, either immediately in the form of dividend or in retained profit which boosts the share price. Suppose it is possible for an investor to earn a return of 5% p.a. in a safe investment like National Savings or gilts. That is the equivalent of a P/E ratio of 20 (calculated as 100% divided by 5%). Any company with a P/E ratio above 20 is expected to perform better than the economy generally. A company with a P/E ratio below 20 is expected to perform less well.

As a rough guide, a P/E of 30 or more means that the market expects the company to perform exceptionally well. You should only invest if you more than share that confidence. A P/E of 4 or less indicates that the market expects the company to perform poorly. It can be profitable to find companies with such low P/E ratios and then subject them to careful scrutiny to see if you believe they will perform better than the market thinks.

Beware of high P/E ratios for young companies. A P/E ratio of 25 or more for a company based on its offer price would typically mean that the company must double its sales in each of the next five years and achieve a net profit margin of at least 9%. Don't believe it. Such stocks are commonly known as glamour stocks. Sock Shop was the investment equivalent of the Bay City Rollers.

Remember that P/E ratios tend to rise during bull markets (when share prices are generally rising) and tend to reduce during bear markets (when share prices are generally falling).

If all companies were expected to perform equally well in the future, they would all have the same P/E. The differences are the clearest indication of how well they are expected to perform relative to each other.

The higher the P/E ratio is, the better investors expect that company to perform. Remember that the share price, which is the P of this ratio, already factors in all known information about that company and its prospects.

You should not invest in a company solely on the basis that it has a high P/E ratio. You should consider how well you expect that company to do, relative to the whole economy or to other companies. Look for companies where you think the P/E ratio is too low. That represents a good investment however high the P/E ratio is.

However the P/E ratio is not just a relative measure but an absolute one also. Until the 1980s, a P/E ratio above 10 was a rarity. Since then much higher P/E ratios have been recorded. If a company has just started to make a small profit but is expected to make huge profits, the P/E can be a huge number. *The Financial Times* does not report P/E ratios above 80 because at that level, the number is pure speculation. It simply represents a company where investors generally expect a massive growth in profits. A P/E below 10 is now generally regarded as one with an expected poor performance, or where the ratio is affected by some unusual factor.

P/E ratios grew during the 1990s without the companies themselves growing by anything as much. P/E ratios in 2002 were up to an average 18.2 against a historic average of 13.7.

A final point about P/E ratios is to be careful when using them for foreign shares. Other countries have different accounting standards which can lead to significantly different P/E figures. Japanese accounts, for example, allow for generous provisions to be deducted from profits, even though the company has earned the money. As a result P/E ratios in Japan can be five or six times that expected for a similar performing UK company. In the USA, P/E ratios can easily be twice the figure for an equivalent UK company.

Only compare P/E ratios for companies operating in the same country or under the same national law.

What is its dividend yield?

Formula: Dividend yield = Dividend per share ÷ Share price

The dividend yield, or simply 'yield', is the percentage of the current share price paid to shareholders. So a company with a dividend of 25p per share which is currently trading at £5, has a dividend yield of 5%. Fairly obviously, the yield can only be calculated for companies currently paying a dividend. For listed companies, the yield figure is quoted in the newspaper listings.

The dividend is the total dividend paid for the financial year. Most companies pay two dividends. The first is an interim dividend before the end of the financial year. The second is paid about six months later after the end of the financial year when the accounts have been prepared. Some companies, such as BP, make four dividend payments each year – three interim and one final. All these dividends are totalled to give the 'dividend per share' figure.

In the UK, dividends are paid net of 10% income tax. That means that if you receive a dividend cheque for £9, you are regarded as having received a dividend of £10 on which you have already paid tax of £1. Accordingly, the amount of dividend received must be increased by one ninth (or 11.1%) to be grossed up to the figure needed for this calculation. A shareholder who pays tax at the higher rate must pay an additional tax on his dividends. Other shareholders pay no further tax.

The share price is calculated as for the P/E ratio, namely the mid-market price at the close of business the previous day.

Dividend yield makes the share dividend comparable with other forms of investments, such as gilts, National Savings, bonds and unit trusts. So a dividend yield of 5% can be compared with the return on a savings account or other investment. However you must always remember that the dividend is just one of the two ways in which shares earn money. The other way is their capital growth. Most other forms of investment do not enjoy this element.

Yields allows companies to be compared, up to a point. The yield is a single figure which measures one of the two elements of the total 'return' on the share. However this is the element that is more certain as it represents money that is actually paid. The capital growth is not 'realised' (that is, turned into cash) until the share is sold. By then, the capital growth could have disappeared.

Shares compete with other forms of investment and tend to be priced at a level which is competitive. As shares enjoy capital growth as well as dividend income, the yield will usually be less than that available from investments with no capital growth, such as a deposit account. However this is not always the case. In 2003, Lloyds TSB had a yield of over 8%, more than double the rate available on any investment products it then had available. In other words you did better buying the bank than any of its products.

Very high yields often indicate that investors expect the dividend to be cut. A high yield dividend is a good investment if you have reason to believe that the dividend will not be cut.

High yields can also indicate that a company is growing slowly, or not growing at all, but is not in trouble. The higher yield compensates for the lack of opportunity for dividend growth.

What is the total return?

Formula: Total return = Dividend yield + Capital growth

Total return is expressed as a percentage, and allows shares to be compared directly not just with other shares but with other investments. It is simply an addition of the two elements which earn money for shareholders.

Dividend yield is the percentage calculated as already explained. Capital growth is simply the percentage increase or decrease in share price over the year.

Total return is sometimes criticised for adding apples to pears and coming up with a meaningless number.

What is its PEG factor?

Formula: PEG factor = P/E ratio ÷ Earnings growth

PEG stands for 'price earnings growth'. It divides the P/E ratio by expected earnings growth. The P/E ratio is itself based on another ratio, while expected earnings can be variously defined. So PEG is a ratio based on a ratio based on another ratio, and adjusted by a variously defined factor. Despite this vagueness, PEG is becoming a popular measure.

The P/E ratio is as previously defined. Earnings growth is variously defined as:

a)   the growth in the last reported year compared with the previous one; or
b)   a long-term average of earnings over any number of years; or
c)   the expected growth for the current year over the previous year; or even
d)   expected growth for any number of future years.

Of these, (d) is the least used as it can be little more than guesswork.

This measure was devised by the investment expert Jim Slater of Slater Walker fame. His preferred method was nearest to (c), though you need to read his book *Beyond the Zulu Principle* to understand the formula fully.

The objections to using (a) or (b) are that we are trying to measure the price for future growth, rather than past growth.

Another curiosity of this ratio is that it is a mathematical nonsense as it divides a number by a percentage. This conceptual problem is probably best avoided simply by saying that we are dividing one number by another number to get a third number which measures nothing but can be used for comparative purposes.

Suppose the P/E ratio is a healthy 20 and the forecast earnings growth is 25%. The PEG factor is 0.8. This is 20 divided by 25.

A PEG below 1.0 is cheap. This is because when the PEG is 1.0, the P/E ratio exactly matches the expected growth. As the PEG rises above 1.0, expected growth ceases to justify the P/E ratio.

As a ratio, PEG has both logic and simplicity on its side. Against that, it is difficult to get the time periods to match so that a proper PEG may be calculated. The combination of both a variously defined factor with a ratio of a ratio of a ratio also introduces many margins of error that can multiply to produce a significant element of error.

Insofar as PEG works at all, it works best for companies which are growing quickly but steadily. It does not work at all if a company is making losses or has falling profits. It works poorly if a company is largely valued on a basis other than profit generation, such as asset value or hope value.

Are there any threats to my interests?

Relevant to

All investors.

Underlying worry

'Is there a possibility that the company will be wrenched in a direction which is not in my interests?'

Who owns the company?

What different types of financial instrument does the company use?

The most fundamental threat to the shareholder is that other suppliers of capital have such a large claim against profits that there is insufficient for a proper return to the shareholders. So we start by looking at financial instruments.

A financial instrument is a means by which a company raises money to support its business. Financial instruments are sometimes called capital instruments or securities. Shares are financial instruments.

As explained in Section 2.6, the many dozens of financial instrument are all variations on one of two themes of *equity* and *debt*. Equity is where the holder of the instrument shares in the profits of the company. Debt is where the holder is paid a fixed rate regardless of the profits. (There are some exceptions, but this is good enough to understand the principle.) The ratio of debt to equity is known as gearing, and is explained in Section 2.6.

Equity instruments

The types of equity instrument are:

Ordinary share capital

This is by far the most common security. It is what is usually meant when the word 'share' is used without any adjectives. The holders of ordinary shares collectively own the company.

A-shares, B-shares etc.

These are ordinary shares but with different votes. Typically A-shares have no voting rights, but that is not always the case. A-shares allow a company to secure ordinary share capital while keeping control. A-shares have become much less common in recent years. One listed company which keeps them is builders merchant Gibbs and Dandy, where the A-shares trade for about half the value of other ordinary shares.

Stock

In the UK shares are individual items of which the shareholder buys a quantity, such as 1,000 shares with a nominal value of 25p each. However US companies prefer simply to express this as an amount of cash and say that the holder owns £250 worth of stock. In the UK there is added confusion because 'stock' can be used in this sense in terms such as stockbroker, stock market and stock-lending, but it can also mean an inventory of a company's products for sale, such as in stock-taking and the current asset of stock.

Founders' shares

These are rarely found now. They are a deferred share which ranks after all other shares in any winding up. It was a means by which a founder of a company persuaded other investors to buy shares.

Deferred shares

These were originally founders' shares, and could be valuable. Today they are more likely to be the opposite – worthless shares. They commonly arise when a company gets into difficulty and so redenominates its ordinary shares. The shareholder gets one share at the lower nominal value, and a deferred share for the rest. Signet plc has A and B deferred shares which it says "are not listed or quoted on any stock exchange and have minimal rights rendering them effectively valueless".

American Depositary Receipts (ADRs) or American Depositary Shares (ADSs)

This is an arrangement where the shares are held by a trustee and the holder transfers the rights to the shares rather than transfer the shares themselves. There are some special tax and legal provisions, but the investment implications are the same as for ordinary shares.

Golden share

When companies are privatised, the government may keep a golden share which allows it to outvote other shareholders. The UK government had golden shares in BT, BAA, Cable & Wireless, PowerGen and National Power. In 2002, the European Court of Justice ruled that such golden shares were only legal to the extent that they were necessary and proportionate to the national interest.

Debt instruments

The main types of debt instrument are:

Preference shares

Preference shares, despite their name, are a loan to a company, usually paid at a fixed rate. They may be traded in the same way as ordinary shares. BAE has 7.75% cumulative preference shares which are traded beside its ordinary shares.

cumulative means that any interest not paid in one year is added to the amount payable next year;

redeemable means that the company may buy the preference share back and thus cancel the loan;

participating means that the holder gets some profit in addition to the interest. This makes the preference share a mixture of debt and equity;

convertible means that the preference shares can be switched to ordinary shares, making the preference share into a share warrant, also a mixture of debt and equity.

Debentures

Debentures are a form of loan, usually secured on specific assets which may be seized if the loan is not repaid. Typically the debenture indicates an interest rate payable by the company, and the date when it may or must redeem the debenture.

Loan stock

Loan stock is simply another form of lending money to the company, usually less marketable than debentures, and not secured in the same way as debentures.

Junk bonds

Junk bonds are issued by low-value companies at high interest rates, and were popular in the 1980s. They either become valuable or worthless.

Financial Reporting Standard FRS 4 introduces a new selection of debt instruments, many of which the author has never seen in any accounts:

- *auction market preferred shares (AMPS)*
  preference shares whose price is fixed by auction

- *capital contributions*
  a temporary loan from a holding company to a subsidiary

- *convertible capital bonds*
  basically convertible preference shares issued by a specially set up subsidiary

- *convertible debt with a premium put option*
  a loan instrument which can be redeemed for more than the loan
- *convertible debt with enhanced interest*
  a loan instrument with a provision for increasing the interest rate
- *debt issued with warrants*
  the debt is paid at the amount lent, and the warrant for the interest can be sold separately
- *deep discount bonds*
  bonds which carry a low rate of interest and therefore sell at a low price
- *income bonds*
  interest is only payable if the issuer has made sufficient profit
- *index linked loan*
  where the interest is determined by a formula
- *limited recourse debt*
  a debt where the security is limited to specific assets
- *perpetual debt*
  where neither the borrower nor lender may demand that the debt be repaid
- *repackaged perpetual debt*
  where perpetual debt that has become worthless is passed to another party
- *stepped interest bonds*
  the rate of interest increases at various times
- *subordinated debt*
  the rights of the lender are less than for other creditors
- *zero coupon bonds*
  deep discount bonds which carry no interest

Derivatives

Both types of instrument, equity and debt, give rise to derivatives, which are neither equity instruments nor debt instruments, but are based on them. These derivatives can usually be sold in the same way as the underlying instruments. The more common derivatives include:

Share warrants

Share warrants give their holder the right to buy shares at a future date for a stated price.

Share options

Share options give their holder the right to buy shares at a future date for a stated price. They differ from share warrants in substance rather than form.

Traded options

Traded options are a type of share option, distinguished from the traditional option described above, in that they represent the right to deal in shares at a future time for a stated price. A call option is the right to buy; a put option is the right to sell, and the (rare) double option is the right to do either. Traded options can assume the nature of a bet as to where a share price or index will be on a particular day.

Financial futures

The holder of a financial future has made a *firm* contractual commitment to buy or sell securities at a future date – far more risky than an option because the holder cannot choose not to proceed with the purchase or sale.

A share investor can find himself with a derivative by accident. For example, a rights issue of, say, one share for every three already held will usually offer the shares at a discount to current price. This means that the right has a separate value from the shares which the investor can sell while keeping his existing shares.

Sometimes a derivative can be a useful means of hedging an investment. Hedging is similar to an insurance policy. Suppose you have £100,000 invested in shares when the stock market stands at 5000. If it fell to 4000, you would lose perhaps £20,000 of your investment. You may be willing to buy an index option which is effectively a bet that if the index falls below 4000 you will receive some cash.

So what is the cost of capital?

It is possible for an investor to calculate the weighted average cost of capital (WACC), by calculating the cost of equity capital, the cost of debt capital, and then providing a weighted average according to their relative amounts. In practice, this is best left to the academics rather than to individual investors.

From the WACC, it is possible to calculate the equity risk premium. This is the amount by which returns from shares exceed the return available from a no-risk investment such as government bonds. One study suggests that the equity risk premium for UK companies has historically been 6.5% to 8%. That means that investors expect shares to provide a return about 7% better than from a safe investment. The premium is to compensate share investors for the risk that share investments can go down as well as up, which is exactly what has happened since 1999.

Another share ratio encountered is the reinvested return on equity (ROE). This attempts to determine the future value of the company on the basis of return. This measures the growth in return over a period, typically five years, and projects it forward, usually for another five years. This measure is speculative and unreliable and is, again, best left for the academics.

Is it part of a group, and what is the ultimate parent company?

Almost all listed companies are now groups. There is a holding company (or parent company) which owns shares in subsidiaries. By owning shares in the holding company you automatically own a similar share in every subsidiary. Sometimes the subsidiaries have sub-subsidiaries.

Every company which is a subsidiary must say who is the ultimate parent company. This is rarely of concern to an investor who usually invests in the holding company.

Usually the annual report lists all the companies in the group. It is worth a look to ask why these companies exist as separate entities. It is normal to have separate companies for different countries or territorial areas, and where there is a clearly separate element of the overall business which justifies independent management. Subsidiaries are likely also to include recent acquisitions which have yet to be assimilated into the group, and older acquisitions which the directors have decided are best run with a significant degree of autonomy.

Subsidiaries which seem to have no clear commercial purpose should be regarded with some suspicion. It could represent delusions of grandeur or unfulfilled plans. Alternatively, it could represent some plan to hive off profitable bits.

Each subsidiary is a separate limited company where the shareholders' obligation is limited to share capital and the subsidiary's own assets. This means that if a subsidiary gets into trouble, the holding company is not obliged to bail it out. The subsidiary can go bust leaving unpaid creditors while the holding company keeps its assets. It is very rare (though not unknown) for a holding company to do this because of the damage to the holding company's reputation.

What is the investor profile of the company?

There is no law which requires a company to provide any profile of who owns its shares, other than to disclose holdings by directors, and anyone holding more than 3%. However some companies volunteer the information. National Grid's 2001 accounts tell us that its shares are owned thus:

	%
banks	0.03
nominee companies	77.99
insurance companies	1.50
pension funds	0.01
other corporate bodies	7.42
electricity companies	0.07
other limited companies	2.35
individuals	10.63

This is one of the types of second-hand information available to investors. At first sight, the low holdings by banks, insurance companies and pension funds would indicate that this is a holding to avoid. However a note explains that the nominee companies hold the shares for financial institutions, so the share is well regarded in the market. Individuals are well represented, making up 650,294 of the total 666,573 shareholders.

A further analysis is on the size of the shareholding. As with all such lists, the top and bottom figures are always the most significant. There are 222 shareholders who each hold at least 1 million shares representing 71.28% of the capital, which further underlines that this share is valued by financial instutions. At the other end, 392,493 shareholders have fewer than 100 shares, representing 1.85% of the capital, showing that it also has appeal for small individual investors.

Who has a significant shareholding in the company?

The annual report must list all shareholders who hold 3% or more of the shares. The Stock Exchange rules require that anyone owning 30% of the shares must make a bid for all the shares, which is why you often find references to 29.9% holdings from someone who may be about to mount a takeover challenge. A 30% holding is regarded as a 'controlling interest'.

The Stock Exchange requires that at least 25% of the shares must be available for other shareholders. So when an existing business is floated on the stock market, the original owners cannot keep more than three-quarters of the shares. However, they can move from the Stock Exchange main to the Alternative Investment Market (AIM) where this does not apply, so the proprietor's holding can again rise above 75%. This is exactly what clothing accessory retailer Monsoon did, to the chagrin of other shareholders. The company then decided to cancel the interim dividend.

This list is relevant to an investor in three ways:

- proprietor holding
- fund holding
- family holding

A holding by the original **proprietor**, who is probably now the chief executive is normal and desirable, particularly in young companies. The original directors demonstrate their continuing commitment by still owning many shares in the company. You should be concerned if the directors do *not* own shares in the company.

You should be concerned if the directors are entitled to more shares in option schemes than they already own. This indicates that the directors have little commitment to the company as it is, and merely hope that it will improve.

Fund holdings are generally a good sign. They indicate that the fund managers have confidence in the company. This is secondhand information, as the fund managers will have done their own private research to reach that conclusion. You cannot share that research, but you can share its conclusion. The annual report will say who has a holding of at least 3% of the shares. For the very biggest companies, the answer will often be no-one. For medium-sized and smaller companies, you may be concerned if no fund is listed, particularly if directors are listed.

Family holdings are always problematical for two reasons. First, there is an unspoken assumption that a family member will succeed the founder, even though that family member need not necessarily have management skills. Some companies have survived into a fourth generation over 100 years, but rarely beyond. Good family companies usually bring in outsiders early in their lifetimes. Second, family companies almost always work in concert. Three family members owning 25% each is the same as one member owning 75%. Family shareholdings are often held in a trust, so if you see a name like Skunkfizz Trust owning 70% of the shares, it is probably a family trust.

Shareholders who, possibly together, control more than 50% of the shares can do what they like with the company, subject to a few legal constraints. To some extent this is always true of management, though it must at least be public about it and persuade fund managers. Seymour Price was a cash-rich small finance company listed on AIM which broke itself up for no obvious reason and paid generous golden handshakes to its directors. The remaining shareholders set up an action group.

Other issues

What is the significance of the share premium account?

The share premium account represents the amount that the shareholders have paid in addition to the nominal value of the shares. If a company sells one million 25p shares at £1 each, the company adds £250,000 to share capital and £750,000 to share premium account. This premium is explained in Section 2.5.

By itself, the share premium account tells you very little and does not lend itself to any useful ratios. Suppose a steadily growing company issued shares for £1 when formed in 1910, and subsequently issued further shares of the same class for £2 in 1920, £3 in 1930 up to £10 in 2000. It has a share capital of £10 million and a share premium account of £30 million. What does that tell you? Little, because you do not know when the shares were issued.

There is a share premium account to share capital ratio of 3.0. It could be said that, on average, shareholders were prepared to buy new shares at an average of four times the share price over the lifetime of the company. Not only is this a meaningless concept, but it is almost certainly wrong. The company will have had many reorganisations, acquisitions, disposals and other capital instruments on the way.

The share premium account is simply additional share capital, which the company can use in its normal trade but cannot pay back as a dividend. The share premium account may be used to pay for the expense of any share issue. Otherwise, a company must obtain the permission of the court to use the share premium account.

Chloride Group plc did exactly that in 1991. It recorded a loss of £4 million, plus £13.6 million for a pension credit whose distributability was not legally determined. This deficit of £17.6 million stopped the company paying dividends. However it had a share premium account of £20 million, and applied to the court to use £17.6 million of that to clear its deficit.

When one company acquires another, the general rule is that it must add the acquired company's share premium to its own unless it can claim merger relief. In practice, almost all acquisitions qualify. There are similar provisions for reorganisations, making this is a way of liberating the share premium account.

What is the significance of the capital redemption reserve?

This arises when a company buys its own shares (except when a private company buys its shares from capital). By law, the company must transfer a sum to this reserve to reflect the share capital that is otherwise reduced. This means that the capital base of the company is maintained. Its status is therefore almost identical to the share premium.

Quite why company law is so insistent on maintaining capital is not obvious. The company is free to use the money for trading, and can therefore lose it. So the share capital with its related reserves may not be represented by anything. UK company law assumes that every company is a railway incorporated in 1844 and then makes exceptions for those companies which are not. Company law is now being rewritten so some of these quaint relics may be removed soon.

If one company acquires another by the issue of shares, the accounts may show a merger reserve, which is another form of capital redemption reserve.

What is the significance of current share value to nominal value?

None.

What factors could lead to a significant dilution of shareholders' funds?

The concept of dilution is explained in Section 2.8 in the context of directors' share options. It is also mentioned in Section 2.9 when explaining diluted EPS.

There are four main factors which can affect dilution of funds:

- new issues of shares
- conversion of debt instruments
- share options
- insolvency (discussed at the end of this section)

There are four types of share issue:

- equity issue (also called public issue or IPO)
- bonus issue (also called scrip issue)
- capitalisation issue
- rights issue

Bonus issues and capitalisation issues are when shareholders receive additional shares in proportion to their existing holdings. The difference is that capitalisation issues turn retained profit to capital (so they are rare in practice). Neither of these issues dilute your shareholding. If you owned 0.1% of a company before these issues, you still own 0.1% of the company afterwards.

An equity issue is a new issue of shares. Unless you buy an equivalent number of shares in the issue, this will dilute your holding.

A rights issue is when the company invites existing shareholders to buy more shares in proportion to their existing holdings. To persuade them to do so, the shares are usually offered at less than the current share price. Sometimes this right is itself a saleable commodity, as explained earlier in this section.

For equity and rights issues (whether or not you buy shares), you should always look for the reason. If it is to buy a new company or to build a new plant, you should ask if that new company or new plant is capable of generating *better* profits than the existing business. Beware of an issue which says it is to "raise working capital". This means that the company has frittered away its existing cash and now wants more.

External threats to shareholders

Almost every development in law, tax, economy, politics, technology, fashion and social values affects some companies somewhere. Exactly how is a matter for your judgment on which only a brief methodology can be summarised.

Any **change in law** shifts a burden from one area of society to another. For example, the continuing growth of employment law has a particular adverse effect on companies with large workforces or who deal with employment. Against that, new regulations, such as in money laundering, create new opportunities for suppliers of such services.

Tax can equally be a positive or negative influence. The reduction of what is now stamp duty land tax in deprived areas provides a boost for property companies operating in those areas. Another change (on 1 December 2003) increases stamp duty land tax on leases by up to 700% which can hit retailers.

Politics is a more subjective area. A change of government could lead to additional housebuilding or encouragement for certain types of building. It could even mean businesses closing. Labour party proposals in the 1980s would have outlawed nursing employment agencies.

The economy influences businesses in two main ways: how the business environment is affected and how alternative investments compare to share returns. The two commonest economic influences are interest rates and exchange rates. For example, Morgan Stanley estimates that every one cent decline in the dollar-pound exchange rate costs engineering company Smiths Group £1.5 million in operating profit.

At Bradford & Bingley 61% of new residential loans are for buy-to-let rather than owner-occupier purchaseers. Buy-to-let has been the smart place to invest money while interest rates, stock markets and pensions have been performing badly. However if investor sentiment moves against buy-to-let, the company could be exposed.

For **technology**, the internet provides an obvious example of how new businesses have been created (and some have survived) while other businesses, such as recorded music, have been adversely affected.

Fashion impacts on how promptly companies reflect changing tastes. Companies like Next started to beat Marks & Spencer, which fought back with new ranges like Per Una. However fashion does not just apply to clothing. It applies equally to household products, cars, media, food and many other sectors. The popularity of the Atkins diet in 2003 adversely affected Unilever's Slim Fast products, though the company is still performing well overall.

Social values can have significant impact in such areas as environmental concern and fair trade. Many annual reports now deal specifically with such matters. Huntingdon Life Sciences has been badly affected by protests against its experiments on animals.

The hot summer of 2003 was credited with booming sales for Dobbies garden centres, and falling sales for Thornton's chocolates.

Against this, there have been several factors in recent years expected to have massive effects on shares. These include the single currency in 1999, the 'millennium bug' of 2000, foot and mouth disease in 2001, and the war in Iraq in 2003. In each case, the economic consequence was less than feared.

9/11 attack on World Trade Center - effects on markets

- airlines and insurance stocks were hit hard. British Airways fell 21% in one day;
- oil prices rose on fear of massive retaliation, and then fell of fear of loss of air travel;
- the markets immediately fell by 4% (the New York Stock Exchange near the World Trade Center was closed for four days, and all trade was subdued);
- the UK, EC and USA all cut interest rates to stimulate the economy;
- consumer spending fell as people stayed in to watch television;
- television companies lost revenue as they decided not to show advertisements while reporting events;
- luxury spending was reduced as consumers thought such indulgence was inappropriate.

There is anecdotal evidence that some companies used this attack to justify results from other causes.

All this is before considering the effect of competition. The various Virgin companies grew big by looking at flabby complacent businesses, such as banks and airlines, and setting up a leaner alternative.

The ultimate threat

The ultimate threat to any business is insolvency. Although this is not always fatal to a business, it is always bad news to the investor.

Insolvency law changed in September 2003 when the relevant provisions of Enterprise Act 2002 were introduced. Strictly speaking, insolvency simply means that a company owes more than it is worth. Insolvency is a financial status, which does not stop a company trading if the directors reasonably believe that the situation can be remedied.

What is of concern to an investor is the legal status which may follow from insolvency. The various forms that legal insolvency may take can be put into three categories from the investors' perspective:

- winding up, liquidation
- receivership, administration
- company voluntary arrangement (CVA), debt moratorium, compounding

Winding up, liquidation

The company is finished. The liquidator is like an undertaker who buries the body. The investor usually receives nothing at all.

Receivership, administration

The company is not necessarily finished, but its management usually is. The directors are temporarily replaced by a receiver or administrator, usually with a view to selling the company. The investor may receive a small amount of cash or may receive shares in the company which buys the company.

Company voluntary arrangement (CVA), debt moratorium, compounding

These are arrangements that allow the company to continue while it sorts itself out. The directors stay in post, though subject to restrictions. A moratorium protects a company from creditors for 28 days. In the USA, similar arrangements are known as Chapter 11.

If a listed company suffers any of these fates, its shares will almost certainly be suspended, meaning that you cannot buy or sell them through a stock market.

The new insolvency laws impose a duty on the insolvency practitioner (the accountant who deals with the troubled company) to try to keep the company going, and for any sale to be of a going concern rather than a collection of assets. The priority for paying debts is amended so that holders of secured loans cannot wind up a saveable company for a quick grab of its money. Some funds must be set aside for paying unsecured creditors, such as the company's trade suppliers. The tax authorities lose their right to grab tax before anyone else is paid. These changes are designed to keep companies going where possible, which is good news for investors.

Often in an insolvency, the creditors agree to take shares in lieu of their debts. This leads to a massive dilution of your shareholding. When Marconi did this in what is known as a solvent burial, the creditors took 99.5% of the capital, so that the existing shareholders had just 1/200th of their original holding.

Companies which have suffered may recover and will represent excellent investments if they do. You must always study the reason for the difficulties with the plans for recovery, allowing for directors' ever-ebullient optimism.

For example, we consider hearing aid maker Hearing Enhancement, a company floated on Ofex in 1996 at 30p a share to exploit patented induction loop technology. It was profitable until 2001. The company went into a CVA in May 2003 after losing two major contracts. Shares were suspended at 13.5p. Two subsidiaries paid creditors 50p in the pound, another six creditors (including three directors) accepted shares for their debt. Four institutions contributed

£306,000 in a share placing (equity issue). The company's shares were again suspended on 6 February 2004 at 3p, though no-one had bought any of its shares since 19 December 2003. The company is worth £428,000, about 4p per share, and has net debt of 40% of its value.

So what is the story? From the chairman's statement it seems to be a classic case for technology companies of engineering strength but management weakness. The company developed new products for which the research was "flawed", yet the company had incurred "major expenditure" setting up a call centre and other support. The obvious question about flawed research is not answered. The company tried to sell by direct marketing which it was forced to abort when it unexpectedly lost two contracts, though we are not told why. The company took immediate action including a volunteered 40% cut in directors' pay and 20% cut in staff wages, before all but the chairman and managing director were made redundant. The author invited the company to comment, but it declined to do so.

Anyone with a sufficiently large and sufficiently balanced portfolio has the occasional investment that goes bust and falls to zero. Remember that even this is an asset, as you can offset this loss against other profits for capital gains tax. Knowing that Inland Revenue will refund up to 40% of your loss can sugar the bitter pill. If the share has fallen to a small figure, such as £1,000 worth of Marconi shares now worth £10, this tax loss is crystallised when you dispose of the share, so you should consider timing. Because dealing costs will probably be more than £10, these fag-end holdings are usually donated to Sharegift for whom there are no dealing charges. These tiny holdings are collected together to produce a portfolio applied to charities.

Applying the 10 tests to different types of business

Accounts analysis in context

How does the nature of its business affect my understanding of its accounts?

This section can do no more than introduce you to some of the special factors you need to consider in specific sectors.

Aerospace

Aerospace is the generic term for those in aeroplane manufacture and related industies. All aerospace companies rely on government defence work to survive, so aerospace companies are often not acceptable to ethical investors.

Earnings in the aerospace industry tend to be lower than average. However such companies tend to be stable and asset-based. Be particularly concerned about too much reliance on single customers, heavy gearing and large amounts of intangible assets.

AIM companies

The Alternative Investment Market (AIM) is a less regulated market for smaller companies which generally provides similar opportunities for the private investor. It started on 10 June 1995, replacing smaller markets such as the Unlisted Securities Market (USM). AIM is run by the London Stock Exchange but under less demanding rules. There is no requirement for minimum worth of £700,000 nor for at least 25% of shares to be public, as there is for the main LSE market. AIM companies must provide half-yearly accounts, and must disclose significant transactions and events. An AIM company may increase its issue of any security by up to 10% without submitting any further admission documents.

As smaller companies, they are higher risk and less liquid. This means that their shares are less easy to sell and the difference between buying and selling prices is greater. However AIM has produced some spectacular opportunities both for gain and loss. There is also the practical advantage that holdings in AIM companies attract special advantages for capital gains tax on disposal.

In 2003, the Alternative Investment Market raised almost as much capital as the main market, £1.46 bn against £1.4 bn (excluding the deeply discounted rights issue for Royal & Sun Alliance).

There are also even smaller markets such as Ofex and ShareMark. You can still buy direct from a prospectus, and there is nothing to stop you making private purchases from existing shareholders in a company of any size.

Most of the formulae and other comments in this book hold good for small companies, though, as ever, you should consider the special factors of each company. In very small companies, you may be expected to participate in the management, and you will certainly find your freedom to sell shares severely limited by a lack of market, if not legally restricted by a shareholders' agreement. Beware of very small companies. About one in three new companies fail in their first few years. The average life of all companies is 9.4 years.

Airlines

Airlines are vulnerable to many factors, particularly to do with international politics. War and international tension always has an adverse impact on airlines. Private airlines compete against national airlines of which national governments are protective despite what they may say and what the European Union requires in public. The EU came down heavily on Ryanair in 2004 when it held that a mutually beneficial agreement with Charleroi Airport was anti-competitive.

It is also a vicious market where the big players try to squeeze out the small players, and compromised governments can be ineffective in preventing this. Laker was forced out in 1982. British Airways was found to have played dirty tricks against Virgin in the 1990s.

In looking at commercial performance, it can be useful knowing how much seating capacity it sells. A good airline should manage 70%, possibly selling off the remaining seats at a reduced price, so don't regard crowded aircraft as necessarily indicating a successful airline.

Earnings tend to be low for the high value of business, so airline shares are suitable for investors looking for capital growth and who believe they understand the aviation industry and international politics.

Alcohol and breweries

Alcoholic drink is traditionally a defensive stock which continues regardless of the state of the economy. When things go well, we buy drink to celebrate. When things go badly, we buy drink to drown our sorrows.

Many breweries own a considerable amount of property, so you should pay particular attention to what the company owns and how it runs its business. The best performing brewery stocks are not necessarily the best known companies.

Automobiles

Automobile companies are cyclical in that their fortunes reflect the general economy. Most UK companies involved in the automobile industry were wiped out by trade union activity in the 1970s and 1980s, and car companies now have significant international ownership.

Banks

Banks and building societies have a reputation for being safe, making the crash of BCCI in 1991 all that more memorable. In fact, BCCI was just one of six banks which crashed that year. In contrast, no-one has lost money in a building society since 1945. Poor performing societies have always been taken over first.

Many ratios are not easily applied to banks. For example, there is no obvious basis for gross profit. Banks therefore produce some sector-specific measures, such as HBOS reporting that its *cost to income ratio* is down to 42.1%

Bank shares tend to attract higher valuations than their equivalents in other sectors. Whatever we think of the High Street banks (not much, usually), they have proved adept at increasing profits year on year by expanding into new markets, maximising profits and cutting costs.

As a defensive stock, banks tend to become overvalued when other sectors suffer. They can represent excellent value. Lloyds TSB was at one point in 2003 providing a dividend yield of 8%, far more than you could get on any of its accounts.

Business services

Business services includes advertising, recruitment, training and outsourcing. The most obvious point to note about these companies are:

- their lack of fixed assets; and
- their vulnerability to the general economy.

This can be an advantage when the company is forced to economise (euphemistically called downsizing), as it is fairly easy to shed staff. Headhunting, a sexy sector in the 1980s and 1990s, suffered in 2002 when a third of staff in the 160 companies lost their jobs.

Business service companies tend not to recover well. Because the company consists of little more than a rented office and some clever kids, a company which has laid off staff is unlikely to persuade them to come back. It is more likely that they will set up their own business.

Advertising is the first business to be hit when a recession comes, and the first to recover.

An investor should conduct considerable analysis on how durable the company is and what asset base it has. Earnings tend to be lower than average, and with little prospect for sustainable capital growth, you need to find some really good reasons to invest.

Chemicals

Chemical companies tend to attract low market ratings because of their volatility. They are highly cyclical, which means their fortunes match the general economy.

Many chemicals are oil-based, including plastics and paint, so chemical companies are heavily influenced by the vagaries which affect oil companies.

Most chemical companies are high volume, low cost operations. This means that they have a high sensitivity to price fluctuations. A small price or cost change can have a significant impact on prices. Chemicals are an international product, so chemical companies are subject to foreign competition and currency risks.

Chemical companies which specialise in low volume high price specialist products have a more stable performance.

Construction

Construction is a cyclical industry in that it is particularly affected by the economy, but not in the same way as other cyclical industries like leisure goods. Construction is determined more by policy, particularly government policy.

In the 1991 recession, the construction industry was particularly badly hit. Sometimes construction can become counter-cyclical, in that booming construction can presage bleak times. It can be sensible to consider buying shares in a construction company during a recession provided you believe the company will survive. You should look particularly for a high current ratio.

Construction materials

Construction materials is a separate business from construction itself. Such companies are entirely dependent on the construction industry, so when construction material companies suffer, it is obvious that construction will suffer next.

Construction material companies traditionally attract low valuations relative to their asset values. This means that ratios for construction material companies will usually be less than what would otherwise appear to be comparable companies.

Engineering

This is a cyclical sector which is affected by the general economy. It is one area where accounting ratios give reliable and consistent answers.

Food manufacturing

Food companies are traditionally defensive, which means that they are resistant to changes in the economy. People still eat and drink whatever the state of the economy.

Food manufacturers are vulnerable to basic food prices which in turn are affected by the weather. For example, 2003 saw a summer heatwave in Europe which led to a poor harvest for wheat, so Tate & Lyle, which turns wheat into sugar syrup used for fizzy drinks, saw profits squeezed, and its share price fall by 10%. Finsbury Food has been hit by soaring egg prices, the main ingredient in its cakes.

Earnings tend to be higher than for other sectors.

Food retailing

Most food retailers have now diversified into other household goods, petrol and financial services. The diversifications of the 1990s have tended to be more successful than those of earlier decades. There is a fierce battle for market share, with Tesco the largest food retailer having overtaken Sainsbury in 1993.

This sector is not cyclical and tends to produce above average earnings.

Pay particular attention to profit ratios (Section 2.3) and then cost ratios (Section 2.2). Remember that retailers are so cash-positive that they can safely trade on a current ratio as low as 0.5. This is even lower than for retailers generally as food has a much faster turnover.

Football clubs

Football clubs are a consistently poor investment. The football industry was very badly hit when ITV Digital went bust in 2002, losing them much of their income from television rights. Football players are ludicrously overpaid by any commercial basis, and the clubs are vulnerable to injuries, poaching of players and relegation. Football club shares are also popular among fans which tends to push their price up above their commercial value. Being household names also tends to push up the price.

Sometimes clubs like to represent that they have diversified, but in most cases this diversification consists of little more than a rag bag of fringe activities of sticking their name on a product to sell to fans.

It is always worth looking at who the shareholders are. Even a successful football club like Manchester United had 45% of its shares owned by just three people at the beginning of 2004.

Household goods

Household goods companies tend to attract good valuations which may overstate their investment potential. Investors like businesses they understand, and making saucepans is more understandable than software for psychological profiling.

Household goods companies are cyclical in that their fortunes tend to mirror the general state of the economy. However they tend to produce above average earnings.

This sector is really dozens of mini-sectors, each of which has its own financial profile. For example, the furniture market is fragmented across many companies, whereas carpets are dominated by Carpetright with 25% of the market. Furniture companies such as DBS have suffered in the early years of 2000s through cheap imports from China and possible competition from new entrants like Matalan and Marks & Spencer. Such uncertainties are translating into low P/E ratios, such as 8.2 for Homestyle which should otherwise be much higher.

Insurance

Insurance companies have been unstable, even though insurance itself is a stable business. Insurance companies have been particularly affected by pensions. In the 1990s, it would have been reasonable to assume that the UK success story on private pensions would continue and could be exported to EU countries, which are well behind the UK in terms of pension provision. As it turned out, insurance companies have yet to break into this market while the home market suffered badly, as explained in Section 2.7.

There are strict liquidity rules for insurance companies to ensure they have sufficient funds to meet claims. The slighest concern about liquidity adversely affects share price.

Insurance companies suffered badly from a series of worse than expected claims in many areas, such as from terrorism and natural disasters. In the 1990s, fierce competition led to suicidal premium cutting which is now being reversed. Pay particular attention to cash indicators (Section 2.4).

Internet companies

Internet and technology companies benefit from their own indices, techMARK in the UK and Nasdaq in the USA. These provide reliable sector indications.

In 2000, 210 substantial dotcom companies crashed, of which 121 crashed in the final quarter. Research by webmergers.com, showed that the main reasons was a lack of basic management control such as market research, budgeting and product-testing.

Boo.com easily raised £100 million on flotation to sell branded sportswear on the internet. It crashed just six months later in May 2000 and is a classic case study of how not to run a business. The company launched simultaneously in 18 countries and was the embodiment of the bright young things of the internet revolution. If they had any idea of how to run a business or what customers wanted, it might have lasted as long as seven months.

In 2000, few people had the broadband connections which are essential to making the internet tolerable. Boo.com produced flashy graphics which made navigation difficult and ordering goods impossible. It sought to be entertaining and wacky, ignoring the fact that this aggravates customers facing long download times before the computer crashes. This was compounded by the lack of a proper business plan, lack of financial expertise and extravagant spending by management.

But while mismanagement can be blamed for bringing down Boo.com and other dotcoms, it cannot be blamed for the ludicrous valuations. This is down to the herd instinct of investors. For what it was worth, P/E ratios fell from meaningless highs of 80 or more in 2000 to about 30 one year later. *The Daily Mail* calculated that these dotcom companies would have to maintain 30% growth for 20 years to support their market capitalisations.

If anything, investor sentiment has now probably swung too far the other way. The Boo.com lessons have been learnt and broadband is now widely available. There is no reason to exclude the surviving dotcom companies provided they pass the accounting tests. Lastminute.com is prospering into 2004.

Investment trusts

Investment trusts are not trusts at all but companies which invest in other companies. They are similar in operation to unit trusts, but less restricted.

A curiosity of investment trusts is that they tend to be valued at less than their net asset value, with a discount of 15% not uncommon. The New Opportunities Investment Trust (launched September 2002) managed to trade at a 59% discount in May 2003 (price 24p; nav 58.5p). All this should make ITs a good investment, except that you would probably have to accept that same discount when you come to sell them. Investment trusts have consistently outperformed unit trusts, but tend not to get suggested by IFAs as they pay less commission.

Investment trusts often run savings plans whereby you can invest a monthly sum as small as £50 a month (though some start at £20). This is a good simple way to make money. First the charges are much lower, typically 0.2% commission rather than 1.5% from a stockbroker. Second, regular investment means that you always buy at a price better than average because of pound cost averaging.

Pound cost averaging is best illustrated by a simple example. Suppose a share price in five consecutive months is 90p, 95p, £1, £1.05 and £1.10. The average price is clearly £1. If you invested £1,000 in shares at this average price, you would have 1000 shares. Suppose you invested £200 in shares each month. You would buy the shares listed at the prices over the page –

222 shares at 90p
211 shares at 95p
200 shares at 100p   1005 shares at an average 99.5p
190 shares at 105p
182 shares at 110p

You will find that pound cost averaging always beats the average price, however the prices move or when they move.

Leisure industry

The leisure industry is the most cyclical of all shares. This means that its performance magnifies the state of the general economy. The more luxurious and extravagant the products, the more cyclical is the company's share.

It is easy to see why. Suppose an individual earns £2,000 a month after tax of which £1,700 pays the mortgage and other household expenditure. That individual has £300 a month free money for luxuries. If taxation or mortgage interest rates increase his expenditure to £1,900 a month, his free money reduces by two-thirds to £100. Conversely, if rates fall to £1,500, his free money increases to £500. There is therefore a gearing effect between the health of the economy and the prosperity of leisure companies.

The generic term 'leisure' covers a wide range of different activities, so it is essential that you find out exactly what the company does. Each type of leisure business will have its own specific measures which are particularly relevant. Look for them in the accounts:

Betting: *market share*

Gambling tends to have a finite market as so many people shun it for its obvious addictive cash-losing qualities. This sub-sector is boycotted by ethical investors. The success of a betting operator therefore depends on how much of the market it has. Betting companies consistently return good profits. It takes some skill to lose money as a casino operator or bookmaker.

Health clubs: *non-use and retention rate*

This country is full of fatties who join a gym, attend at least twice in the first two weeks and then are too busy but do not cancel because that would be an admission that they are not serious about losing weight. Whatever that says about the nation's health, it is good news for the company's wealth. Retention rate is how many customers a health club manages to keep. The two measures (non-use and retention rate) indicate the same factor, so only one needs to be disclosed.

Hotels: *occupancy rate*

If a tailor fails to sell a suit today, he can still sell it tomorrow. If a hotelier fails to sell a room one night, that sale is lost forever.

Many leisure companies have realised this and tried to diversify, which is not usually wise. Some hotel companies in the boom 1980s tried to diversify into conference centres, holiday attractions and retail. They were usually over-geared and consequently suffered in the 1991 recession. Hotels that stuck to their knitting, like Stakis, coped much better during the recession. Stakis is now part of the Hilton group.

Among companies which have successfully moved are Esporta, which moved from holiday attractions (mostly in Blackpool) to health clubs. Another example is Zetters which moved from football pools to financial services and gaming.

Be careful of 'hobby' companies, which are similar to football clubs in being over-valued because of fans subscribing. The Flying Scotsman company, listed on OFEX, ran the historic 1923 locomotive. The shares were sold for 38p and were suspended at 30.5p in June 2003 while they tried to find a buyer for the locomotive. If you fancy owning a share in a steam locomotive, fine, but don't kid yourself it is an investment.

Media

Media is a ragbag which covers such completely different activities as books, newspapers and films. They have different investment profiles.

You should always ask what is the future for publishing. Generally, publishers have suffered from the 1990s onwards as people buy fewer books. Publishers are competing with internet publishing and more television channels. Some significant mergers have failed to reverse this trend.

Remember that most publishing companies are dependent on another sector. Newspapers depend on advertising, for example. Books depend on how well the sector at whom the book is aimed performs. Fiction and coffee table books are really a leisure product.

Commercial publishing is usually the second industry (after advertising) to be hit when a recession comes, and the second to recover.

Films are heavily influenced by tax policy. The government introduced a scheme to provide generous tax relief and then withdrew it because they realised people were paying less tax as a result. (Think about it.)

Earnings tend to be lower than average. This sector is not cyclical, it just has problems of its own.

Mines

Mark Twain said that a mine is a hole in the ground with a liar at the top.

Mining is the ultimate basic industry, as the companies are literally selling the ground we stand on (or parts of it). They tend to have a higher P/E ratio than their equivalent-sized companies in other industries. This reflects the value of mineral in the ground which is not included in the company's assets. This makes mining a unique sector, highly cyclical but generally stable.

Many products, such as diamonds, are dominated by particular countries or companies. Turmoil in South Africa in the 1980s introduced unwelcome volatility to trading in diamonds and precious metals.

You should always know exactly what the company is mining and what it is used for. For example, gold has uses in electronics, aeroplane windscreens and jewellery as well as being an asset in its own right. Gold has its own value which tends to move in the opposite direction to everything else. When investors fear that everything else is about to do badly, they buy gold.

When the mineral is a commodity it is useful to know the unit cost of production. For example in 2004, Peter Hambro Mining say they can mine gold at $150 an ounce. With gold selling at around $400 an ounce, that shows a very healthy gross profit margin and plenty of safety if the gold price falls.

To understand mines and quarries, you must understand what the material is used for. Central African Mining moved from mining to tantalum to copper. You need to know how each metal is used, and why the move was made. The most common use of silver, for example, is still in photography, though silver is usually mined with other metals such as zinc.

Oil industry

Oil companies tend to have higher P/E ratios than their equivalent-sized companies in other industries. This reflects the fact that the real asset of an oil company is the oil in the ground.

Valuing oil in the ground is notoriously difficult. Shell recently had to reclassify 20% of its reserves as probable rather than proven. In 1983, BP spent $130 million drilling a hole in Mukluk, Alaska, which proved to contain only water. Badluk.

You must consider financial data against the economic and political risk. Oil prices are governed by OPEC through the regulation of production. In 1973 OPEC trebled oil prices causing havoc in oil-consuming countries like the UK, but has become more responsible since. The political risk comes from how you read the situation regarding terrorism, the clash of East and West and the rise of fundamentalist Islam.

Oil companies tend to have lower than average earnings and understated asset values.

Pharmaceuticals

Pharmaceuticals are companies which develop drugs. There are huge research & development costs to find products, many of which are never marketed. Then there is a long and expensive period of accreditation while clinical trials take place. Finally, the company receives a 20-year patent during which time it alone can make or license that product. You should always find out how much longer there is to run on the patents for the company's money-spinners. Even when a patent has expired, a company can still earn money from supplying that product, as it has a 20-year head start on its competitors.

At first sight, it would seem that such companies must suffer massive price sensitivity. A company may spend £1 million developing ten products, of which one goes to clinical trial, costing another £1 million to be approved. This product has arguably already cost either £2 million or £11 million. It might then be produced at a unit cost of a few pence, forcing the company to recover its costs within 20 years. To compound problems the National Health Service has a monopoly on many products.

The reality is not as bad as the theory. Pharmaceutical companies can produce a steady pipeline of new products and are able to negotiate prices which allow recovery. Pharmaceuticals are seen as a defensive non-cyclical sector.

Always look at the figure for research & development. Although written off to profit and loss account, this really represents a hidden asset.

Pharmaceuticals have a high negative sensitivity of 6.4 to interest rates, meaning that a 1% decrease in interest rates leads to a 6.4% increase in profits.

Property

Property companies are sometimes called real estate, an American term. P/E ratios are almost meaningless for such companies, for which asset value indicators (Section 2.5) are more appropriate. It is quite common for shares to trade at a discount to net asset value, even a 30% discount does not necessarily indicate any problems. British Land was 34% below by 2004. The sector average is around 19%.

Housebuilding companies usually quote a figure for land bank, and equate this to plots and years' worth of build. So Ben Bailey Construction said in 2004 that it has 1,400 plots, enough for three years' build.

Property companies have banked land which is often held on the books at cost rather than revaluation, indicating that asset values can be significantly understated. Sometimes property companies refer to **triple net asset value**. This is the value of net assets after allowing for tax on disposals, marking debt to market value, and dilution if all share options are exercised.

Income is usually secure as rental income flows easily. Property is readily resaleable, and rent increases often just a formality. The 1991/92 recession did hit property companies, but most recovered. If you believe that there could be another recession, pay particular attention to a property company's borrowings and gearing.

For the medium term, you should consider the domestic economy such as mortgage rates and house price inflation, and how long such trends will continue. The house boom has allowed property companies to show some impressive statistics. Bellway has achieved growth of 23% a year for a decade, but its EPS is up only a third and its P/E ratio is only around 6. This indicates that the market does not think this property growth can continue. If you believe it will, here is a good investment for you.

A small investor will often own his or her own home and know how property values increase and represent a good investment for the individual. Do not be deceived. Property values have not produced anything like the return from shares.

Retailers

For investment purposes, food retailers are generally regarded as having a separate sector profile from all other retailers. Retailers tend to have lower than average earnings but are generally not cyclical unless they are well into the luxury market. Most listed general retailers are sufficiently diversified down-market.

For retailers, you must always ask what competition there is and what new competition there may be. WH Smith underperformed the market by 60% in the ten years to 2004 because it was undercut by other retailers, including supermarkets and internet retailers like Amazon.

Pay particular attention to profit ratios (Section 2.3) and then cost ratios (Section 2.2). Remember that retailers are so cash-positive that they can safely trade on a current ratio below 1.0.

Shell companies

Shell companies are those with no trade at all. They have sold their businesses and are now just a name with a stock market listing with perhaps some cash and an office.

The conventional measures of valuing such companies are meaningless as income is unlikely to be more than interest on deposits, and expenses just a few overheads. You need to consider who is running the company, why it sold its business and what plans it has.

The most famous and most notorious shell company was Polly Peck. This was an obscure East London clothing company bought by Asil Nadir. He used it as a listing for his fruit packing business. The shares traded at 3p in 1976 and soon soared to £36. The company was suspected of fraud, the shares fell and were suspended at 108p. Nadir fled the country. The company went into administration with debts of £1.3 billion. Shareholders will see none of their money.

Technology companies

When a new product becomes available, there is usually a host of companies offering the product, of which most disappear and a few survive.

In 1846 the London Stock Exchange quoted 280 railway companies, then the largest businesses in the country. By 1850 there were 160. During the 20th century, 2000 car-making companies started in the USA. Only three remained at the end of the century. A similar phenomenon can be seen for record companies in the 1920s and computer companies in the 1980s.

Spotting the survivors is the key to success, but this is not easy. A good product is not a guarantee of good success. Apple's operating system is technically superior to Microsoft's; Betamax video superior to VHS; and BSB broadcasting superior to Sky. Yet in each case, the latter company prevailed because of better management. It is not true that the world will beat a path to the door of the person who invents a better mousetrap.

It can be difficult to spot what technology will take off. It was expected that eight-track cassettes, video discs and household management software would all be successful, but no-one wanted them. Against that, there is a string of inventions that were dismissed as unsaleable from the telephone through to Post-It notes and fax machines. Edison invented the first recorded sound machine in 1877 but saw no practical use for it for 11 years.

Brilliant technology does not mean a brilliant business, as the Channel Tunnel and the Concorde aeroplane both demonstrate. Even when a technology company survives because it has achieved the magic combination of technological and commercial success, there is no guarantee that it will continue to maintain the stream of technological brilliance. Sinclair pioneered a brilliant little computer at the start of the 1980s but followed this with the disastrous C5 toy car. Many companies such as RAC and Amstrad were highly innovative and commercially successful, but could not sustain their success.

Sometimes companies can become their own worst enemy. Record companies promoted sales of cassettes and then complained they were losing revenue when purchasers illegally copied their records. The lesson was not learned as 20 years later it became easy to download recordings from the internet. Record sales plummeted during 2002 and 2003, yet the unexpected success of the Mac iPod has shown that consumers are prepared to pay for the legal downloading of music.

You must always question what future there is for any technology company, and remember that you are not likely to get it right. It can be a successul investment strategy to ignore most accounting ratios completely, and instead concentrate on having a wide portfolio of small holdings in many technology companies. In such a strategy you must monitor the companies closely and be ready to sell quickly.

Technology companies tend to pay a low rate of dividend.

Telephone companies

In current investment jargon, telephone, media and technology companies are often lumped together as 'TMT companies'. This is because they are seen as converging. Advances in cable and satellite technology has seen the growth of companies which provide you with television channels, internet line and telephone. However this convergence has not been as complete as had been predicted.

Telephone companies have fought a brave fight against the might of BT which had the considerable advantages of a 50-year head start, national monopoly (except in Hull for some reason) and owning the vast national infrastructure. BT has mounted a tough fight back. As with the utility companies mentioned below, an attempt to provide the benefit of competition to a monopoly has been made by introducing a regulator (Oftel for telecoms) with power to overrule the monopoly's commercial decisions which are seen as being anti-competitive.

The biggest issue for telecommunication companies is where future growth will come from when everyone who wants a telephone has one. An answer is that we will all have two. Oftel clearly thought so when it reordered telephone numbers so that there were enough numbers available for exciting new products. Most telephone numbers now contain 11 digits which provide enough numbers for every man, woman and child in the UK to have over 1,600 telephones.

Part of the answer is the runaway success of mobile telephones. The immediate future depends on the success of the 3G technology which includes camera and internet facilities. Telecom companies paid a total of £22 billion to buy their 3G licences for new telephones which transmit pictures. Companies now recognise that they paid too much, and some have written off this amount in their accounts.

In addition mobile telephone companies are under pressure to keep reducing costs. The Competition Commission ruled in January 2003 that costs to consumers should reduce by 15% each year until 2006. This is based on the Commission's calculation on a return on capital, which completely ignored the £22bn licence fee.

Whether you should invest in telecoms depends more on your view of the future rather than what is in the accounts.

Television companies

The television sector is dominated by a handful of companies following mergers. While broadcasters are confined to big companies, there are hundreds of small television-based companies, such as independent producers and service providers.

You should pay particular attention to the capital structure of television companies, particularly to what shares are in issue. They can issue A-shares without voting rights so they can attract equity investment without losing control.

Television companies tend to pay low earnings, are non-cyclical and have a poor record of survival.

Tobacco companies

Tobacco companies tend to trade at low values with high yields. They have been heavily boycotted by ethical investors and many fear the risk from damaging lawsuits from those damaged by smoking. British American Tobacco's website is dominated by corporate responsibility statements to counter negative publicity.

Tobacco companies are heavily affected by the amount of duty imposed and how much smuggling there is to avoid the duty. Smoking is steadily declining in the UK, so you should ask where is the growth potential. The answer is either in promoting smoking in new overseas markets or by diversifying. The former raises ethical questions while the latter begs the question of why should a tobacco company make a go of a different business? That is why tobacco companies are undervalued.

Tobacco companies are not cyclical and pay above average earnings.

Utilities

Utilities are mainly the telephone, electricity, water and gas companies privatised in the 1980s. These shares were priced low to encourage the general public to take them up. This was certainly successful as privatisations trebled the number of individual shareholders to 9 million. Such investors were known as Sids, from the television advertisement promoting British Gas shares. One quarter of these shares were immediately sold for a profit, a process known as stagging. It is estimated that there are now 12 million Sids.

Many utilities, particularly water companies, attract lower values than equivalent accounts would justify in other sectors.

Wholesalers and distributors

In investment terms, the main difference between wholesaling and retailing is that the former is highly cyclical whereas the latter is non-cyclical. It would seem obvious that they should share the cyclical profile as one simply supplies the other, but that is not actually so.

Wholesalers enjoy high quality earnings. They trade on low liquid asset ratios, though anything less than 1.0 should cause some concern. Pay particular attention to profit ratios (Section 2.3).

The reliability of reports & accounts

The main financial statements

A simple guide to understanding accounts

The rest of this book assumes that you understand the conventions of company accounts. If you do not, this sub-section can be read while no-one is looking.

As a shareholder you will receive an annual report and accounts, sometimes in separate documents, sometimes bound together.

The two most important financial statements are the balance sheet and profit and loss account. They are both made up to the same date, known as the balance sheet date. This is the last day of an accounting period, usually of one year.

Expressing amounts

Financial statements only record amounts of money. UK accounts are presented in £, but sometimes accounts may be presented in other currencies such as the US dollar $, or the euro €. To avoid cluttering the page with £ signs, the columns of numbers are headed with the currency symbol. To avoid large numbers, companies often express the accounts in multiples of thousands or millions of pounds. The column indicates the currency and its multiple. So £5 million can be shown as:

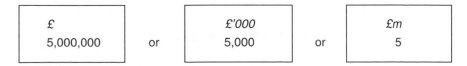

£		£'000		£m
5,000,000	or	5,000	or	5

Most financial statements have two columns of figures, where the second column is the comparative figure for the previous year. Usually the current figure is on the left and is printed in bolder type or otherwise made more obvious.

If a figure is the opposite to what is expected for the item, the number is shown in brackets. So suppose a company showed the following in its profit and loss account:

	Note	**2005** **£m**	2004 £m
Operating profit	7	**4.7**	(2.3)

This means that the company made a profit of £4,700,000 in the year to its balance sheet date in 2005, but made a loss of £2,300,000 in the previous year.

Accounts are always immediately followed by pages of notes which are numbered in order. In this case we are told that note 7 will tells us something about the operating profit, such as how it has been calculated or what has been included.

Layouts

When Charles Dickens was alive, accounts were produced with various indented columns whose sub-totals and totals were offset, so it was clear which numbers were being added and subtracted. So part of the balance sheet may read:

	£	£	£
Fixed assets			1,000
Current assets			
Cash	400		
Stock	600		
Debtors	300		
Total current assets		1,300	
Current liabilities		(200)	
Working capital			1,100
Net assets			2,100

A single underline indicates the end of the column to be added or subtracted. A double underline indicates the end of the addition or subtraction.

Today, all numbers are listed in a single column. Sometimes single underlines are used to indicate that the number is separated from those below. Sometimes a box is drawn round numbers which make up the figure which appears immediately below. However these conventions are not universally adopted.

Also graphic designers now prefer sans serif typefaces.

Under the modern convention, the balance sheet above might look like this:

	£
Fixed assets	1,000
Current assets	
Cash	400
Stock	600
Debtors	300
Total current assets	1,300
Current liabilities	(200)
Working capital	1,100
Net assets	2,100

The exact forms of layout are specified in Companies Act 1985 Sch 4 Part I which provides alternatives.

The Balance Sheet and Profit and Loss Account

The **balance sheet** is a snapshot of one moment in time – the end of trading on the balance sheet date. It comprises two columns of numbers which add up to the same figure, in other words they "balance". The first column adds up everything the company owns which can be expressed as an amount of money (assets) and subtracts what it owes (liabilities). The second column lists how this is represented in terms of where the money came from (capital). Historically these columns were printed side by side. Now they are usually printed one over the other.

The **profit and loss account** is a history. Unlike the balance sheet, it covers a period of time, usually one year. It says how much money the company earned as turnover from sales. From this, it deducts its costs and expenses to arrive at various figures of profit. The figure for operating profit is particularly important to investors. From this, further deductions are shown for tax and dividends paid to shareholders. The last figure is retained profit. This is the amount of profit the company keeps for its own use. (Strictly speaking this statement should be called a 'profit *or* loss account', but the 'and' name has stuck.)

Reflecting transactions

Although this book is only concerned with companies, a balance sheet and profit and loss account can be produced for any business of any size. Suppose on 1 January 2005, Archibald Maltravers decides to put £10,000 into a business selling widgets. He can immediately draw up the two main financial statements.

Archibald Maltavers Balance sheet as at 1 January 2005		Archibald Maltravers Profit and loss account for the period of 1 January 2005	
	£		£
Fixed assets	–	Turnover	–
		Cost of sales	–
Current assets:			
cash	10,000	Gross profit	–
	10,000	Expenses	–
Current liabilities	–	Operating profit before tax	–
		Tax	–
Net assets	10,000		
		Operating profit after tax	–
Represented by:			
Capital	10,000		

He then decides that his business should be a company, so on 10 January 2005, he sets up Maltravers Widgets Ltd. He buys a company for £50, which leaves £9,950 in the bank. He buys two shares for £1 giving a share capital of £2 paid to the company. The £10,000 he provided is a loan from him to the company. Notice that a company has a separate legal identity from its shareholders and directors. Archibald has 'given birth' to the legal person of a limited company.

The accounts now look like this:

Maltravers Widgets Ltd Balance sheet as at 10 January 2005		Maltravers Widgets Ltd Profit and loss account for the period from 1 January 2005 to 10 January 2005	
	£		£
Fixed assets	–	Turnover	–
		Cost of sales	–
Current assets:			
cash	9,952	Gross profit	–
Total current assets	9,952	Operating expenses	(50)
Current liabilities	–	Net profit/(loss)	(50)
Net assets	9,952		
Long-term liabilities: loan from A. Maltravers	(10,000)		
Net assets	(48)		
Represented by: Sharecapital Retained loss	2 (50)		
	(48)		

The profit and loss account shows that the company has made a loss of £50 by incurring an expense for that amount with no turnover. The balance sheet shows that the company is now worth a negative sum of £48, and calculates this in two ways. First it shows the amount of cash the company has less the amount it owes. Second, it shows that this is represented by a share capital of £2 less the retained loss of £50.

On 14 January 2005, the company buys 100 widgets at £7 each and receives an invoice payable in 30 days time. The accounts now show:

Maltravers Widgets Ltd Balance sheet as at 14 January 2005		Maltravers Widgets Ltd Profit and loss account for the period from 1 January 2005 to 14 January 2005	
	£		£
Fixed assets	–	Turnover	–
Current assets:		Cost of sales	–
cash	9,952		
stock	700	Gross profit	–
		Operating expenses	(50)
Total current assets	10,652		
		Net profit/(loss)	(50)
Current liabilities:			
Trade creditors	(700)		
Net assets	9,952		
Long-term liabilities:			
loan from			
A. Maltravers	(10,000)		
Net assets	(48)		
Represented by:			
Sharecapital	2		
Retained loss	(50)		
	(48)		

On 21 January 2005, the company sells 20 widgets at £10 each. This means that it issues an invoice for £200 to its debtor (customer) payable in 30 days time. It also means that its stock has reduced by £140, representing the 20 lots of £7 it paid to buy the widgets.

The financial statements now look like this:

Maltravers Widgets Ltd Balance sheet as at 21 January 2005		Maltravers Widgets Ltd Profit and loss account for the period from 1 January 2005 to 21 January 2005	
	£		£
Fixed assets	–	Turnover	200
Current assets:		Cost of sales	140
cash	9,952		
debtors	200	Gross profit	60
stock	560	Operating expenses	(50)
Total current assets	10,712	Net profit/(loss)	10
Current liabilities:			
Trade creditors	(700)		
Net assets	10,012		
Long-term liabilities:			
loan from			
A. Maltravers	(10,000)		
Net assets	12		
Represented by:			
Sharecapital	2		
Retained loss	10		
	12		

You note that the company is now worth £12. The balance sheet calculates this figure in two ways, and they give the same answer.

By 21 February 2005, the company has paid £700 to the supplier, the customer has not yet paid his bill but has bought another £200 worth of widgets which cost the company £140. The financial statements now show:

Maltravers Widgets Ltd Balance sheet as at 21 February 2005		Maltravers Widgets Ltd Profit and loss account for the period from 1 January 2005 to 21 February 2005	
	£		£
Fixed assets	–	Turnover	400
Current assets:		Cost of sales	280
cash	9,252	Gross profit	120
debtors	400	Operating expenses	(50)
stock	420		
Total current assets	10,072	Net profit/(loss)	70
Current liabilities:			
Trade creditors	–		
Net assets	10,072		
Long-term liabilities:			
loan from			
A. Maltravers	(10,000)		
Net assets	72		
Represented by:			
Sharecapital	2		
Retained loss	70		
	72		

This process could be repeated every time any transaction at all happened. In reality, companies record all transactions such as sales, purchases, payments, receipts and other adjustments in day books (or their computer equivalents); and enter the totals from those day books into a nominal ledger, from which the final accounts are eventually produced.

The entries to the nominal ledger are made using double-entry bookkeeping (invented in 1340) where every debit has an equal credit, so the debits and credits always come to the same figure. That is what ensures that the balance sheet always balances. Double-entry bookkeeping acknowledges that every financial transaction affects two items, for example:

Transaction	first effect	second effect
Buy stock	increase stock	increase creditors
Pay creditors	reduce cash	reduce creditors
Sell stock to customer	reduce stock	increase debtors
Customer pays you	increase cash	reduce debtors

And so on. (Incidentally, 'bookkeeping' is the only word in English with three consecutive double letters.)

Both the balance sheet and profit and loss account are statements of opinion, not fact. Although there is not much scope for opinion in the examples above, as soon as it starts depreciating fixed assets or valuing premises or deciding which debtors may not pay, an element of opinion enters the figures.

"Represented by" on balance sheet

Before moving on, it is worth noting what the net assets can be represented by. The list is:

- share capital
- share premium account
- reserves
- profit and loss account.

Share capital is sometimes described as called-up share capital or issued share capital, or something similar. A company may be authorised by the legal documents which set it up to issue, say, one million £1 shares, but decide only to issue 100,000, so only £100,000 has been received from shareholders and appears in the accounts. Sometimes, the shareholders do not have to pay the whole amount in one go. Most of the privatisations in the 1980s had three 'calls' of perhaps 30p, 30p and 40p in the pound, payable every six months. After the second call, the called up capital would be £60,000, and that figure would appear in the accounts.

Share premium account is the extra money received from shareholders. The share may be issued for £1, but after it has been trading, shareholders may be willing to pay £3 for additional shares. Each £1 is added to share capital, and the £2 is added to share premium account. Any expenses of issuing shares may be deducted from the share premium account.

Reserves are amounts of profit. They is sometimes called 'other reserves' as the share premium account and profit and loss account, legally, are also reserves. There are specific rules about what reserves may be included. Reserves also arise when fixed assets, such as buildings are revalued.

Profit and loss account can also be called retained profit or revenue reserves. It is the accumulated profits and losses made by the business since it started and which have not been allocated to another reserve. In our example, this was the same as the net profit from the profit and loss account, but that was only because this was the first accounting period. In future years, the profit and loss account figure will be the previous year's cumulative total to which the current figure is added.

The Cash Flow Statement

After the balance sheet and profit and loss account, the next most important statement is the cash flow statement.

A cash flow statement is a statement of fact, not opinion. It looks at how much cash has flowed into and out of the company. It is unconcerned with such things as bills yet to be paid. It tells us nothing that we cannot already determine from the balance sheet and profit and loss account. A cash flow statement for the above accounts would show:

Maltravers Widgets Ltd

Cash flow statement for the period 1 January 2005 to 21 February 2005

	£
Net cash outflow from operating activities	(750)
Financing:	
Issue of ordinary share capital	2
Loan from A Maltravers	10,000
Increase in cash	9,252

The net cash outflow comprises £700 paid to the supplier and £50 to set up the company. The final figure is the increase in cash, from zero to its current balance of £9,252. This statement tells us nothing about how much profit the company has made, what fixed assets it owns, nor how much it owes or is owed.

The Statement of Total Recognised Gains and Losses

The fourth financial statement is the newest, the statement of total recognised gains and losses. This was introduced by Financial Reporting Standard FRS 3 in 1992.

Various accounting standards allow or require items to be written directly to reserves. All that the statement of recognised gains and losses does is to provide a separate financial statement so that you can see what changes there have been to reserves during the year. In our example, the only change is the £70 operating profit which goes to profit and loss account or revenue reserves.

Other statements

Company law and accounting standards prescribe the minimum amount of information which must be disclosed by the company. Companies are free to produce other statements and tell us anything else they wish.

Additional statements often include a longer historical perspective, over five or ten years. Much additional information is often offered in the notes to the accounts.

Accounting principles

The terms accounting principles, concepts, policies, practices and bases have been variously used in standards and law to describe the assumptions that are made in the accounts unless the opposite is specifically required and stated in the accounts.

The most fundamental principle of all is that the accounts must represent a 'true and fair' view, which is explained further below.

The matter is now regulated by Financial Reporting Standard FRS 18 which prescribes five accounting principles. These are:

* *going concern*
  the business will continue to trade for the foreseeable future;

* *accruals*
  revenues and costs are matched so they both relate to the same period;

* *consistency*
  the same items are accounted for in the same way from one accounting period to the next;

* *prudence*
  revenue and profits are not anticipated, but only included when reasonably certain. Liabilities are included when reasonably certain or at a best estimate;

* *separate valuation of assets and liabilities*
  where a company gives one figure as a total for assets or liabilities, it must determine the value of each item separately.

You may assume that all five of these principles have been followed unless the accounts expressly say otherwise. The commonest exception is to consistency, when the accounts may explain that something has been accounted for differently, such as when a new accounting standard is introduced.

Accruals means that accounts are adjusted so that only the income and expenditure which relates to the period covered by the profit and loss account appear in it. Telephone bills issued on 1 March and 1 June may each involve the prepayment of three months rent, and three months' calls charged in arrears. In preparing the accounts to 31 March, the accounts will include only one month's prepayment from the 1 March bill and will accrue two months' calls from the 1 June bill.

Sometimes the accruals and consistency concepts conflict. A consistent depreciation or amortisation policy may become out of step with the income to which it relates. This is what happened in artist management company Sanctuary, where the writing down of artists' advances happened more slowly than the income many generated, enhancing reported profits in the early years.

Prudence requires that all liabilities are included, even if they have to be estimated, but that profits are only included when reasonably certain. This means that accounts are cautious or even pessimistic, and may understate profit and value.

Accounting policies are decisions which the company has made, such as the period for depreciating fixed assets. The policies must be stated in the notes to the accounts.

Are accounts reliable?

What is 2 times 2? The answer will tell you the man's job:

Engineer	–	approximately 4
Scientist	–	4.0
Statistician	–	4 (provisionally)
Salesman	–	at least 4
Director	–	leave it with me and I'll let you know
Consultant	–	the answer that is right for you
Politician	–	that's not the real issue
Accountant	–	what do you want it to be?

The point is that accounts are malleable at the hands of the skilled accountant, who can mould the figures to make it look how he wants.

What are accounting standards?

This question is best introduced with a little history.

UK accounting standards started in 1971. Those old enough are likely to remember this year for Concorde, decimal currency, hot pants, The Industrial Relations Act and *Bridge Over Troubled Water*. More significantly for us, it was also the year that Rolls-Royce went bust after producing audited accounts showing that it was in a healthy state.

The company was working on the RB211 aeroplane engine to power Lockheed's new Tristar wide-bodied jets. The expenses it incurred on developing this engine were not written off in the profit and loss account but were capitalised. In other words, the company said that all this knowledge was an asset, just like its factory building, and therefore was part of the company's value. Unfortunately the engine had the slight drawback that it didn't work. And, unlike a factory, expenditure on an engine that did not work has no value. The massive overspends and delays dragged down Rolls-Royce and Lockheed, both of whom had to be bailed out by their governments.

Rolls-Royce and Lockheed survived after takeovers, and even the RB211 engine's problems have been resolved. It now powers Boeing 757 jets. But long before that happened, there were questions asked about how a company could produce accounts showing it was healthy one day and go bust the next.

Until 1971, UK accounts were entirely subjective. It was often impossible to compare figures for one year with the equivalent figure for the next because accountants were largely free to include and exclude what they liked, and to present the figures however they wished. (In 1875 Justice Quain referred in a court judgment to "an ignorant set of men called accountants".) The Institute of Chartered Accountants in England and Wales published 'recommendations' which accountants were not compelled to follow.

The accounting bodies realised this could not continue.

In 1970 the Scottish and Irish institutes of chartered accountants joined the English institute to form the Accounting Standards Steering Committee. In 1971, they were joined by what are now the Association of Chartered Certified Accountants and the Chartered Institute of Management Accountants. The body became known as the Accounting Standards Committee (ASC).

The first statements of standard accounting practice (SSAP) were produced by ASC, but issued by the accounting boards. Enforcement was solely by the accounting bodies disciplining any members who ignored the standards without good reason. (There is no known example of such disciplining.) There was no law requiring accounts to be prepared by a qualified accountant, so there was no enforcement for accounts prepared by an unqualified person. Indeed the law still is that the tea lady may prepare the accounts but only a qualified accountant may audit them. Despite these drawbacks, SSAPs attracted meek compliance and provided an effective block on the worst excesses.

In 1976, the Chartered Institute of Public Finance and Accountancy (CIPFA) joined ASC. In the same year the Consultative Committee of Accounting Bodies (CCAB) was formed of which the ASC became a sub-committee.

On 1 August 1990, ASC was replaced by the more powerful Accounting Standards Board (ASB). This is a subsidiary of the Financial Reporting Council (FRC), also set up in 1990. FRC includes not just accounting bodies but the Department of Trade and Industry, Bank of England and London Stock Exchange. Standards are now issued by the ASC directly. They were given statutory authority under a new law which is now Companies Act 1985 s256(1). The Act also incorporated many provisions previously contained only in standards.

The ASB adopted the extant SSAPs which are slowly being replaced by Financial Reporting Standards (FRSs), though a few SSAPs still remain in force. A Financial Reporting Standard starts life as a Financial Reporting Exposure Draft (FRED), proving that if you make up enough acronyms one will eventually spell a name. A FRED is a proposal on which comments are invited during the exposure period. These are considered before the FRS is issued.

Two other bodies were also set up in 1990. The Financial Reporting Review Panel (FRRP) monitors published accounts for compliance with standards. In particular it looks at departures from FRSs to consider whether the departure is justified. If not, FRRP can obtain a court order for the accounts to be amended. Apparent discrepancies must be referred to the FRRP as it does not otherwise trawl through all published accounts.

To date, the FRRP has not obtained a single court order. In practice, what happens is that the company agrees to amend the accounts in line after discussion with FRRP. In 2003, Kingfisher Group agreed to amend how it reported certain mortgage transactions to comply with FRS 5 on reporting financial transactions.

Also in 2003, FRRP ruled that Finelot plc was wrong to capitalise pre-production work on a lifestyle magazine as research & development. This expenditure did not come within the scope as defined in SSAP 13. Again the company accepted the findings without the need for a court order. Previous instances may be found by looking at the FRRP website.

The Urgent Issues Tax Force (UITF) issues 'abstracts' which deals with particular issues which suddenly arise and says how they should be shown in accounts. Thus UITF 13 dealt with the newly introduced employee share option plan (ESOP) trusts, UITF 21 dealt with issues from the introduction of the euro, and UITF 29 prescribes how to account for the costs of setting up a website.

From 1 January 2005, the European Union has ruled that listed companies must comply with international accounting standards (IASs). These are issued by the International Accounting Standards Board (IASB) formed in 1973 by 13 countries, though 90 countries now use IASs. The USA is the largest exception. The UK has played a significant role in developing IASs, and many FRSs and IASs are compatible.

From 2003, the IASB issues International Financial Reporting Standards, of which IFRS 1 was issued on 19 June 2003 to be effective in 2004. It deals with issues arising from the first-time adoption of international accounting standards.

The ASB has decided that all companies should use the same standards. Rather than simply adopt IASs, which are often less detailed than FRSs, the ASB has adopted a policy of amending existing FRSs to comply. Despite these noble efforts, the two sets of standards are not yet fully harmonised.

In addition to accounting standards, the London Stock Exchange has listing rules. From 2000, these are issued by the UK Listing Authority which is controlled by the Financial Services Authority (FSA). Previously the exchange issued the rules itself in what was commonly known as 'the Yellow Book'.

How much reliance can I put on accounting standards?

Quite a bit, even though accounting standards have lost their way over the decades. The early standards in the 1970s were short and simple. They said what you must do and must not do. Statement of standard accounting practice SSAP 5 on accounting for VAT was issued in 1974 and is still in force unamended. It comprises ten short paragraphs written on two pages. It says that VAT must be excluded from amounts when reclaimable, and the amount owed to Customs is a creditor. And that's it.

The other extreme is Financial Reporting Standard FRS 13 on financial instruments. This is a book running to 165 pages, in three parts and seven appendices. The rules themselves are contained in 135 paragraphs. This is one of the shorter and less profound paragraphs:

> 48. If the estimated difference between the carrying amount of a financial asset or financial liability (or of a category of them) and its fair value is not material, the carrying amount may be used as the fair value.

In other words, if when you calculate one figure, you find it is the same as another, you can use the other. Think about it.

Of more consequence than their greater length and complexity, are the acres of concepts, analysis and other theology which now enwraps them. Accountants must now consider the meaning of life in deciding what number to use.

Accounting standards still differ from law in that they set objectives which must be met, rather than rules which must be followed regardless of whether an objective is met, and that is the salvation of UK accounting. The 'true and fair' override provides a long stop against maverick accounting.

It is worth remembering that there are many aspects of accounting which have yet to be included in any standard.

How significant is any departure from accounting standards?

Probably not very significant at all.

Any departure must be clearly stated in the notes to the accounts. This is a legal requirement under Companies Act 1985 Sch 4 para 36A, applicable from 1990. If the reason is not valid, the accounts will break the 'true and fair' override, and the Financial Reporting Review Panel will be on to it.

A legal opinion obtained by the Accounting Standards Board and reproduced in the Foreword to Accounting Standards states that "in general compliance with accounting standards is necessary to meet the true and fair requirement".

Are different standards used in preparing accounts of overseas subsidiaries?

Yes, but they must be adjusted back to UK accounting standards for UK companies.

BP's 2002 accounts are prepared using UK accounting standards, but a separate statement shows what the figures would be if USA GAAP (generally accepted accounting principles) were followed.

Item in accounts	UK standards	USA standards
Profit for the year	£6,845m	£8,395m
Value of company	£69,409m	£66,999m

The main difference in profit relates to the additional £1,302 million goodwill which USA standards may include. The main difference for company value is the additional £2,286 million which USA standards require for pension liability.

Both UK and USA standards are intended to give a true and fair view of the company's position. That the USA profit figure is 22.6% higher shows how subjective that concept is.

The Auditor's Report

How much reliance can I put on the auditor's report?

None.

An auditor's report is an opinion on part of another accountant's opinion, and nothing more. The auditor's report provides no guarantee that the accounts are correct, that the business is trading legally or indeed at all, or that there is no massive fraud going on.

The auditor's report is a complete curiosity. Under English company law, anyone may prepare company accounts. The directors can appoint the village idiot if they wish, but the auditors must be professionally qualified accountants. The professional bodies then impose their own exacting standards with a practising certificate and inspection system.

This system of controlling the inspector rather than the producer of accounts would provide a measure of security were it not for the fact that:

- the report is limited to two narrow issues; and
- the real report is given to the person being inspected.

An auditor states that the accounts are true and fair, and comply with the Companies Act 1985, and that is all. If the company is involved in crooked dealings and has been ripped off, it will still get a clean audit report, provided those dealings and rip-offs are properly accounted for.

> If the Auditing Practices Board were the police, it would confine its activities to telling burglars whether their shoelaces were undone.

The audit report typically occupies a whole page of the annual report. But any investor who bothers to read them will notice remarkable similarities between them. Only the last paragraphs ever differ. The reason is that the auditor does no more than select one of several standard reports from Statement of Auditing Standard SAS 600, published by the Auditing Practices Board. And that is all the shareholders get for the millions they pay to the auditors they appoint.

All the real work from the audit report is put into a letter of weakness which is given to the company's management – who are the very people the shareholders pay the auditors to check. The terms of the letter of weakness are given in Statement of Auditing Standard SAS 610.

If the Auditing Practices Board were the police, it would confine its activities to telling burglars whether their shoelaces were undone.

If you invest in small companies, you could find that the accounts have not been audited at all. The turnover threshold for compulsory audit is increased from £1m to £5.6m from 30 March 2004.

How much reliance can I place on the accounting concept of 'true and fair'?

Much. Under UK law, a company's accounts must be 'true and fair'. This law is now contained in Companies Act 1985 s228. You will find this expression buried in one of the final paragraphs of the auditor's report, and probably nowhere else, yet this is the most fundamental accounting principle of all.

Ultimately it is a matter for the courts to decide whether a company's accounts are true and fair. In the case *Lloyd Cheyham v Littlejohn* [1987], Woolf J held that accounting standards were "very strong evidence as to what is the proper standard which should be followed". This was before these standards became statutory.

Accounts may depart from any standard or any detailed provision of Companies Act 1985 (found in Sch 4) if compliance means that the accounts cease to be true and fair. In particular, 'true and fair' can require additional disclosure.

This proved to be a battleground. The Department of Trade statement on Argyll Foods back in February 1982 said:

> The true and fair view requirement is, if possible, to be satisfied (if provision of the statutory information is insufficient for the purpose) by giving additional information in the balance sheet or profit and loss account or the notes. Only when this is impossible is departure from other requirements permitted.

This view was not accepted by Sir David Tweedie, later chairman of the Accounting Standards Board. Writing in *Auditor's Factbook* in 1987, he said:

> Personally, I disagree with this view. It is never impossible to provide further information... but can the do-it-yourself approach reveal a true and fair view if the additional information simply informs the reader that the accounts themselves are not fairly presented?... If the user has to take out a pencil and paper to derive the true picture of an entity's performance or financial position by adjusting the financial statements, then, in my view, the accounts themselves should be changed rather than additional information provided. The accounts per se must not be misleading.

It is worth noting that Tweedie's view has prevailed.

The position is now stated in an appendix to the foreword to accounting standards, published in 1993 and written by Mary Arden QC, drawing on the joint opinions she wrote in 1983 and 1984 with Leonard Hoffman QC (now Lord Justice Hoffman). This makes clear that, since accounting standards were given statutory backing in 1990, compliance with accounting standards is necessary for a true and fair view. This includes compliance with UITF abstracts.

It is edifying to consider what this expression really means, how it came to be adopted and how it has been applied in contentious areas.

First, truth and fairness are both opinions rather than facts. This reflects that a set of accounts is an opinion and not a statement of fact. A valuation of freehold property is subjective in that any figure between, say, £50 million and £60 million may be considered true and fair. It is only when a valuation departs significantly from that range, that anyone could say it was untrue and unfair.

Second, there are two conditions to be met. Truth relates to correctness of belief. The published accounts comply with the accounting records and the directors believe them. None of this guarantees that it is free from mistake or fundamental misunderstanding. Fairness relates to the overall impression conveyed by the accounts. Suppose a hopelessly optimistic chairman of a struggling company says "some say that we are going bust but I believe that we can survive and prosper".

Journalist A reports "the chairman said 'we are going bust'". That is true but unfair.

Journalist B reports "the chairman said the company is struggling". That is untrue but fair.

When the concept of the joint stock company was developed during the middle of the 19th century, there was such a close rapport between investors and managers that there was little need for formal accounts and so a laissez-faire attitude was common. The other extreme is strict prescription where rules dictate how every last item must be accounted, regardless of how it impacts on the accounts.

Prescription can be a particular problem regarding disclosure. If a company is required to disclose vast quantities of information down to how much it has spent on biscuits and paper clips, the important information is buried in a mass of trivia. Accounts are designed to present a picture, and therefore need to be concerned about how much detail is provided, as well as how little.

The concept of 'true and fair' was introduced by Companies Act 1947 to replace the previous concept of "true and correct" which implied a spurious accuracy. This concept strikes a balance between the laissez-faire attitude and strict prescription, giving UK accounts the best of both worlds. The concept has survived the consolidated Companies Acts of 1948 and 1985, as well as the amending Acts of 1967, 1976, 1980, 1981 and 1989. It was adopted by the European Union in 1978 in its 4th directive on company law, and is now the common standard throughout Europe.

No-one has attempted a legal definition of 'true and fair' though the courts have commented on it in specific situations.

Accounts present a picture representing the company's financial state. Just as different artists produce different pictures of the same object, so different accountants can produce different accounts of the same company at the same time. 'True and fair' permits that subjectivity.

True and fair controversies

The concept of 'true and fair' has triggered some separate controversies.

Probably the first was the 'substance over form' debate, initially introduced by Institute of Chartered Accountants in England and Wales (ICAEW) in Technical Release TR 603. This said that accounts must reflect the substance of an arrangement in preference to its legal form. It was an attack on arrangements whereby loss-making subsidiaries could be kept out of consolidated accounts by manipulating their legal form. This approach was immediately attacked by the Law Society who maintained that legal form is preferable as they provide "a clear point of reference" rather than "a subjective evaluation". They concluded that substance over form was "dangerous and undesirable", but substance over form has prevailed. Substance over form has been the basis for many specific standards, particularly regarding leases.

Another issue was whether unrealised gains from revaluation should be shown in the profit and loss account (as introduced by New Zealand in the 1980s) or not (as was the UK position). The UK has now solved it by introducing a statement of total recognised gains and losses which, in effect, is a halfway house between the two historic positions.

Yet another issue concerned inflation. Is it reasonable to regard £1 of sales or expenses at the beginning of a year as being worth the same as £1 of sales or expenses at the end of the year if there has been 20% inflation during the year, so that the latter £1 is only worth 80p of the former? Annual inflation in the UK peaked at 26.9% in August 1975. It was above 10% as recently as October 1990.

Accounting standards have had two stabs at addressing this problem. Statement of standard accounting practice SSAP 7 introduced current purchasing power (CPP) which was withdrawn before it took effect. This was followed by statement of SSAP 16 which introduced current cost accounting (CCA). This added four adjustments to the accounts to re-express the historic figures at their value on balance sheet date. CCA was widely ignored and ceased to be mandatory in 1985. In the 20 years since then, there has been one abandoned further attempt and some guidance notes only. Companies Act 1985 permits inflation accounting to be used as "alternative accounting rules", though the normal historic accounts must still be given. No significant use has been made of this provision. Sometimes accounts include some inflation-adjusted figures, but with inflation down to 3% or less, no-one is much bothered.

There is an international accounting standard IAS 29 which deals with hyperinflationary economies, defined as where the currency loses half of its value in three years, such as in Argentina and much of Africa. In such cases, the accounts must either use CCA or be expressed in a stable currency.

Legitimate ways for companies to 'improve' their results

What scope is there for companies to 'massage' their figures?

Plenty.

A set of accounts is an opinion, not a statement of fact, and different accountants will form different opinions on the same set of facts. That is why accounts are never said to be 'correct'. An opinion is acceptable if it falls within a range. Eventually an opinion can become so unreasonable that it ceases to be acceptable, but the exact point where this happens is debatable.

Unfortunately, as the figures get larger, the scope for different opinion becomes larger. A simple example is to consider the different types of asset held by a company.

First, we consider petty cash. On 31 March 2003, the petty cash box is found to contain £147.26. It does not matter who counts it nor how many times they count it, there is no argument on how much it contains. If someone else counts it and finds £147.16, someone has mislaid 10p and the entire accounts department can spend all afternoon looking after it. At least, that is what used to happen.

Second, we consider stock. On 31 March 2003, the store is found to contain 1,429 old widgets. Again, it does not matter who counts them or how many times, there is no argument on how many are there. But how much are they each worth? They cost £10 to buy, but they are not selling well and will probably have to be sold at a loss, perhaps for £8 but it could just be as low as £5 each. So what figure do we use for the value? Depending on our opinion, the answer could be anything from £7,145 to £14,290. Suddenly the 10p missing from petty cash does not look very important.

Third, we consider the premises. These were bought for £10,000 in 1948. They were last valued two years ago for £120 million, but the director believes the site could now be worth anything up to £200 million. Suddenly, neither the petty cash nor the stock looks very important.

To massage figures, all an accountant has to do is to form an opinion which is most favourable to the company's position.

What are the most common ways in which companies massage their figures?

There are many ways in which figures can be massaged. A distinction should be made between deliberate deception and favourable presentation. The former should be of serious concern to the investor (usually don't invest at all), while the latter is something to consider.

Forms of deliberate deception are limitless in number, but three themes are particularly popular:

1.	Anticipating profits
2.	Capitalising expenditure
3.	Off balance-sheet expenditure

Each of these is considered in turn overleaf.

Anticipating profits

Anticipating profits is where a company takes profits before they are due. Consider the following sequence of events in a straightforward sale:

Step	Date	Event
1	2 January	A customer orders a cement mixer from you.
2	9 January	You receive a written confirmation of the order.
3	1 February	You provide the cement mixer.
4	4 February	You send an invoice for the cement mixer.
5	20 March	The customer sends you a cheque to pay the invoice.
6	21 March	You pay the cheque into the bank.
7	24 March	The cheque clears.
8	1 August	The deadline for returning faulty goods passes.

At what step has the company earned the profit and may include it in the accounts? A case could be made out for any of the eight steps above. In law, the answer is 3, though most companies in practice will use 4, and some may use 5.

Selling a cement mixer is a simple matter. Selling holidays or capacity on a cable service is less obvious. Here are some recent examples:

• Ahold (Dutch company, world's third largest retailer) overstated profits for 2001 and 2002 by £315 million, because of "overstatements of income related to promotional allowance programmes". When announced in February 2003, shares fell by 67%, and the chief executive and finance director resigned.

• My Travel (tour operator, previously Air Tours) included income from travel insurance when sold rather than the later day of departure.

• Allied Carpets (carpet retailer) indulged in 'pre-despatching', by booking carpets as sold when the order was placed rather than when supplied. Profits were overstated by £6.3million. Director Ray Nethercott was jailed for three months for misleading auditors.

Capitalising expenditure

If a company buys fittings for £10,000, it regards them as a fixed asset, shows them as such on the balance sheet and writes off perhaps only £1,000 each year in its profit and loss account. But suppose the company makes fittings. For £1,000 worth of materials and £2,000 worth of labour, it may be able to make the same fittings. Should it be allowed to include those fittings on its balance sheet for £10,000 and write them off at £1,000 a year, as if it had sold them to itself?

The answer is no, because a company cannot make a profit by selling to itself. But there is no reason why it cannot treat the £3,000 worth of fittings as a capital item, and write off just £300 a year in the profit and loss account rather than the whole £3,000.

This process of regarding expenditure as a fixed asset is known as 'capitalisation'. By capitalising this expenditure, the expenses in the profit and loss account are reduced. Instead of showing £3,000 expenditure in the profit and loss account, you show just £300 depreciation. The reported profit for that year is thus increased by £2,700. Also the company can show another £2,700 worth of fixed assets, increasing its net asset value. So there are two incentives to capitalise expenditure.

In our example, such capitalisation is justified, but sometimes it is not. Suppose a company has spent millions of pounds developing an aeroplane engine. For its money it has acquired machinery and a vast amount of 'know-how'. It might decide to capitalise all that expenditure and say that it has this asset of its know-how to produce engines. After all, know-how is as much part of the manufacturing process as machinery. That is exactly what Rolls-Royce did, leading to its collapse in 1971.

In June 2002, WorldCom admitted that $3.6 billion (£2.4 billion) of expenses had been capitalised as assets, inflating its profits for the last five quarters. This was found by internal auditors (the company's own employees) one month after the external auditors accepted the accounts. The external auditors were Andersens, who were already facing oblivion after their less than successful audit of Enron. WorldCom shares fell by 60% on the news, triggering large falls in stock markets round the world. WorldCom has issued $30 billion in debt instruments. Of this less than $2 billion has been identified, leading to fears that insurance companies and pension funds may have massive exposure, and massive losses, which they have yet to admit.

Off-balance sheet financing

Suppose individuals A and B own company C which has subsidiaries D, E and F. By law, the accounts must consolidate the results of C, D, E and F into a single set of group results as if they were a single company. If C creates any more subsidiaries, they will also have to be consolidated. But suppose A and B decide to create a new company G which they will own directly. That company is not consolidated into the C group, as it is not owned by C even though it is controlled by the same people.

Now suppose you are about to launch some new product which could make a big profit but could make a big loss. All that C needs to do is ask A and B to set up G and for the product to be developed there. C may invoice G for a "management charge", which improves C's figures regardless of how well G is doing, because G is a completely independent customer in the eyes of the law.

Another popular method was to set up a subsidiary but where less than 50% of the shares are held by the holding company, so it is not consolidated. The subsidiary can then quietly disappear taking with it any inconvenient liabilities. This has now been outlawed by new accounting rules which include such controlled companies as subsidiaries.

Setting up a new company with the same shareholders is just one form of off-balance sheet financing. Other methods use joint ventures and consortia. This was the method used by Enron to hide their problems until the structure came crashing down in January 2002. Enron was the USA's seventh largest company.

In 2002, a French media company, Vivendi, was accused of hiding losses. The news prompted an immediate 26% drop in its share price.

Also in 2002, US company Tyco was found to have hidden a $20 million fee to a director and various acquisitions. The company was found to have debts running into billions of dollars.

Other methods

Ignoring expenses

The corollary to anticipating profits is deferring expenses:

* HP Bulmer (cider makers) announced in October 2002 £3.8 million of previously unidentified promotional costs, namely discounts to retailers.

Inclusion in sales

Sales may be inflated by non-trading income:

* Wickes (DIY chain) overstated profits by £18 million during the 1990s by including cash rebates and supplier discounts as sales.

Forgery

Forgery is not in itself a means for massaging accounts, but it can be a means by which falsification may be covered. It is surprising that there is no auditing standard on checking the veracity of documents. Modern computers with scanners and artwork software make it a simple matter to produce false documents. This is made easier because auditors may only see a photocopy or faxed copy on ordinary A4 copy paper. The original document could provide hints, such as the quality, size and colour of the paper, whether the ink has been printed on a press rather than computer, the quality of artwork in any logo, whether there are perforations from a pad, and so on.

In 2004, the Italian dairy conglomerate Parmalat collapsed when it was discovered that its assets were overstated by €3.9bn (about £2.1 bn) in its 2002 accounts. The company submitted a document dated 6 March 2003 apparently from Bank of America confirming that Parmalat subsidiary Bonlat had £2.1 billion with the bank. When the auditors asked the bank to confirm this, it replied that it had no current relationship with Bonlat. The company failed to reimburse a bond on 19 December 2003, though it apparently had plenty of cash to do so. The company went bust four days later.

Forgery also played a part when rogue trader Nick Leeson brought down Barings

Bank in 1995. He had outstanding notional futures positions on Japanese equities and interest rates of US$27 billion when the bank's worth was only $615 million. The bank even transferred $835 million to its Singapore branch to help Leeson meet its margin obligations in Singapore. When the auditor questioned whether a transaction was for a client, she was satisfied with a faxed copy of a client note which Leeson forged using scissors, paste and a photocopier. Leeson's reported activities represented half of all Barings' reported profits in the 1994 accounts. The bank paid him a bonus of $720,000 for reportedly making a profit of $46 million when he had actually made a loss of $296 million.

Falsifying documents was also an element in how in 1974 Marc Colombo, aged 28, managed to lose £33 million for Lloyds Bank at Lugano, Switzerland through currency dealing.

Enron went even further, deceiving investors by creating a completely false dealing room manned by actors talking into unconnected telephones.

How do I know if the accounts have been massaged?

Sadly, you do not.

There is some limited protection in that it is almost impossible for accounts to be massaged so that all ratios and statements still stand up. That is why you should always analyse results and read reports with a quizzical eye. If something seems to be too good to be true, it probably is.

Should I read the notes to the accounts?

Yes. That is where all the juicy detailed information is hidden.

It is worth reading the notes through completely, and not just going to the relevant section as you read the main financial statements. You will be surprised what significant information is contained in small type at the end of a note.

Fraud

How do I know whether the company is a victim of fraud?

You don't.

The directors are responsible for preventing and detecting fraud. Your first view should be whether you trust the competence of the directors.

Supporting information from outside the accounts

Updating the information in the accounts

Does it matter that the information in a set of report and accounts is historic?

No, because what else can a company report?

There is only limited truth in the statement that the past is no indication of the future. The accounts state:

* what the company intends to do; and
* what the company has done.

The former says what the future is likely to hold while the latter indicates how likely the management will deliver it.

Few corporate disasters were unforeseeable from the previous reports if only investors understood how to read and understand them.

Although the accounts are drawn up to the balance sheet date, they are not signed by the directors until many months later. Every company is required to disclose significant post-balance sheet events which happen between the balance sheet date and the date of signing. These will usually be buried in the notes to the accounts. Make sure you find the note and read it.

Can I ask the company itself for updated information?

Yes, but this is only appropriate for specific concerns. General information is found through other means such as the various stock market news services.

A letter should be addressed to the company secretary. Emails and telephone calls tend to be ignored. For small companies, such as those listed on AIM, the author's experience is that a targeted question is likely to lead to a detailed answer. Even a phone call from the chairman to a holder of fewer than £1,000 worth of shares is not unknown.

Shareholders also have the right to ask questions at the annual general meeting. For large companies, this right is likely to be limited in practice. Companies have got wise to objectors who try to take over AGMs. For small companies, hardly anyone attends, so you might find yourself welcome as they are delighted to have a shareholder to talk to.

The court case *Peskin v Anderson CA [2001] 1 BCLC 372* established that directors of a company have no duty to individual shareholders to inform them regularly of matters which might affect the shareholders' interests, unless there is a special relationship requiring them to do so. The case concerned a member of the Royal Automobile Club Ltd who resigned two months before the demutualisation which would have realised £34,000 for him.

How can I make sure that I receive official announcements made by the company between reporting dates?

By subscribing to a news service. The London Stock Exchange's own news service is RSN. However, from 2 April 2002, the Financial Services Authority authorised four other bodies: Business Wire Regulatory Disclosure, Newslink Financial, PimsWire, and PR Newswire Disclosure.

Probably the easiest way for the individual investor to access such data is on the website http://www.uk-wire/com. This gives all official announcements made by companies. They include such announcements as:

- new listing of a company;
- cancellation of listing;
- transactions in a company's own shares;
- changes in shareholdings of more than 3%;
- publication of annual or interim accounts;
- directors' dealings in shares;
- information issued to shareholders;
- offers for other companies;
- declaration of a dividend;
- grant of options;
- appointment or resignation of director.

There is a facility that allows you to enter details of the companies in which you are interested, and to receive alerts about official announcements relating to those companies. All companies have an EPIC code, which is an abbreviated form of the company name in a few letters. Your stockbroker may also offer a service.

Companies must be concerned about ensuring that price-sensitive information is released first through an official channel. Manchester United was rebuked for letting news agencies know first that it was letting David Beckham go. (The share price rose on the news.)

If a company announces a profits warning, how significant is that?

Very. This means that the directors know that there is some bad news.

As an investor, you can do nothing about it, as the share price will reflect the news as soon as it is announced. Your response is simply to consider whether this changes the reasons why you continue to hold the share. However the market tends to overreact to any news, good or bad.

The EU has produced a Transparency Directive which allows companies to publish price-sensitive information on their own websites only.

What about takeover documents?

An uncontested takeover usually occurs when the old management has given up. The share price will probably have fallen, the new owners will almost certainly be better and the investor is usually best advised meekly to accept the inevitable.

A contested takeover is much more exciting. You will be bombarded with claims and counter-claims as each side explains why you should sell your shares to them or not sell them at all. Suppose White Shark Investments is trying to take over Lazy Trout Trading which has these profits:

1999 - £10m   2000 - £2m   2001 - £5m   2002 - £7m   2003 - £9m

White Shark will tell you that the company is doing badly because its latest profit is down 10% on four years earlier. Lazy Trout will tell you how well it is doing, because its profits have risen by 350% over three years.

And so on. This book has shown you how many ratios a company can use and how apparent facts may not be what they seem. In a contested takeover, you can watch the professionals put their own spin on the same facts and counter the other side. They go into 'gramophone mode' – wind them up and they give the record a spin.

As a quick rule of thumb, takeover bids are good news for investors in the target company, who see the share price soar. Takeovers are not always such good news for the company making the bid.

The London Stock Exchange lays down a strict timetable for takeover bids. The bidder sends an offer document to shareholders within 28 days of making the bid. The day of posting is day 0. The timetable is:

Day	Event
0	offer documents posted to shareholders
14	last day for target company to reply
39	last day for target company to issue defensive material
46	last day for bidder to increase offer
60	bidder must have secured 50% of shares to succeed

If a counter-bidder turns up, he starts a new clock running. The investor has 42 days after the initial bid to change his mind, unless the bidder has already gained control.

Takeovers can take much longer when clearance is needed from the various regulatory authorities (Competition Commission in the UK). One of the longest running bids was when Air Products of USA and Air Liquide of France started bidding for BOC in summer 1999. The companies were unable to get the clearances in the time allowed, so the bid lapsed in May 2000. BOC's share price fell back from a takeover high to £14.60 to £9.

In 1991, Hanson and ICI, then the fifth and ninth largest UK companies were planning a merger to make them the second largest (after BT), even though Hanson had acquired a stake of only 2.8% in ICI. Instead Hanson split four ways, and ICI demerged its pharmaceuticals company Zeneca to boost profits. Zeneca fared better and overtook ICI. It subsequently merged to form AstraZeneca.

What is volatility?

Formula:

volatility = [highest share price – lowest share price] ÷ 2 x current share price

Most ratios are intended to advise on how well the company is performing. Volatility measures how predictable it is that the company will perform as well as suggested. Most portfolios are a balance between low-risk and high-risk companies. Volatility is one of the measures by which the investor can determine how much risk there is to the share. It is a simple measure which calculates how far the share price has strayed from its current price over the last 12 months.

Suppose a share is currently selling for £1. The figures for the 12-month high and low show that it has traded between £1.40 and 80p during the last year. The formula requires you to divide 60p by £2, showing volatility of 30%. Many share information services calculate volatility for you.

The problem with this measure of volatility is that:

- it measures past performance which is no indication of how the share will perform in the future;

- one year is a very short period to consider volatility when many investments are held for longer periods;

- it does not indicate whether the price is going up or down (for which a graph provides a better indication); and

- it does not distinguish share-specific factors from economy-specific factors (known as the beta) such as the three-year bear market from 2000.

Independent research

Where can I get independent research on a company?

The most independent research on a company is what you do yourself, following the three-point plan of:

- analyse the accounts;
- then read the reports;
- then read other people's comments.

Market analysts can command high salaries and doubtless work hard, but their results are little better than random selection, particularly over the long-term. Much of the analysis is understanding the company, and deciding what is an appropriate investment for your circumstances and your investment views.

Magazines such as *Investors Chronicle* and *Shares* provide useful insights into companies, such as working out many of the key ratios for you, and distilling salient facts. The best way to use them is to consider the arguments being offered, but to ignore their recommendations to buy, sell or hold. Newspapers, particularly *The Financial Times,* contain many articles and company profiles which provide useful information.

Newspaper articles about companies are largely written by PR agencies for the companies and say what the company wants you to know. In the unlikely event that a newspaper unearths some new significant fact about a company, you can be sure that the share price will reflect that before you have finished reading the article.

Never buy a share tipped in last Sunday's newspaper. Share prices are influenced by supply and demand, so retail stockbrokers on Monday are inundated with orders for Whizzo plc because it was tipped in yesterday's Sunday Times, and it briefly rises in price, simply confirming the investors' views – until he sells. If you believe the share is good value, wait at least a month before buying.

There are many software systems now for managing share portfolios. Many of these include facilities for giving information about companies. The internet has made this process much simpler. Although most share prices offered free by websites are quoted subject to a 15-minute delay, many also offer real-time prices to paying subscribers.

There are also many bulletin boards where people can post their comments. The quality of information on these boards is notoriously unreliable, as many contain comments of aggrieved individuals. You should regard them as generating ideas to consider rather than conclusions to accept. In the case *Totalise plc v Motley Fool Ltd. QBD. The Times 15 March 2001*, the investment website Motley Fool was obliged to identify Zeddust who posted defamatory comments about Totalise.

Do analysts have access to information that ordinary shareholders do not?

Yes. And large shareholders can have private meetings with directors.

Some of the information derived by analysts and fund managers can be acquired as second-hand information. This includes:

- directors' dealings;
- fund managers' dealings; and
- share price movements.

Directors' dealings are explained opposite.

If fund managers start buying a share, it could indicate that they have found out something privately or by analysis which is not obvious to the rest of the market. Jim Slater, a famous investor, reversed a gold-mining company into what is now called Galahad Gold. On the strength of his name, the share price almost immediately doubled. Some magazines follow such activities.

Share price movements are themselves a source of second-hand information. The way share prices move can reflect the collective wisdom of investors. For this reason, there are many systems of charting and similar indicators which look at the way prices move.

How much reliance you place on second-hand information is a matter for your judgement. The methods outlined in this book are collectively known as fundamental analysis. Charting and similar methods have devoted followers. You may decide to use them to test your conclusions.

Can I trust independent research?

For facts – yes; for opinions – no.

Researchers usually get their facts right. However their opinions are no better than yours.

At the start of 2002, the FTSE 100 index stood at 5217. Predictions on where it would be at the end of the year ranged from a low of 5200 (Charterhouse Securities) to a high of 6350 (Gerrard). The index actually ended at 3940, meaning that every forecaster was wrong by between 30% and 58%.

£10,000 invested in *Investors Chronicle's* ten "must have" shares at the start of 2003 lost more than 20% of their value in the next 14 months. Only four even kept their value. One of them, Po Na Na, lost 96.4% of its value. And I shall spare the reputations of financial journalists by not printing their comments about Marconi in 1999 and 2000.

Section 2.2 looked at Scottish & Newcastle in some detail, outlining the facts behind whether the company will prosper again. At the start of 2004, 19 research firms were pessimistic against five who are optimistic.

Directors' dealings

Directors' dealings are one of the most popular forms of second-hand investment information. These dealings are routinely announced in the share information services, and are published in magazines like *Investors Chronicle* and *Shares*.

Directors are best placed to know what is going on in their company and will buy and sell according to their own judgment. Significant purchases and sales can therefore indicate possible increases and decreases. Sometimes such actions become self-fulfilling prophecies. If enough people notice that a director buys shares in his company, they will assume it must be doing well and will therefore buy shares which itself pushes up the price. Unless grounded on company fundamentals, such price increases are quickly reversed.

Relying on directors' dealings as an indicator of share price movement is far from foolproof. First, you never know the reason for a director's purchase or sale. It could be that they simply want some cash to extend their house. Also, directors are not infallible.

An example of how following directors *can* be successful, however, is software company Xansa. Various directors sold shares at a high of 240p in April 2002, bought shares at a low of 44p in October 2002 and sold in August 2003 at then highs of 114p and 103p. The shares rose to 126p in November 2003, but then started falling and were worth around 100p by February 2004.

Summary

10 signs of a company in good health

10 signs of a company in trouble

Summary of key accounting ratios and measures

10 signs of a company in good health

1. It includes financial highlights within the first two pages of the annual report.

2. The annual report gives equal prominence to both sales and finances.

3. The share price is less than two-thirds of its net assets divided by the number of shares.

4. The company owes less than half the amount it is worth.

5. The number 100 divided by the P/E ratio gives a number which is at least three points higher than the current bank base rate.

6. A current assets ratio of at least 2.0 (1.0 for a major retailer).

7. Total return over the last five years is at least five percentage points above inflation.

8. Steady increase in EPS above the stock market average.

9. Dividend cover of at least 3.0.

10. A flexible dividend policy.

10 signs of a company in trouble

1. It includes more than three photographs of its chairman or chief executive.

2. The accounts are difficult to find, follow or read.

3. It mentions EBITDA.

4. The chairman's or chief executive's report talks of "difficult conditions", "economic downturn", or "challenges".

5. The chairman or chief executive tells you that he is confident the company will meet these challenges.

6. It has an exceptional item for reorganisation in two consecutive years.

7. Gearing of more than 200%.

8. A long explanation under "going concern" in the notes to the accounts.

9. Significant amounts shown as exceptional items.

10. It has a flagpole or fountain at its head office.

Key accounting ratios and measures

Ratio	Formula	Page
acid test	(current assets – liabilities) ÷ current liabilities	31
burn rate	cash ÷ monthly operating expenses	83
creditor period	(trade creditors x 365) ÷ cost of sales	57
current ratio	current assets ÷ current liabilities	31
debtor period	(trade debtors x 365) ÷ sales	57
diluted EPS	net profit ÷ (issued shares + shrs which may be iss'd)	136
discounted cashflow	sum of cashflows for each year	86
dividend cover	EPS ÷ dividend per share	133
dividend yield	dividend per share ÷ share price	139
EBITDA	pre-tax profit + interest + depreciation + amortisation	51
enterprise value	market value + total debt – cash	63
EPS	net profit ÷ issued shares	135
gearing	(total borrowings – cash) ÷ shareholders's funds	99
gearing balance point	net profit after tax ÷ total capital	101
gross margin	gross profit ÷ sales	41
gross profit	turnover – cost of sales	23
interest cover	(pre-tax profit + net interest) ÷ net interest paid	96
internal rate of return	(can only be calculated by an iterative method)	87
liabilities ratio	liabilities ÷ costs and expenses	105
market value	issued shares x share price	59
net assets	fixed assets + current assets – liabilities	76
net margin	net profit ÷ sales	41
net profit	gross profit – expenses	23
P/E ratio	share price ÷ EPS	137
PEG factor	P/E ratio ÷ earnings growth	140
premium or discount	(market capitalisation – net assets) ÷ net assets	77
price to book	share price ÷ shareholders' funds per share	64
return on capital employed	(profit before interest and tax x 100) ÷ net capital employed	49
stock turn	sales ÷ stock	81
total return	dividend yield + capital growth	140
volatility	(highest share price – lowest share price) ÷ 2 x current share price	202

Appendix 1

Sources of Company Accounts

Shareholders

If you are a shareholder in a company, and your holding is registered in your own name, the company will automatically send you its report and accounts. It may offer you abbreviated accounts. Always ask to receive the full accounts.

Having your shareholding registered in a broker's nominee account instead of your own name has advantages when it comes to settlement of transactions, but one of the disadvantages is that you will not automatically receive copies of reports and accounts because the company will not have your name and address on its register. One way round this is to become a member of CREST which allows you to register shareholdings in your own name, and so receive copies of reports and accounts, but at the same time have the advantages of electronic settlement. For more information, visit www.crestco.co.uk.

Shareholders *or* non-shareholders

Whether or not you are a shareholder, you can easily get free copies of a company's reports and accounts, online or in printed format.

Online

Almost all accounts are now available on the internet. Type 'Marks & Spencer accounts' into Google, for instance, and www.marksandspencer.com comes up as the first search result. On the company's site you can reach the most up to date report and accounts in two clicks. You can also download the document to your computer as a PDF file and then review it offline. Most quoted company websites have similar areas for investors. The links to look for on the Home Page are 'Investors' or 'Investor Relations' or 'About the Company'.

An alternative to using a company's own website is to go to one of the services which offers access to financial information on hundreds of companies – for instance, WILink (see below), or the Carol World website at www.carolworld.com.

Printed copies

WILink offers a free annual reports service for selected companies. You simply tell WILink which companies or sectors you are interested in, and they send you the latest company reports to your home or office free of charge.

On the following page is a form which you can photocopy and send to the address at the foot of page 213. If you prefer to request copies online, visit **http://gi.ar.wilink.com.**

A final option is simply to telephone the company directly and ask for the company secetary's department. They will usually send you a copy of the accounts with no fuss.

WILink request form for annual reports & accounts

1. Photocopy this form
2. Tick the boxes of the sectors which you are interested in.*
3. Fill in your delivery address opposite
4. Post the form to the address at the bottom of the page opposite

☐	Aerospace and Defence	6 reports
☐	Agriculture, Paper & Packaging	4 reports
☐	Automotive	12 reports
☐	Banks, Financial Services & Insurance	66 reports
☐	Building & Construction	46 reports
☐	Business & Support Services	57 reports
☐	Chemicals	17 reports
☐	Closed End Funds & Investment Companies	200+ reports
☐	Computers, Technology & Internet	49 reports
☐	Consumer & Retail Products	42 reports
☐	Electronics & Engineering	48 reports
☐	Food Manufacturing & Products	23 reports
☐	Healthcare & Pharmaceuticals	35 reports
☐	Industrial & Manufacturing	8 reports
☐	Leisure & Entertainment	17 reports
☐	Metals & Mining	17 reports
☐	Oil, Gas & Energy	21 reports
☐	Publishing & Media	29 reports
☐	Real Estate	35 reports
☐	Telecommunications	5 reports
☐	Transportation	18 reports
☐	Utilities	9 reports

*If you do not want to receive ALL the reports in a sector, you can pick and choose reports of specific companies by ordering from the website:

http://gi.ar.wilink.com

1. Your contact details

Name

Address

Postcode

2. Daytime phone no. (we may need to verify your details)

3. Email address (we may need to verify your details)

Important notes

1. **The reports and the WILink service is completely free of charge.**

2. If you are ordering more than 4 reports they will be delivered by carrier and will normally take 3 working days. It may not be possible to deliver to a P.O. Box number or a BFPO address, so please provide a full personal or business address.

3. WILink will use the information you provide on this form in acccordance with your wishes. That means it will send you the reports you have requested and, if you agree, provide further services. Please indicate by ticking the appropriate boxes below whether you wish to receive further services.

☐ I do NOT wish to receive information about products and/or services from WILink.

☐ I do NOT wish to receive information by post from carefully selected third parties.

☐ YES, I would like to receive information via electronic communication about other products and services from carefully selected third parties.

Send this form to:

WILink Annual Reports, Unit 1/HQ3, Hook Rise South, Surbiton, KT6 7BR

GI1103

Appendix 2

Software for investors

There are various software packages which help investors to manage their portfolios. Two of the leading packages are:

Updata

Updata is a leading provider of software for investors, with a range of products covering company analysis, portfolio management and technical analysis. With these systems Updata also provides a broad range of company data from Balance Sheet and Profit & Loss accounts through to news, directors' names, directors' shareholdings and company information. The company provides data going back 20 years as well as price information from over 30 international stock exchanges. The company also offers a series of training courses in line with these investing techniques.

Updata plc
Updata House
Old York Road
London
SW18 1TG

+44 (0)20 8874 4747
sales@updata.co.uk
www.updata.co.uk

Sharescope

ShareScope is an award-winning stock market data and analysis package produced by Ionic Information. You install the software and data on your PC, and then get updates of price and company information as part of the subscription package. The data package provides daily prices for over 3,000 shares, historic daily prices going back over 10 years, up to 12 years' historic companies results and 3 years' forecast results, analysts' conssensus buy, hold and sell recommendations, directors' dealings, AFX News, a capital gains tax calculator and tax planner, and advanced data mining tools. There is a one-off membership fee of around £80 per year, with monthly ssubscription fees of £12 for standard end-of-day prices. Real-time prices are available at extra cost.

Ionic Information
19-23 Wedmore Street
London
N19 4RU

+44 (0)20 7561 6000
orders@sharescope.co.uk
www.sharescope.co.uk

Example of Sharescope fundamental data: Excel plc

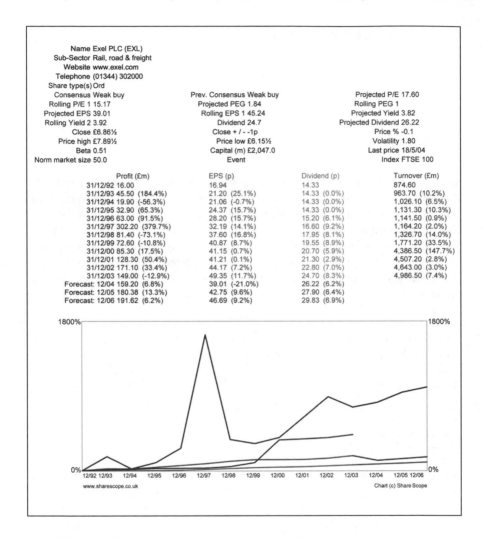

Name Exel PLC (EXL)
Sub-Sector Rail, road & freight
Website www.exel.com
Telephone (01344) 302000
Share type(s) Ord

Consensus Weak buy	Prev. Consensus Weak buy	Projected P/E 17.60
Rolling P/E 1 15.17	Projected PEG 1.84	Rolling PEG 1
Projected EPS 39.01	Rolling EPS 1 45.24	Projected Yield 3.82
Rolling Yield 2 3.92	Dividend 24.7	Projected Dividend 26.22
Close £6.86½	Close + / - -1p	Price % -0.1
Price high £7.89½	Price low £6.15½	Volatility 1.80
Beta 0.51	Capital (m) £2,047.0	Last price 18/5/04
Norm market size 50.0	Event	Index FTSE 100

Profit (£m)	EPS (p)	Dividend (p)	Turnover (£m)
31/12/92 16.00	16.94	14.33	874.60
31/12/93 45.50 (184.4%)	21.20 (25.1%)	14.33 (0.0%)	963.70 (10.2%)
31/12/94 19.90 (-56.3%)	21.06 (-0.7%)	14.33 (0.0%)	1,026.10 (6.5%)
31/12/95 32.90 (65.3%)	24.37 (15.7%)	14.33 (0.0%)	1,131.30 (10.3%)
31/12/96 63.00 (91.5%)	28.20 (15.7%)	15.20 (6.1%)	1,141.50 (0.9%)
31/12/97 302.20 (379.7%)	32.19 (14.1%)	16.60 (9.2%)	1,164.20 (2.0%)
31/12/98 81.40 (-73.1%)	37.60 (16.8%)	17.95 (8.1%)	1,326.70 (14.0%)
31/12/99 72.60 (-10.8%)	40.87 (8.7%)	19.55 (8.9%)	1,771.20 (33.5%)
31/12/00 85.30 (17.5%)	41.15 (0.7%)	20.70 (5.9%)	4,386.50 (147.7%)
31/12/01 128.30 (50.4%)	41.21 (0.1%)	21.30 (2.9%)	4,507.20 (2.8%)
31/12/02 171.10 (33.4%)	44.17 (7.2%)	22.80 (7.0%)	4,643.00 (3.0%)
31/12/03 149.00 (-12.9%)	49.35 (11.7%)	24.70 (8.3%)	4,986.50 (7.4%)
Forecast: 12/04 159.20 (6.8%)	39.01 (-21.0%)	26.22 (6.2%)	
Forecast: 12/05 180.38 (13.3%)	42.75 (9.6%)	27.90 (6.4%)	
Forecast: 12/06 191.62 (6.2%)	46.69 (9.2%)	29.83 (6.9%)	

reproduced with the permission of Ionic Information

Example of Sharescope charting: Excel plc

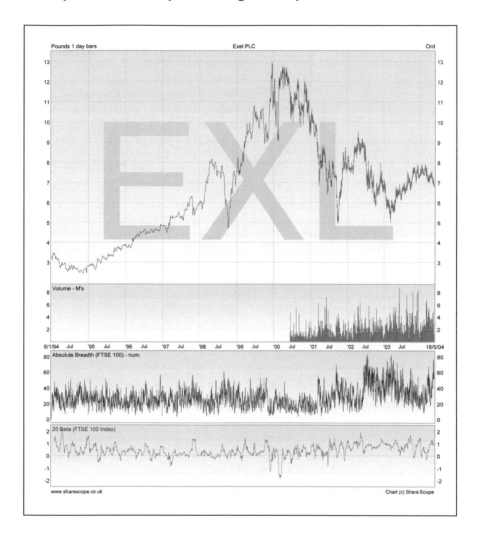

reproduced with the permission of Ionic Information

Appendix 3

Glossary of accounting terms

This appendix gives simple understandable explanations rather than strict definitions.

A-share	ordinary share with some difference in shareholder's rights
accrual	cost of the current period which is paid in a future period
accruals concept	principle that related income and expenditure are shown in the accounts for the same period
acquired goodwill	amount paid for a business above the value of net assets
acquisition cost	amount paid to acquire something
adjusted profit	net profit from profit and loss amended according to tax laws
administration	process whereby insolvent company is externally managed
amortisation	annual expense of using up acquired goodwill
asset stripping	practice of buying a company for its assets, not its business
asset	something with a money value
associated company	company in which parent owns between 20% and 50%
audit	limited annual check on the accounts
bad debt	debt that has been written off
balance sheet	statement of how much business was worth on a particular day
bankruptcy	legal insolvency of an individual
budget	management statement of required income and expenditure
call	demand on shareholders to pay instalment on new shares
called-up capital	amount of shares paid so far by the shareholders

capital	money used for purposes other than general spending
capital allowance	deduction from taxable profits given instead of depreciation
capital employed	how much a business is worth
capital gain	profit on sale of fixed asset
cash	money in readily accessible form
cashflow	statement of how money flows in and out of the company
chargeable gain	another name for capital gain
close company	company owned and run by five or fewer people
Companies Act	laws which govern how companies are run
consistency	fundamental accounting principle that the same methods are followed from year to year
consolidated accounts	accounts for a group prepared as if they were one company
consortium	when several companies own one company without its being anyone's subsidiary
control	the right to dictate what a company does
conversion	making something into something else, usually preference shares into ordinary shares
corporation tax	payable by companies on adjusted profit
cost of capital	equivalent interest rate for how much the company's capital costs it
cost of sales	amount incurred in producing goods or services sold
creditors	people to whom the business owes money
cum div	with the next dividend payable
current asset	asset which is expected to be consumed within one year
current liability	obligation to make a payment within one year
debenture	a form of debt instrument
debt instrument	form of capital which is not equity
debtors	people who owe the business money
deferred share	usually a worthless share
deferred taxation	taxation payable in a future year

defined benefit	pension scheme investors should be concerned about
defined contribution	pension scheme investors should not be concerned about
depreciation	annual expense of using a fixed asset
dilution	effect (usually on earnings per share) if everyone who could acquire shares did so
discounted cashflow	cashflow adjusted to allow for inflation or cost of capital
distribution	dividend, and similar payments from company to shareholders
dividend	payment to shareholders by company from its profits
doubtful debt	amount of debtors the company expects not to be paid
earnings per share	net profit expressed as an amount per one share
EBITDA	theoretical profit if you ignore interest, tax, depreciation and amortisation
equity	share capital, as opposed to debt instruments
ex div	with the next dividend not payable
exceptional item	particularly large or unusual trading transaction
external audit	audit by someone not employed by the company
extraordinary item	most unusual non-trading transaction
fair value	a value required by accounting standards which is considered more accurate than value otherwise determined
final dividend	dividend payable on basis of the whole year's accounts
final salary	pension scheme investors should be concerned about
fixed asset	asset with an expected life of more than one year
forecast	management statement of expected income and expenditure
gearing	ratio of debt to equity
going concern	assumption that a business will continue trading
goodwill	value of a business above the value of its net assets

gross profit	turnover minus cost of sales before expenses
group	holding company and its subsidiaries and associated companies
holding company	company which owns other companies
inflation	percentage measure of by how much prices increase
insolvency	owing more than you are worth
intangible assets	assets which have no physical existence, such as goodwill and brand names
intellectual property	copyright, patents and similar; forms of intangible asset
interim accounts	accounts prepared halfway through the year
interim dividend	dividend payable on basis of first six months' trade
internal audit	audit by the company's own employees
joint venture	two or more companies working together on a project
leverage	American term for gearing
liability	obligation to make a payment
liquidation	process of selling a company's assets
loan stock	a form of debt instrument
long-term liability	obligation to make a payment in more than a year's time
matching concept	another name for accruals concept
materiality	big enough to affect the accounts
merger	two companies becoming one
minority interest	the amount of subsidiaries not owned by the holding company
money purchase	pension scheme investors should not be concerned about
net assets	value of assets minus liabilities
net liabilities	value of liabilities minus assets
net profit	gross profit minus overheads of running a business
off-balance sheet	accounting transactions which are kept outside the published accounts
operating profit	net profit from trading operations

ordinary share	the real shares of the business representing ownership
parent company	company which owns subsidiaries
preference share	a form of debt instrument
private company	company in which members of the public may not invest
profit and loss	statement of how much profit has been earned during a period
profit	money earned from trading
provisions	amounts of profit kept for a specific purpose
prudence	assumption that caution has been exercised in valuing figures
public company	company in which members of the public may invest
realisation	turning an asset into cash
redeemable	process of turning something into cash
research & development	expenditure written off but really a hidden asset
reserves	amounts of retained profit
retained profit	profit a company keeps for its own use
return	total amount received from an investment
solvent	able to pay debts as they fall due
spread	difference between buying and selling prices
straight line basis	depreciation method dividing acquisition cost by expected years of life
subsidiary	company in which parent owns at least 50%
sub-subsidiary	subsidiary of a subsidiary
takeover	one company buying another
tangible assets	assets which have a physical existence, such as buildings
taxation	amount of corporation tax payable in current year
turnover	income from trading activities
winding up	process of ending a company's existence
working capital	readily realisable assets minus current liabilities
write off	process of regarding an asset as worthless

Appendix 4

Common abbreviations in accounts and investment

a/c	account
AASB	Australian Accounting Standards Board
AAT	Association of Accounting Technicians
AB	aktiebolag (Swedish for "limited company")
ACAS	Advisory Conciliation and Arbitration Service
ACCA	Association of Chartered Certified Accountants
ACT	advance corporation tax (now abolished)
ADR	American depositary receipt (or alternative dispute resolution)
ADS	American depositary share
AF	Accountancy Foundation
AG	Aktiengesellschaft (German equivalent to public limited company)
agm	annual general meeting
AIM	Alternative Investment Market
AMPS	auction market preferred shares
APB	Auditing Practices Board
APD	airport passenger duty
arb	arbitrageur (someone who makes profits on small price differences)
AS	Aktieselskab or Aksjeselskap (Danish and Norwegian for public company)
ASB	Accounting Standards Board
ASC	Accounting Standards Committe (now replaced by ASB)
AVC	additional voluntary contributions (to company pension)
BA	Benefits Agency
BBA	British Bankers' Association
bn	billion
CAA	Capital Allowances Act 2001
CAC	Central Arbitration Committee
Cap	capital (fund of investment trust)
CBI	Confederation of British Industries
CC	Competition Commission
CCA	current cost accounting
CCAB	Consultative Committee of Accounting Bodies
ccc	cwmni cyfyngedig cyhoeddus (Welsh for "public limited company")

cd	cum dividend (with the dividend payment)
CEO	chief executive officer
CFC	controlled foreign company
CGT	capital gains tax
CIMA	Chartered Institute of Management Accountants
CIOT	Chartered Institute of Taxation
CIPFA	Chartered Institute of Public Finance and Administration
co	company
COMPS	contracted out money purchase scheme (pension)
COP	code of practice
cosec	company secretary
COSRS	contracted out salary related scheme (pension)
cr	credit (to)
CT	corporation tax
Cv	cumulative (preference share)
cva	company voluntary arrangement (in insolvency)
cyf	cyfyngedig (Welsh for "limited")
DCF	discounted cash flow
DG	director general
DGFT	Director General of Fair Trading
DLT	development land tax (now abolished)
DM	deutschmark (old German currency)
dr	debit (to)
DSS	Department of Social Security
DTI	Department of Trade and Industry
DWP	Department of Work and Pensions
EB	early bargain
EBIT	earnings before interest and tax
EBITDA	earnings before interest, tax, depreciation and amortisation
ED	exposure draft
EEA	European Economic Area
EEIG	European Economic Interest Group (type of company)
egm	extraordinary general meeting
EIS	enterprise investment scheme
EMI	enterprise management initiative (tax scheme for employees)
ENI	employer's national insurance
EPS	earnings per share
ESOP	employee share option plan
ETF	exchange-traded fund
EU	European Union

FD	finance director
FFr	French franc(s)
fmcg	fast moving consumer goods
forex	foreign exchange
FRED	financial reporting exposure draft
FRRP	Financial Reporting Review Panel
FRS	financial reporting standard
FRSSE	Financial Reporting Standard for Smaller Enterprises
FSA	Financial Services Authority
fsavc	free-standing additional voluntary contributions (to pensions)
FSB	Federation of Small Businesses
FT	The Financial Times
FTSE-100	FTSE 100 index (of share prices)
GAAP	generally accepted accounting principles
GB	Great Britain (England, Wales and Scotland)
GBP	pound sterling
GDP	gross domestic product
GmbH	Gesellschaft mit beschränkter Haftung (German for limited company)
HCC	historic cost convention
HICP	Harmonised Index of Consumer Prices (measure of inflation)
HSE	Health and Safety Executive
IAS	international accounting stands
IASB	International Accounting Standards Board
ICAEW	Institute of Chartered Accountants in England and Wales
ICAI	Institute of Chartered Accountants of Ireland
ICAS	Institute of Chartered Accountants of Scotland
ICSA	Institute of Chartered Secretaries and Administrators
ICTA	Income and Corporation Taxes Act 1988
IFRS	International Financial Reporting Standard
iht	inheritance tax
IMF	International Monetary Fund
Inc	incorporated (USA equivalent to "Ltd")
Inc	income (fund of investment trust)
IOD	Institute of Directors
IP	insolvency practitioner
IPO	initial public offering (of shares)
IR	Inland Revenue
IRR	internal rate of return
IRS	Internal Revenue Service (American tax collection body)

ISA	individual savings account
IT	information technology, or investment trust
ITEPA	Income Tax (Earnings and Pensions) Act 2003
IVA	individual voluntary agreement (in insolvency)
JV	joint venture
LIBOR	London Inter Bank Offering Rate (interest rate)
LIFFE	London International Financial Futures Exchange
llp	limited liability partnership
LSE	London Stock Exchange
Ltd	Limited (company)
m	million
MBO	management buy-out
MD	managing director
MFR	minimum funding requirement (for pensions)
MI	minority interest
MMC	Monopolies and Mergers Commission (now replaced by Competition Commission)
NAO	National Audit Office
NAV	net asset value (of company)
NBV	net book value (usually cost less depreciation)
NCE	net capital employed
NCIS	National Criminal Intelligence Service
ned	non-executive director
NI	national insurance
NIC	national insurance contributions
NL	no liability (Australian equivalent to "plc")
NMW	national minimum wage
NPV	no par value
NSO	National Statistics Office
NV	Naamloze Vernootschap (Dutch stock corporation)
NYSE	New York Stock Exchange
ODPM	Office of the Deputy Prime Minister
OEIC	open-ended investment company
OFR	operating and financial review
OFT	Office of Fair Trading
ono	or near offer
OPRA	Occupational Pensions Regulatory Authority
OTC	over the counter (ie not purchased through a recognised stock market)
OY	Osakeyhito (Finnish limited company)

p	penny or pence
P&L	profit and loss account
P/E	price/earnings ratio
para	paragraph
PAYE	Pay As You Earn (income tax collection system)
PEG	price/earnings divided by growth
PEP	personal equity plan (now abolished)
Pf	preference (share)
PFI	Private Finance Initiative
PI	proprietor's interest (capital of sole trader)
PILON	payment in lieu of notice
plc	public limited company
PN	Practice Note
PRP	profit-related pay (particularly tax-saving scheme, now abolished)
PRT	petroleum revenue tax
PSBR	Public Sector Borrowing Requirement
PSO	Pension Schemes Office
R&D	research & development
RDA	Regional Development Agency
RI	Revenue Interpretation (on a point of tax law)
RNS	new service used by London Stock Exchange
ROACE	return on average capital employed
ROCE	return on capital employed
ROE	return on equity
RPI	retail prices index
RPIX	retail prices index less mortgages
s	section
S&P	Standard and Poor's (US ratings agency)
S&U	sources and uses (old name for cash flow statement)
S2P	state second pension
SA	Sociedad Anonima (Spanish for limited company)
SA	Société Anonyme (French for limited company)
SAS	Statement of Auditing Standard
SAYE	Save As You Earn
Sch	Schedule
SDLT	stamp duty land tax
SDRT	stamp duty reserve tax
SEAQ	Stock Exchange Automated Quotations System
SEC	Securities and Exchange Commission (US regulatory body)

SERPS	State Earnings Related Pension Scheme
SETS	Stock Exchange Trading System
SFO	Serious Fraud Office
SI	statutory instrument
SIP	share incentive plan
SIPP	self-invested personal pension
SME	small and medium-sized enterprises
SORP	statement of recommended practice
SP	statement of practice
SpA	Societá per Azioni (Italian public company)
SSAP	statement of standard accounting practice
STRGL	statement of total recognised gains and losses
TCGA	Taxation of Capital Gains Act 1992
TESSA	tax-exempt special savings account (now abolished)
TMT	technology, media and telecoms (shares)
TR	technical release (old statement on accounting matters)
TUC	Trades Union Congress
TUPE	Transfer of Undertakings (Protection of Employment) Regulations 1981
UCITS Securities	Undertakings for Collective Investment in Transferable
UITF	Urgent Issues Task Force (for accounting standards)
UK	United Kingdom (Great Britain plus Northern Ireland)
UKLA	United Kingdom listing authority
US	United States
USM	Unlisted Securities Market (now replaced by AIM)
USP	unique selling point
VAT	value added tax
VATA	Value Added Tax Act 1994
VCT	venture capital trust
vfm	value for money
WACC	weighted average cost of capital
WDV	written down value (cost less capital allowances for tax)
WTO	World Trade Organisation
Wts	warrants
xd	ex dividend (without the dividend payment)
ZBB	zero-based budgeting

Appendix 5

Companies mentioned in this book

Appendix 6

Further reading on company accounts

Accounting For Growth
Stripping the Camouflage from Company Accounts
by Terry Smith
Arrow, 1996, paperback
Code 0052, £14.99

Valuegrowth Investing - How to Become a Disciplined Investor
by Glen Arnold
FT Prentice Hall, 2001, paperback
Code 14314, £21.99

FT Guide to Selecting Shares that Perform
10 Ways to Beat the Index
by Richard Koch
FT Prentice Hall, 2001, paperback
Code 12832, £21.99

Magic Numbers for Stock Investors
How to Calculate the 25 Key Ratios for Investing Success
by Peter Temple
John Wiley & Sons, 2003, hardback
Code 16461, £19.95

Investor's Guide to Analyzing Companies & Valuing Shares
by Michael Cahill
FT Prentice Hall, 2003, paperback
Code 16299, £21.99

The Economist Guide to Analysing Companies
by Bob Vause
Economist Books, 2001, hardback
Code 12505, £20.00

Key Management Ratios
How to Analyse, Compare and Control the Figures that Drive Company Value
by Ciaran Walsh
FT Prentice Hall, 2002, paperback
Code 0620, £21.99

Determining Value
Valuation Models and Financial Statements
by Richard Barker
Pearson Higher Education, 2001, paperback
Code 13955, £33.99

The Financial Numbers Game
Detecting Creative Accounting Practices
by Eugene Comiskey
John Wiley & Sons, 2002, paperback
Code 14894, £25.95

Security Analysis
by Sidney Cottle, Roger Murray and Frank Block
McGraw-Hill Professional, 1987, hardback
Code 0139, £63.99

Screening the Market
A Four-Step Method to Find, Analyze, Buy and Sell Stocks
by Mark Gerstein
John Wiley & Sons, 2002, hardback
Code 15503, £34.95

All the books mentioned, and over 5,000 other titles can be bought at 15%-35% discount from Global-Investor.com, the UK's leading financial bookshop.

Global-Investor Bookshop
43 Chapel Street, Petersfield, GU32 3DY
www.global-investor.com
+44(0)1730 233870, fax +44(0)1730 233880, bookshop@global-investor.com

Index

Harriman House

About Harriman House

Harriman House is a UK-based publisher which specialises in publishing books about money – how to make it, how to keep it, how to live with it, how to live without it. Our catalogue covers personal finance, stock market investing, trading and spread betting, and property investment.

Some recent titles

Superhobby Investing

Peter Temple, the FT columnist, reveals the secrets of making money out of wine, stamps, gold, classic cars, forestry, rare books, coins, art, antiques and banknotes. Choose prudently, follow the golden rules, and these assets can far outperform the stockmarket and other types of savings.
2004, pb, 264pp, £14.99, Code 16666

The Midas Touch
The Stategies that Have Made Warren Buffett the World's Most Successful Investor

The story of how Warren Buffett, the world's second richest man, amassed his $35 billion fortune through investing. John Train looks at Buffett's spectacular record, and explains his sytem for picking winning shares. Short, lucid and written with style and wit, *The Midas Touch* is regarded as a classic investing text. 2003, hb, 208pp, £14.00, Code 15842

500 of the Most Witty, Acerbic & Erudite Things Ever Said About Money

A slim, wickedly entertaining collection of the most memorable quotes on money, wealth, investment, and success. Superb conversational ammunition! 2002, pb, 64pp, £4.99, Code 14896

Logic Problems for Money Minds

42 conundrums, problems and riddles designed to be fun as well as instructive. Some are straight numeracy tests, some are word plays, some are logic traps, and some require lateral thinking. A few are easy, most demand mental exertion, one was devised by Einstein. The best part is, having tested your own mental agility, you will have an arsenal to inflict on friends and colleagues. 2003, pb, 96pp, £5.99, Code 14902

The Beginner's Guide to Financial Spread betting

Spread betting is growing fast in popularity. You place your stake on the direction of a share, predicting whether it rises or falls. The more right you are about its direction, the more money you make. It's easy, you do everything online, and gains are tax-free. This UK guide explains how it works, and how to make money at minimum risk.

2004, pb, £12.99, Code 16699

The eBay Book

eBay is the auction website on which you can buy and sell collectables, consumer goods, CDs, DVDs, electronics, sports equipment, cameras . . . you name it, eBay has it. 9 million people in the UK use eBay on a regular basis for fun and profit. This is the first book to explain how eBay works, how to improve your bidding, and how to maximise the value of what you're selling. It is full of tips, tactics and tricks that the author has learned from his own trading over the last 5 years

2004, pb, 160pp, £9.99, Code 19434

The Investor's Toolbox

'Buy-and-hold' is no longer a valid strategy in the stockmarket. The real money is being made by investors who know how to manage risk and reward by using spread bets, CFDs, covered warrants and other leveraged tools that allow you to make money whether the market is going up or down. For too long, there was never a book to explain how these instruments actually work. Peter Temple, a regular FT columnist, has written it.

2003, pb, 272pp, £21.99, Code 15802

Free catalogue of books on money

If you would like a copy of Harriman House's full catalogue, please ring us on 01730 233870, or go to the 'Free Stuff' section of the Global-Investor website:

http://books.global-investor.com

Global-Investor is the UK's only specialist money bookshop. We stock over 5,000 books on money and most are offered at a discounts of 15%-35%. As the Times put it – 'Global-Investor is the home of finance books on the web'.